GREENBERG'S®
GUIDE TO
STAR TREK®
COLLECTIBLES

VOLUME 1   A - E

CHRISTINE GENTRY
&
SALLY GIBSON-DOWNS

Greenberg Publishing Company, Inc.
Sykesville, Maryland

Greenberg Publishing Company, Inc.
7566 Main Street
Sykesville, MD 21784
(301) 795-7447

First Printing

Manufactured in the United States of America

Greenberg Publishing Company, Inc. offers the world's largest selection of Lionel, American Flyer, LGB, Marx, Ives, and other toy train publications as well as a selection of books on model and prototype railroading, dollhouse building, and collectible toys. For a complete listing of Greenberg publications, please call or write at the above address and request a current catalogue.

Greenberg Shows, Inc. sponsors *Greenberg's Great Train, Dollhouse and Toy Shows*, the world's largest of its kind. The shows feature extravagant operating train layouts, and a display of magnificent dollhouses. The shows also present a huge marketplace of model and toy trains, for HO, N, and Z Scales; Lionel O and Standard Gauges; and S and 1 Gauges; plus layout accessories and railroadiana. It also offers a large selection of dollhouse miniatures and building materials, and collectible toys. Shows are scheduled along the East Coast each year from Massachusetts to Florida. For a list of our current shows please call or write at the above address and request our current "show schedule."

Greenberg Auctions, a division of Greenberg Shows, Inc., offers nationally advertised auctions of toy trains and toys. Please contact our auction manager at (301) 795-7447 for further information.

ISBN 0-89778-208-9

Library of Congress Cataloging-in-Publication Data

Gentry, Christine.
    Greenberg's guide to Star trek collectibles / by Christine Gentry
and Sally Gibson-Downs.
        p. cm.
        Contents: v. 1. A-E
        ISBN 0-89778-208-9 (v. 1 : pbk.) : $29.95
        1. Star trek (Television program)--Collectibles. 2. Star trek
films--Collectibles. I. Gibson-Downs, Sally. II. Title.
PN1992.77.S73G46 1991
791.45'72--dc20
                                                                91-19672
                                                                    CIP

DEDICATION

With love once again to our husbands and children.
Doug and Milo, without your support this book would have been impossible.
Alesha, Courtney, and Jack, without you this book would have been improbable.

ACKNOWLEDGMENTS

Special thanks to the following individuals and groups who in the present or past contributed information or photographs to this ongoing guide:
Audrey Anderson
Ruth Berman
David Bostwick
Bradley Time, Division of Elgin Industries
Betsy Caprio
Loch David Crane
Douglas Downs
Ken Dumas
Ernst Limited Editions
General Mills, Inc.
John F. Green
Hollywood Wax Museum
Robert Jaiven
K-Tel International, Inc.
Cynthia Levine
Kathi and Rick Mingo
Rocketships and Accessories
Milo Rodriguez
Running Press
June Stoops
David Thompson
Uncle Hugo's Science Fiction Bookstore
Robert Wilson

Great thanks must be given to the Memory Alpha Collection for supplying both information and the opportunity to photograph the very rare and unusual Star Trek memorabilia shown in these volumes. Other items pictured are from the collections of the authors. The photograph of the Star Trike is used by permission of Loch David Crane.

Christine Gentry and Sally Gibson Downs
July 1991

I would like to thank the staff at Greenberg Publishing Company for all their support and advice, especially the book's editor, Marsha Davis, who coordinated the book's typing, editing, and compilation; our photographers Brad Schwab and Bill Wantz; our patient artist Maureen Crum, who was responsible for the book's cover as well as preparing it for the printer; our proofreader Donna Price; and Donna Dove and Samuel Baum, who helped with this project through its completion.

Bruce C. Greenberg, Publisher
July 1991

Items pictured on the cover

Front cover (from left to right): Star Trek Telescreen Console by Mego Corporation, mug from *Star Trek: The Motion Picture* Dish Set by Deka Plastics, and Spock Decanter by Ceilo.

Back cover (clockwise from left): *Star Trek: The Next Generation* 1989 Calendar by Pocket Books, bowl from *STTMP* Dish Set, and *Star Trek* porcelain collector dolls by R. J. Ernst Enterprises.

Original cover art by Maureen Crum.

TABLE OF CONTENTS

Star Trek Lives! _____ ?

Reference Guide _____ 9

Abbreviations
Classic Cast
Star Trek: The Next Generation Cast

Glossary Of Collectible Terms
Classic Episode Abbreviation Guide

The Collectibles _____

A _____ 1?

Action Figures And Accessories
Action Figure Sets
Activity Pads
Address Books
Address Labels

Animation Cels
Animation Drawings
Art Prints
Audio Cassettes

B _____ 4(

Badges And I.D. Cards
Banks
Bed Linens
Belt Buckles
Belt Pouches
Belts
Binoculars
Blueprints
Board Games
Bookcovers
Bookmarks

Bookplates
Books
Book Sets
Books (Translations And Foreign Editions)
Books (Trek-Related)
Bop Bag
Brush And Comb
Bumper Stickers
Business Cards
Buttons (Photo)
Buttons (Slogan)

C _____ 116

Cachets
Calculators
Calendars
Card Games
Car Hangers And Kinetic Passengers
Certificates
Chairs
Charms
Checkbook Covers

Chess Sets
Clocks
Coaster
Coins
Colorforms
Coloring Kits
Comic Books
Comic Books (Foreign And Translations)
Comic Premiums

Comic Specials
Comic Syndications
Communicator Kits And Props
Communicator Toys
Computer Prints
Computer Software

Contests
Convention Booklets And Bags
Costumes
Credit Cards
Cups And Cup Holders
Curtains

D _____ *173*

Decals
Decanters And Accessories
Decorations
Diplomas

Dish Sets
Dolls And Play Sets
Doorknob Hangers And Signs

E _____ *184*

Earrings
Ears
Eight-Track Tapes

Erasers
Events
Exhibits

Star Trek Lives!

The market feeler coupon excerpted below was printed in 1967 by *T.V. Star Parade Magazine*, ushering in a quarter-century of advertising zeal for promoters involved in selling Star Trek.

"Is there anything Star Trek has that you would like to have? The people concerned with your favorite show Star Trek and "T.V. Parade" have received many requests as to where they can purchase copies of the shirts worn on the show by Bill Shatner, Leonard Nimoy, DeForest Kelley, James Doohan, and George Takei. They even have requests for Nichelle Nichols' yeoman costume. So we've been asked to have all of you write in to us on the coupon below telling us whether or not you'd be interested in a nylon velour exact copy of the U.S.S. Enterprise crew's shirts. And what price you'd be willing to pay? Do you have favorite colors you'd like to select from? Would you like HIS and HERS shirts? Is there anything else on the show which appeals to you and which you'd like to see on the market? Write and let us know. We'll pass the information along and who knows? Maybe some day real soon you'll be able to buy your favorite item."

In truth, official promotions for Star Trek began even before the airing of the premiere television episode "The Man Trap" on September 8, 1966 and, in one form or another, Star Trek has continued to be promoted for twenty-five years. Now, not only is the original *Star Trek* series still alive and well, but *Star Trek: The Next Generation* has added yet another chapter to the success story penned by Gene Roddenberry so long ago.

Even during the lean decade of the 1970s, when studio and network promotion for the canceled series ebbed to its lowest point, there was always some latent, newsworthy spark of interest about the Trek universe that kept attracting media attention.

Occupying a unique and enviable position in the entertainment field, the "Star Trek Phenomenon" owes its evolution to the very unusual double nature of both Trek promotions and the TV show's concepts and moral philosophies, which appeal to people in virtually all walks of life.

There have always been twin forces at work keeping public interest keenly attuned to the fan slogan, "Star Trek Lives!" The first force is a direct and measurable one stemming from the practical business side of the coin. There has always been a series of media campaigns specifically designed to direct public attention to Star Trek's success, resulting in a media event of remarkable longevity. There has been no end to the publicity releases, press kits, contests, premiums, and offers during all phases of Star Trek's evolution from television series to movies to series again.

There has also been a second very powerful force of continuous promotion for Star Trek — the tireless operations of devoted fans. The allegiance of Star Trek fans to their cause is a most mysterious thing and even science fiction experts shake their heads at this devotion in wonder. What exactly is it about Star Trek that makes it so popular year after year? Is it the functional realism of the universe, its willingness to express thoughts on controversial problems, or the show's tendency to stir the imagination and make meaningful statements?

Whatever the formula, Star Trek fans of all colors, shapes, ages, and dispositions once rallied to save *Star Trek* from cancellation in 1967 merely through the number of letters written to NBC President Julian Goodman requesting the show not be given a premature burial. Throughout the United States and Canada, thousands of *Star Trek* followers watched the show and came loyally to its rescue.

Nowhere else are the twin forces of Star Trek more evident that at those special occasions where live performances bring the stars and their fans together. Fan conventions serve a critical part in the continuing popularity of Trek. For the Trek actors and actresses, the phenomenon has created vast fan interest in all other non-Star Trek activities in which they participate as well.

Star Trek has given fans the emotional feeling of "belonging" and this is the special glue that really binds together the official and unofficial sides of Star Trek's double nature. Anyone who enjoys Star Trek in any of its entertainment mediums is considered a fan. Those who preserve the artifacts of the Star Trek phenomenon are collectors. Between them both lies the answer as to why Star Trek will be eternally in our thoughts.

How To Use This Book

This handbook has been designed for all types of *Star Trek* and *Star Trek: The Next Generation* collectors, new and old. The format is in encyclopedia-style to allow for easier reading and quick reference. It is a source of information for as many collectibles as was humanly possible to catalogue and which are, for the most part, readily available to the average collector.

In listing the items, the wording on the actual packaging and/or items has been used. For example, some books contain the term, "Star Fleet," in their titles, used as two words; others combine the term into one word, "Starfleet." Item descriptions reflect these varied uses of terminology. In the listings and text, we have tried to differentiate between Star Trek, or Trek, as a genre and the term *Star Trek* as used in naming the television shows or movies. The italic form is used only when referring to the shows or movies (e.g., *Star Trek, ST, Star Trek: The Next Generation, STTNG,* etc.)

Included in this guide is the original **Issue** price for an item, if known. This is important because it allows a collector to see how much an item has escalated in price since its date of manufacture, production, or publishing. The **Fair** and **Mint** price ranges represent merchandise in poor condition up to a pristine mint condition. The prices reflect a fair market value for each. Intermediate conditions fall between the two ranges accordingly.

USE this book before you shop for Trek wares. It will help you to know if the item you want exists.

USE this book to determine if variations of a collectible exist, such as reissues and reprints, which may have different price ranges.

USE this book to note the price ranges and to compare them to what you see out in the Trek marketplace.

USE this book when you go shopping and have the important merchandising details at your fingertips.

USE this book to help catalogue your collection. If you don't know what it is, we do.

Condition

The condition classifications that follow will help collectors match a collectible's appearance to its cost. Originally, the ten-point scale below was derived for comic collectors in the *Comic Book Price Guide* by Robert Overstreet, but the general guidelines for merchandise condition can be applied to Star Trek collectibles.

Pristine Mint — Designates a non-circulated item. Surfaces are flawless. Any pages are white and crisp.

Mint — In new or newsstand condition. Any defects are attributable to a cutting, folding, or stapling process.

Near Mint — Almost perfect. There may be some discoloration. Published materials have a tight spine with clean pages.

Very Fine — Slight wear signs and some creases. Otherwise very clean merchandise.

Fine — Stress lines may appear around sealed edges or along staples, spines, and glue points. There may be minor flaking and discoloration.

Very Good — Staples present may be loose, but there are no tears. Written materials may have browning pages and cover gloss may be absent.

Good — An average used copy or tampered-with piece of merchandise. Has minor creases or tears. With published wares, the spines may be rolled.

Fair — Package or collectible is soiled or has multiple wrinkles and tears. May not have original packaging. A heavily-read copy of a book, magazine, etc.

Poor — A damaged piece of merchandise. Soiled and technically unsuitable for collector purposes.

Coverless — Almost worthless published collectible. The cover alone can be worth more than the text.

Reference Guide

Abbreviations

IDIC = Infinite Diversity in Infinite Combinations
PPC = Paramount Pictures Corporation
SFC = Star Fleet Command
ST = *Star Trek*, the classic television series
STTMP = *Star Trek The Motion Picture*, the first movie
ST II = *Star Trek: The Wrath of Khan*, the second movie

ST III = *Star Trek: The Search for Spock*, the third movie
ST IV = *Star Trek: The Voyage Home*, the fourth movie
ST V = *Star Trek: The Final Frontier*, the fifth movie
STTNG = *Star Trek: The Next Generation*, the new syndicated television series
STTOFC = Star Trek The Official Fan Club
UFP = United Federation of Planets

Classic Cast

William Shatner — plays Captain James T. Kirk
Leonard Nimoy — plays Mr. Spock
DeForest Kelley — plays Dr. Leonard "Bones" McCoy
James Doohan — plays Montgomery "Scotty" Scott
George Takei — plays Lieutenant Sulu

Nichelle Nichols — plays Lieutenant Uhura
Walter Koenig — plays Ensign Pavel Chekov
Majel Barrett — plays Nurse Chapel
Grace Lee Whitney — plays Yeoman Rand

Star Trek: The Next Generation Cast

Patrick Stewart — plays Captain Jean-Luc Picard
Jonathan Frakes — plays Commander William Riker
Brent Spiner — plays Lieutenant Commander Data
Marina Sirtis — plays Counselor Deanna Troi
Denise Crosby — plays Lieutenant Tasha Yar

LeVar Burton — plays Lieutenant Geordi LaForge
Wil Wheaton — plays Ensign Wesley Crusher
Gates McFadden — plays Dr. Beverly Crusher
Michael Dorn — plays Lieutenant Worf

Glossary Of Collectible Terms

Abridged — An interior text which has been altered in some way through deletions or typesetting processes. An abridged text is shorter than an unabridged text.

Amateur Band Recording — Independently manufactured records which usually make their debut as 45 RPM singles and first appear at science fiction conventions.

Annotated Script — The most valuable of Trek scripts. They appear as typed originals containing heavy personal commentaries or annotated notes by actors, directors, and producers. These scripts are more valuable than original scripts of episodes never produced.

Blister pack — A hard, molded plastic cover which is bubbled over a retail item, especially toys. Usually attached to a cardboard backing.

Blurb — The small paragraphs and phrases on the cover of a book intended to stir a reader's interest. They may be nothing more than direct reprints of some inner portion of the manuscript, abridged quotes, or plot summaries.

Book cover jacket — A cardboard or plastic slipcover that fits over children's book and record sets,

9

adult records, books, or even computer software packages.

Brass — An alloy composed of copper and zinc of variable proportions.

Bronze — A copper-based alloy containing variable amounts of tin.

Buttons — Messages laminated with a thin plastic and then crimp-pressed around a metal disk to which a latch clip is attached. Button clips may be either horizontal clasps, safety pin style, or cheaper stick pin varieties. The most common size is the circular pin of 2¼" diameter. However, they range in sizes from 1½" to 6".

Cast recording — Records (singles or LPs) or tapes produced by Trek cast members as commercial endeavors.

Cellophane wrap — A thin, lightweight plastic covering shrink-wrapped over a retail item to protect it from moisture or bending.

Classic Trek — A relatively new term which has appeared since the start of *Star Trek: The Next Generation* in 1988. Anything "classic" refers to its association with the original *Star Trek* series, characters, or cast.

Con — A fan convention.

Cover art — Artwork which appears on a book cover and which usually originates from a commissioned drawing or oil canvas. Once photographed by offset lithography (a process used since 1950) and cropped, the artwork is used as a visual condensation of a book's plot.

Draft — The successive rewrites of an outline as it proceeds through the filming of a TV series or movie.

Episode score — Music specifically designed for *Star Trek* episodes during the 1960s. Most were borrowed from classical and popular compositions, but a few were original music scores written for particular scenes.

Fanzines — Self-published manuscripts by Trek fan clubs and fan enthusiasts, which feature fiction and nonfiction themes. They also include original fan artwork and are a complete literary genre of their own, comprising an elaborate media network of collectors. Also called **Zines**.

Filled — In jewelry, a process where gold or silver metal actually surrounds a center made of a baser metal, as in "gold-filled."

Film clip frame — Individually cut celluloid frames from TV or movie out-takes. These first appeared in 1968 marketed by Star Trek Enterprises and features classic 35mm frames from the *Star Trek* syndicated series. Beginning with *Star Trek The Motion Picture*, these clips were 70mm in size.

Final revision — The alteration of a script outline until it is considered an Incompleted Final.

Funny money — Assorted personality bills with Trek affiliations, spoofing real currency. Of notable importance is the set of uncirculated U.S. tender bills which sported faces of classic Trek characters and which was advertised in *Starlog* magazine.

Gimmick promotions — A sales tactic created by advanced graphics and printing processes. Decorative enhancers such as foil stamping, embossing, cutaways, and sidestep gatefolds are used on paper stock items. The Pocket Star Trek book covers employ these techniques quite often, but they may be found on I.D. badges and buttons as well.

Gold — A precious metal that occurs in prescribed units of fineness (purity) called karats. One karat equals 1/24th part of real gold, 12K = 50%, 14K = 58%, 22K = 92%, and 24K = 100% gold.

Half-sheet — A theater poster, usually sized 22" x 28" or 22¼" x 30".

I.D. badges. — Cardstock calling cards of assorted colors and sizes. They may be slipped into clear plastic name tag holders, or sold separately in sets. Usually 2½" x 3" or 2¾" x 3½".

I.D. card — See **I.D. badges**.

Imprint — A distinguishing name or symbol on the cover or spine of a book that delineates a particular line of books. Pocket Book's newly created *Timescape* editions featuring science fiction books is an example. Not to be confused with a logo.

Incompleted final — This is the last formal layout before a final draft is considered to be a shooting script.

Insert poster — A theater poster with the dimensions of 14" or 36" or 14¼" x 38".

ISBN — Abbreviation for International Standard Book Number. This is the ten-digit code which appears on all commercial texts and which identifies the copyrighted property for inventory purposes.

Lobby card — A set of theater promotion cards depicting scenes and characters from a movie. These are printed on 11" x 14" cardstock panels and were designed to be inserted into plastic pockets inside theaters. Today, poster one-sheets or half-sheets are more commonly used.

Logo — A mascot-type identification placed on the spine or cover of a book. For instance, Pocket Book's wallaby has undergone many changes over the years. Gertrude, as the wallaby was named by designer Frank J. Lieberman (in honor of his mother-in-law) has appeared reading a book, hopping, and was even drawn once by Walt Disney. Reprint editions of Trek novels now sport two different wallaby logos.

embership I.D. — Small cardstock cards indicating fan affiliation. May or may not display a photo in rt relating to an actor's or actress's personal fan ub.

arrative cover — Book covers containing neither otos nor cover art. There is only a bold editorial-yle print with the book title and author's name on e front. It is rarely found in Trek literature.

arrative recording — A behind-the-scenes ex mination into Trek philosophies, biographies, live rformances, and literary recordings by the Trek cast embers reproduced on tape or record.

ext Gen — Anything associated with the *Star Trek: ue Next Generation* series, characters, cast, or its ndom.

ickel — A metallic element allied to iron and cobalt. is used chiefly in alloys and in electroplating.

ne-sheet — A theater poster, usually sized 27½" x ".

riginals — New typewritten scripts often produced bulk (and sometimes by the hundreds for produc- n purposes), which individually are considered one- -a-kind. These scripts carry identifying copy mbers written on their covers as well as special tes of revision. Some original scripts may contain otocopied sections which doesn't effect the sale ice. A first draft original is no more valuable than final original.

arody specials — A comic satire of Star Trek, its aracters, and technology as spoofed through pen d ink cartoons in commercial periodicals.

tch — Clothing novelties sewn onto apparel. The edia motif is of thread design with a heavy cloth cking. Some patches may be nothing more than th cut-outs. They vary in size and shape.

oto glossy — Star Trek glossies began as TV me clips or pre-mounted slides reprinted as 5" x s or 8" x 10"s. They appear as color or black-and-ite photos processed from film footage. They are ually action scenes or character studies.

oto sheet — Photo lithographs produced on slick nd or glossy stock paper products. These first ap- ared in the 1970s when Langley Associates oduced an extensive line of top quality, color sheets turing scenes, planetscapes, and character profiles.

oto still — Developed in the mid-1970s. These e color photo reproductions of Trek scenes printed bond paper with a flat finish. They usually appear wallet-sized photos (2½" x 4½"), photo cards (4" x , or as photo montages (8½" x 11") in prescribed s lacking identifying legends on the reverse.

astic pocket — An envelope-style covering made heavy gauge plastic often seen on role playing ex- nsions.

Plastic sealed — A heavy gauge plastic covering which is not blister-packed.

Plated — In jewelry, a brass, nickel, or silver layer of metal placed electrically over the top of a baser metal.

Prozine — Professional-quality periodicals originating from fan factions. These are slick publications dealing with Trek interests and may be issued monthly, quarterly, or biannually. The word **prozine** originates from professional-style formats with a fanzine background.

Reel — 8mm projector-style films of archival quality much superior to commercial videos in durability and photographic clarity after successive showings.

Reprint — Any subsequent printing of an original first edition manuscript, no matter how delayed. A reprint should contain the same text and essentially the same cover style without a major alteration.

Rhodium — A metal from the platinum family used to prevent corrosion when used in electroplating.

Script copy — Mimeographed or photocopied scripts. Some may bear Paramount Pictures Corporation trademarks. Those produced in the 1960s are worth more than their newer counterparts and the cleaner the better.

Script outline — The beginning format of any TV or movie project that is a written synopsis of a story submitted by a writer to the producer for initial review.

Script partial — These are combination scripts which contain partial dialogues from several different drafts of the same story. An original script partial can be valued the same as a typed original even if the story is fragmented.

Second edition — A reprint of an original first edition. The content of the interior text may differ because of updating or the outside cover has been drastically altered in some way. Usually a second edition manuscript has different cover art, cover photos, or a different ISBN.

Shooting script — A hand-carried movie or TV script kept during filming where changes are constantly being made before it reaches a final draft.

Slide — Individual transparencies reproduced from frame clips or existing photo glossies. Usually mounted on a 2" x 2" cardstock holder designed for use in slide projectors. Those produced by Langley Associates in 1976 are notable photographic memorabilia.

Soundtrack — Original TV and movie score on record or tape. Soundtracks may be issued as volume sets.

Spotlight periodical — Any magazine of commercial status which gives column inches to Star Trek topics from 1970 to the present.

Star Trekkers — The name given to Star Trek fans during 1966-1969. It identified about 20 million fans.

Sterling silver — In jewelry, a metal with a unit of fineness equal to 0.925 real silver.

Sticker — Any peel and stick design featuring a slogan or picture which bonds to a flat surface. This includes bumper stickers and sticker sets.

Symbolic cover — The most common style of book cover among Trek literature. This consists of a single scene artwork drawing on the front and a dramatic blurb on the rear.

Tabloid — Star Trek coverage as it appears in newspapers. Usually newspaper articles in syndicated papers chronicle information and movie reviews, but there have been fan newspapers as well. *Trek Magazine* originally started out as a newspaper and the much-celebrated *Monster Times* was a science fiction fanzine in tabloid format.

Taped interview — Vintage recordings of television interviews given by Trek cast members. Usually available on cassette from small commercial sources.

Theme song anthology — LPs, cassettes, or compact discs which include Trek scores among their numerous space theme collections.

Tradepaper — Oversized softbound book.

Transfer — May be of either the decal or iron-on variety. Decal transfers reproduce a reverse image onto cloth via heat-sensitive dyes. Iron-on transfers attach an original design to a cloth surface with heat bonding glues. Photographic transfers also exist which recreate actual film footage.

Trekkie — This term appeared in 1971 in several professional magazines. The term encompassed Star Trek fandom as one united group. It was derived from the term "groupie" as a few teen tabloids had referred to Trek fans as Star Trek groupies. The word can also trace its origins directly to the greatly successful Star Trek Con of 1972. The pseudonym appeared simultaneously with convention coverage in the *TV Guide*. A Trekkie was a fan who haunted conventions all over the country.

Trekker — Trekkers are generally acknowledged the workers and doers of Star Trek fandom. They organize, promote, and supervise most conventions and clubs. They also feed information and literature to a hungry fandom with private and commercial Trek-related materials. Trekkers may also be personally loyal to the original series since its airing in 1966.

Trekkist — This is a rare term which applies to a person who may follow syndicated Trek on occasion or attend a few conventions, but who isn't actively involved in collecting memorabilia or in the fan movement.

Trekster — This term has been created from the Star Trek of the movies. A Trekster is a fan from the 1980s who enjoys Trek in the theater and returns to see the movies over and over again.

Typographic cover — This is found primarily in nonfiction books. A front cover is composed of editorial print, along with photo inserts. Typographic styles are used to pinpoint well-defined Trek audiences interested in specific nonfiction topics.

Vignette cover — The rarest of Star Trek book covers. This occurs when cover artwork extends from the front of the book to the back, creating one continuous scene.

Vintage periodical — Magazines which appear during the years 1966-1969 and gave media coverage to TV Trek during its initial premiere.

Wax board — In older retail items, this is a distinctive heavy cardboard backing material or box with a waxy surface.

Window box — A clear see-through panel on a box which allows viewing of the interior contents.

Window card — A theater poster, 14⅛" x 22⅛" size or 14⅜" x 24⅛".

Zinc — An element resembling magnesium which is used in making alloys.

Classic Episode Abbreviation Guide

The abbreviated references to specific episodes listed here and used throughout this guide follow in accordance with those developed by Bjo Trimble as they appear in her *Star Trek Concordance* (published by Ballantine Books). These abbreviations are used frequently herein to indicate the classic *Star Trek* episode from which a particular photograph has been taken or when an episode is mentioned.

All Our Yesterdays (AY)

Alternative Factor, The (AF)

Amok Time (AT)

Apple, The (Ap)

Arena (Ar)

Assignment: Earth (AE)

Balance Of Terror (BT)

Bread And Circuses (BC)

By Any Other Name (AON)

Catspaw (Cp)

Changeling, The (Cg)

Charlie X (CX)

And The Children Shall Lead (CL)

City On The Edge Of Forever, The (CEF)

loud Minders, The (Cms)

nscience Of The King, The (CK)

orbomite Maneuver, The (CMn)

ourt-Martial (Cml)

agger Of The Mind (DMd)

ay Of The Dove (Dv)

eadly Years, The (DY)

evil In The Dark, The (DD)

oomsday Machine, The (DMa)

aan Of Troyius (ET)

npath, The (Em)

nemy Within, The (EW)

nterprise Incident, The (EI)

rand Of Mercy (EM)

or The World Is Hollow And I Have Touched The
   Sky (FW)

riday's Child (FC)

alileo Seven, The (GS)

amesters Of Triskelion, The (GT)

nmunity Syndrome, The (IS)

Mudd (IM)

There In Truth No Beauty? (TB)

urney To Babel (JB)

et That Be Your Last Battlefield (LB)

ghts Of Zetar, The (LZ)

an Trap, The (MT)

ark Of Gideon (MG)

enagerie, The (Me)

etamorphosis (Mt)

iri (Mi)

irror, Mirror (MM)

udd's Women (MW)

aked Time, The (NT)

Obsession (Ob)

Omega Glory, The (OG)

Operation: Annihilate! (OA)

Paradise Syndrome, The (PSy)

Patterns Of Force (PF)

Piece Of The Action, A (PA)

Plato's Stepchildren (PSt)

Private Little War, A (PLW)

Requiem For Methuselah (RM)

Return Of The Archons, The (RA)

Return To Tomorrow (RT)

Savage Curtain, The (SC)

Shore Leave (SL)

Space Seed (SS)

Spectre Of The Gun (SGn)

Spock's Brain (SB)

Squire Of Gothos, The (SG)

Taste Of Armageddon, A (TA)

That Which Survives (TWS)

This Side Of Paradise (TSP)

Tholian Web, The (TW)

Tomorrow Is Yesterday (TY)

Trouble With Tribbles, The (TT)

Turnabout Intruder (TI)

Ultimate Computer, The (UC)

Way To Eden, The (WEd)

What Are Little Girls Made Of? (LG)

Where No Man Has Gone Before (WNM)

Whom Gods Destroy (WGD)

Who Mourns For Adonis? (WM)

Wink Of An Eye (WE)

Wolf In The Fold (WF)

THE
COLLECTIBLES

A - E

A

Action Figures and Accessories

Star Trek: The Motion Picture **Action Figures:** Mego Corporation, 1980. *STTMP* vintage 3¾" plastic molded figures with movable hands and legs. These are painted and mounted on a 6" x 9" cardstock backing with a plastiform bubble mount. The front package features cartoon illustrations. The rear shows photos of the characters as they appeared in the movie. Collectors should note that *STTMP* alien figures were primarily released in Europe and are very hard to find in the United States. Any U.S. stock available probably came from Italy.

	Issue	Fair	Mint
(A) #91200/1, Captain Kirk	**2.99**	**20**	**30**
(B) #91200/2, Mr. Spock	**2.99**	**20**	**30**
(C) #91200/3, Decker	**2.99**	**20**	**30**

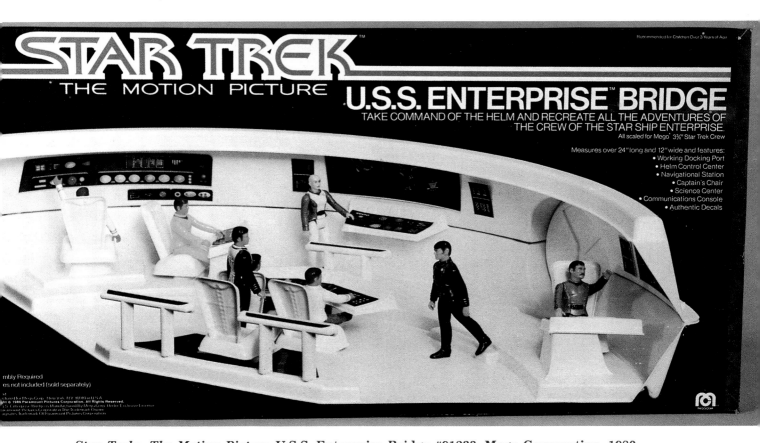

Star Trek: The Motion Picture U.S.S. Enterprise Bridge #91233, Mego Corporation, 1980.

Galoob's *Star Trek: The Next Generation* Action Figures, 1988: Data, Worf, and Yar; along with Galoob's Shuttlecraft Galileo, #5362, 1988.

	Issue	Fair	Mint
(D) #91200/4, Ilia	2.99	10	15
(E) #91200/5, Scotty	2.99	20	30
(F) #91200/6, Dr. McCoy	2.99	20	30
(G) #91200/7, Klingon (with skull ridges)	2.99	10	25
(H) #91200/8, Zaranite alien (split skull with respirator)	2.99	100	150
(I) #91200/9, Betelgeusian (blue-skinned samurai)	2.99	100	200
(J) #91201/1, Acturian (scaled)	2.99	100	150
(K) #91201/2, Meganite (hooded with folds on face)	2.99	100	150
(L) #91201/3, Rigelian (pink-skinned reptilian)	2.99	100	150

Star Trek: The Motion Picture Enterprise Bridge: #91233, Mego Corporation, 1980. Bridge replica play set for the *STTMP* action figures. Contains a 12" x 24" theater with working dock port, helm, navigation console, communication and science stations, and the Captain's chair. Plastic shell snaps together at top and bottom and uses sticker press tabs. The play set becomes very fragile after the applied paper tabs are used and is not designed to be a carrying case. 14" x 28" boxed. **9   100   150**

Star Trek III: The Search for Spock Action Figures: Ertl Company, 1984. *ST III* vintage 3¾" plastic molded figures with posable arms, elbows, knees, and legs. Each figure included individual accessories within a cardstock backing with plastiform bubble wrap. Figures are painted.

➤ #331, Mr. Spock with phaser

	Issue	Fair	Mint
➤ #332, Captain Kirk with communicator			
➤ #333, Scotty with phaser			
➤ #334, Kruge with Klingon dog			
Price for each.	2.95	8	1(

Star Trek: The Next Generation Action Figures #5340, Lewis Galoob toys, 1988. Posable 3¾" action figures from the TV series with moving arms and legs. Each painted figure comes with an accessory and is mounted on a cardstock backing with a plastiform bubble wrap. Most collectible are Yar, Data, and the aliens, because a lower stock run was made. Because Galoob has ceased production of its *STTNG* wares, all these figures are good investments.

	Issue	Fair	Mint
(A) Captain Jean-Luc Picard	2.95	4	5
(B) Commander William Riker	2.95	4	5
(C) Lieutenant Geordi LaForge	2.95	4	5
(D) Lieutenant Worf	2.95	4	5
(E) Lieutenant Commander Data	2.95	15	25

Note: Due to several different production runs of the above figure, assorted complexion anomalies exist. In general, the basic price of any Data figure should be standard because of its relative rarity when compared to the vast numbers of the other *STTNG* figures which were produced. Complexion types include white face, blue face, light green face, light skin with gold speckles, dark face with gold speckles, and dark tan face.

| (F) Lieutenant Tasha Yar | 2.95 | 15 | 20 |
| (G) Antican (voracious alien enemy) | 2.95 | 25 | 35 |

ore Galoob *STTNG* Action Figures: Antican, Selay, Ferengi, and Q; plus Galoob's Ferengi Fighter, #5362, 1988.

	Issue	Fair	Mint
I) Selay (snake-like alien enemy)			
	2.95	25	35
) Q (powerful alien enemy)	2.95	40	55
) Ferengi (alien enemy of the Federation)			
	2.95	40	55

tar Trek: The Next Generation Action
dioramas: #5360, Lewis Galoob Toys. Set of three
ardstock punch-and-build dioramas, which were
ever produced by Galoob despite heavy promotion to
ie contrary. All three sets were designed for connec-
on to one another to form one large diorama. They
re listed here as curiosities.

- U.S.S. Enterprise Starship Bridge, detachable battle section.
- U.S.S. Enterprise Transporter Room, action figures
  can beam down from transporter.
- U.S.S. Enterprise Starship Alien Planet, works as
  stand for all three action dioramas.

rice for each.	5.95	N/A	N/A

tar Trek: The Next Generation Ferengi
'ighter: #5362, Lewis Galoob Toys, 1988. Plastic 9"
essel designed for play with *STTNG* alien figures.
eatures fold-up phaser weapons, opening canopy,
'ing tip phaser cannons, and seats two figures.

	11.95	25	35

	Issue	Fair	Mint

Star Trek: The Next Generation Shuttlecraft
Galileo: #5362, Lewis Galoob Toys, 1988. Plastic 9"
vessel designed for play with Enterprise crew figures.
Features gull-wing hatches, pop-up sensor unit, slide-
out phaser cannon, and carries six action figures.

	11.95	20	30

Star Trek: The Next Generation U.S.S.
Enterprise Starship Action Play Set: #5368,
Lewis Galoob Toys, 1988. This was Galoob's most
desired, but never produced, toy for use with the
STTNG action figures. This was a large plastic toy
in the shape of the Enterprise with open bridge area.
Saucer section with bridge interior has viewing
screen, navigator, and helmsman stations with swivel-
ing chairs and swing-out consoles, plus sliding doors
to the turbolift and transporter room. The Captain,
Commander, and Counselor stations include consoles
that lift to reveal circuits and seats that slide out-
wards. The battle section of the play set, which includes transporter and shuttlecraft landing bay
interiors, has lever-activated rotating transporter
platform to "beam away" figures. There is also a
removable transporter console, slide-out landing bay
pads, and a landing area for the Shuttlecraft Galileo
vehicle. Approximately 18" long.

	49.99	N/A	N/A

Action Figure Sets

tar Trek Classic Action Figures: Hamilton Gifts
Enesco), 1991. Lifelike 11½"-high vinyl figures of

Kirk and Spock painted in full color and standing on

insignia-shaped bases.	15	10	15

	Issue	Fair	Mint
Price for each figure.	3.95	4	5
Price for complete set.	—	45	50

Star Trek **Classic Figures:** Hamilton Gifts (Enesco), 1991. Set of thirteen 4¼" figures similar to the above set. Vinyl, with insignia bases on the crew figures and natural terrain bases for the alien figures.

➤ Kirk
➤ Spock
➤ McCoy
➤ Sulu
➤ Scotty
➤ Chekov
➤ Uhura
➤ Klingon
➤ Mugato
➤ Gorn
➤ Andorian
➤ Tellarite
➤ Talosion

Star Trek V: The Final Frontier **Figures:** #5350 Lewis Galoob Toys, 1989. Set of five 8"-high limited edition, plastic figures featuring characters from *ST V* in action poses. Each figure comes with a deluxe display base and an illustrated backdrop scene. Officially licensed by Paramount, these figures are also individually numbered as collector items. However, fans should note that there is a discrepancy between issue prices offered by a limited group of retail outlets and most independent distributors, which has played havoc with their collectible value. The figures come in a 9½" x 10½" x 5" box with a cellophane window.

➤ Captain James T. Kirk with phaser drawn, in front of rock outcropping with moon.
➤ Mr. Spock with tricorder, in front of desert landscape.

Star Trek V: The Final Frontier Action Figure Set #5350, Lewis Galoob Toys, 1989.

	Issue	Fair	Mint

➤ Dr. Leonard "Bones" McCoy with communicator, in front of fortress wall.

➤ Sybok, leader of the Nimbus III, in front of fortress archway.

➤ Klaa, Klingon captain, with disruptor pistol drawn and rock outcroppings in background.

Each (reduced price through retail outlets).

	19.95	30	40

Each (through distributors).

	29.95	30	40

Activity Pads

Star Trek Play Pad: Cliveden Press, Finland, 1985. Unusual foreign collectible. This is a tape-bound activity pad for kids with theme games, coloring pages, etc. Paper is newsprint stock. 5⅞" x 9⅛".

	—	5	8

***Star Trek III: The Search for Spock* More Movie Trivia Play Pad:** A Magic Answer Book. See **Books**.

***Star Trek III: The Search for Spock* Trivia Play Pad:** A Magic Answer Book. See **Books**.

Address Books

Star Trek Address and Telephone Book: Reed Productions, 1983. Checkbook-sized A-Z address book with special telephone number and area code sections. Includes second pocket for slipping in notes and papers. Clear vinyl plastic cover has black and white photo insert from TV, showing Scotty, Chekov, McCoy, Chapel, Uhura, Sulu, and Spock standing around Kirk in command chair. 3½" x 6½".

	4.99	5	6

Star Trek Address Book / Checkbook Covers: See **Checkbook Covers**.

***Star Trek: The Next Generation* Address Book:** ReedProductions, 1991. Checkbook-sized A-Z book with additional telephone number and area code sec-

The unusual Star Trek Play Pad by Cliveden Press, 1985.

	Issue	Fair	Mint

tions. Includes pockets for notes and papers. Clear plastic slipcover shows color photo of *STTNG* cast on the bridge: Wesley, Pulaski, Riker, Worf, Picard, LaForge, Troi, and Data. 3½" x 6½".

	4.49	4	5

Address Labels

Star Trek Address Labels: T-K Graphics, 1984. Customized, self-adhesive labels with assorted Trek designs and slogans. These have four lines to personalize them. Sets include four packs with twenty stickers to a pack. 1" x 2¾".

➤ Beam me up Scotty. This place has no intelligent life.

➤ U.F.P. Janus head emblem

➤ U.F.P. pennant design

➤ U.S.S. Enterprise Command insignia

➤ U.S.S. Enterprise, ship schematic style

➤ U.S.S. Enterprise, ship silhouette

Price for each set.

	4	4	5

Star Fleet Command Intelligence Division: T-K Graphics, 1988. New style of self-adhesive and personalized label. Come as four packs with twenty stickers per pack. 1" x 2¾".

	4	4	5

Classic *Star Trek* Address and Telephone Book; *Star Trek: The Next Generation* Address Book, both by ReedProductions, 1983 and 1991.

Animation Cels

Animation celluloids or cels are original, hand-painted drawings made on celluloid/acetate film. They are designed to be overlaid on art board mattes containing the background scenes and are the end product of animated drawings and storyboards used in the creation of animated films and cartoons. This is the technique used by Filmation Studios in producing the Star Trek animated TV series.

While animated drawings, art boards, storyboards, and cels are each collectible in their own right, cels are by far the most desirable collectible of all the different art mediums necessary to produce a polished animated film. Prices for a cel will vary according to its general availability (whether it has been reproduced for distribution in great quantity by laser techniques or is a limited hand-painted original). Also, as is true for all works of art, the marketability

of any particular cel depends upon its unique esthetic appeal. Animated cels can attain high values over time. One oddity of this collectible genre is the fact that cel reproductions offered with certificates and registration numbers often sell for far more than original works of hand-painted celluloid art. Most likely this phenomenon is due to the fact that cels with certificates confirm bona fide collectible authenticity, whereas celluloids of unmarked identity are hard to catalogue and authenticate.

Animation Cels — Original Releases: An assortment of original cels have been offered through private collectors and film houses. Generally, these are matted works measuring 11" x 14" to 12" x 16" with the size of the hand-painted image overlay being anywhere from a miniature 6" x 5" background stud to a close-up character portrait that fills the ce

Limited edition reproduction cel (Tuttle & Bailey #ST-16, "Beyond the Farthest Star").

Issue Fair Mint

Prices for such untitled, un-certificated works of original art ranged from $18 to $30 at issue. Present value: — **200 300**

Note: Glass frames can add $50 or more to the price of individual mounted cels. Collectors should remember this is a finishing cost which does not increase the value of the actual cel.

Animated Cel Reproductions: Reproductions of animated art on clear acetate film. These are **copies** of the original drawings made by the studio animators. The cels listed here are those that have been authorized and advertised for distribution. Many unadvertised cels exist.

Limited Edition Filmation Studios Reproduction Cels: Tuttle & Bailey Galleries, Ltd., distributor, 1977. High quality reproductions of original hand-painted cels. Paintings are on transparent celluloid and individual cels are overlaid on colorful background mattes, mounted in a holder. Each bears a studio seal and/or limited edition issue number. Mat size is 14" x 18". Prices shown below are for the limited edition, sealed and numbered cels. Cels with the studio seal only were $5 less (or $15) at the time of issue.

➤ #ST-00, title scene. Small Enterprise with TV title logo credit showing.

➤ #ST-1A, the crew of the Enterprise. Spock with a camera and six crew members.

➤ #ST-4, the Enterprise escapes from a fiery exploding planet in the background.

➤ #ST-5, "Yesteryear." Spock pointing finger at winged Aurelian named Aleek-Om.

Original hand-painted animation cel ("Albatross," from Filmation Studios).

Issue   Fair   Mi

➤ #ST-6, "More Tribbles, More Troubles." Bridge scene with tribbles from the cartoon episode.

➤ #ST-8, the Enterprise encounters a Klingon ship with green planet in the background.

➤ #ST-9, "The Ambergris Element." Sursnake (a red serpent creature) and green aliens called Aquans.

➤ #ST-11, "Jihad." Composite of Aliens. Crew members with one female crew member.

➤ #ST-12, "Yesteryear." Spock as a boy atop L'-Chaya. Young Spock atop pet Sehlat faces a Vulcan mountain cat.

➤ #ST-14, "The Time Trap." Enterprise in a space ship graveyard in space.

➤ #ST-15, the Enterprise and the Aqua (underwater) shuttle as it leaves the hangar bay.

➤ #ST-16, "Beyond the Farthest Star." Enterpris entrapped by a giant pod-like ship.

➤ #ST-20, Kukulkan and the Enterprise as the sta ship faces off the Aztec serpent-ship.

➤ #ST-22, "Time Warp." Blue, red, and yello Enterprise going through a black hole.

➤ #ST-23, about to battle a Klingon, the Enterpri in deep dive on left with enemy on right, gree planet.

➤ #ST-24, Star Trek's famous scene of Enterprise i front of a large red planet.

➤ #ST-25, "The Counterclock Incident." Enterpri from rear approaching alien ship and a purp planet.

Price for each.   **20   300   40**

Issue   Fair   Mint

Note: In November 1977 selected issues of the above cels were advertised with a cardstock insert between pages 84 and 85 in Blish's paperback novel *Star Trek 12.* Cels 1A, 4, 5, 8, 9, 12, 14, 15, 16, and 20 were available through mail order for $21.50.

Lincoln Enterprises Reproductions:

A) Crew Portraits, 1976. Ten standing poses including Kirk, Spock, McCoy, Scotty, Uhura, Sulu, Chapel, Lt. M'Hress, Lt. Arex, and the Enterprise. Cels are 1" x 8", unmounted.   **4   7   10**

B) Enterprise, 1979. Overlay of the TV starship designed to mount over any backdrop of your own creation. Measures 10" x 14". Unmounted.
                    2.50   7   10

Royal Animation Studios Reproductions: STTOFC, 1990. Recently a large selection of laser reproductions made from the original cels used to produce the series have again become available. Individual cels may or may not come with full-color Xerox backgrounds included.

➤ #1 Head-to-waist shot of Spock and Kirk. No backing.

➤ #2 Slanted head-to-waist view of McCoy.

➤ #3 Close-up front view of running Spock.

➤ #4 Standing Scotty with hieroglyphics.

➤ #5 Head-to-waist shots of McCoy and Kirk facing each other with a computer bank backdrop.

➤ #6 Head-to-waist shot of Spock, bust of Kirk on transporter.

➤ #7 Close-up of Lt. Arex, head-to-waist shot of Scotty.

Issue   Fair   Mint

➤ #8 Helmeted alien and crewman over computer.

➤ #9 Head-to-waist shot of Kirk holding communicator.

➤ #10 Head-to-waist shot of Sulu, no backing.

➤ #11 Close-up front view of Sulu with hand on chin.

➤ #12 Close-up of Scotty with hand on chin.

➤ #13 Head-to-waist shots of Kirk and McCoy with hypodermic.

➤ #14 Head-to-waist shot of Spock with alien machine.

➤ #15 Bust close-up of Spock over telescopes.

➤ #16 Bust shot of McCoy bisected by railings.

➤ #17 Close-up front view of running Kirk.

➤ #18 Close-up of Kirk.

➤ #19 Action scene, Spock held by reptilians.

➤ #20 Close-up of Chapel and Kirk's face.

➤ #21 Distant standing Kirk, no backing.

➤ #22 Head-to-waist shot of Kirk with standing Spock.

➤ #23 Head-to-waist shot of Scotty on the bridge.

➤ #24 Head-to-waist shot of Kirk with head of Spock.

Price for each.   **250   225   260**

Note: In 1989 the above cel #24 was offered through Paramount Special Effects (PSE) for the price of $150, advertised as limited to 1,000 reproductions. A certificate of authenticity was included. Also in 1989 through PSE, cels #14 and #22 were offered as original hand-painted cels for $250.

Animation Drawings

Animation drawings are the original drawings from which animation cels are made. It follows that there are as many drawings as there were eventually hand-painted celluloids used during the production of the *Star Trek* animated series, although far fewer drawings have surfaced in the secondary collectibles market. Drawings are on paperboard stock and like the cels, they feature close-ups and action poses of the animated characters, aliens, and machines that move. Prices range: **—   30   50**

Art Prints

This section includes artwork that is generally available through catalogue and retail sales and the prices relate to packaged reproductions that are part of a portfolio set. Art prints are usually reproduced on paper or cardstock in large volume runs. The price ranges below do not reflect values of specially commissioned works or "one-of-a-kind" artist originals. Listings are alphabetized by portfolio titles. For other sections pertaining to Star Trek art see **Animation**

Drawings, **Fanzines**, and **Wall Hangings**.

Creation Salutes Star Trek: Artist Chuck Frazier, Creation Con, distributor, 1989. Original cast portraits, 11" x 14½". Includes Kirk, Spock, McCoy, Scotty, Uhura, Sulu, and Chapel. Originally sold loose, later in paper folder.   **—   8   12**

Enterprise Evolution Packet: #P2192, Lincoln Enterprises, 1976. Full-color art rendering of all the various ship designs bearing the name of "Enterprise"

	Issue	*Fair*	*Mint*

from the Star Trek archives. Twelve drawings in set, 11" x 17". **4.95 5 7**

Enterprise Print: Artist Gerald W. Roundtree, Star Trek The Official Fan Club, 1986. 20th Anniversary, limited edition print. Full-color rendition of the movie Enterprise over planetscape. 3,500 signed and numbered. 11" x 17". **15 18 20**

Enterprise With Tribbles: T-K Graphics, 1988. Cardstock print with gold-colored oval picture of rearward starship spewing forth a rocket trail of tribbles. Header reads "Tribble Breeding is a Hairy Experience." Format 8½" x 11". **1 2 3**

Kirk / "Master and Mistress": Solar Winds, 1988. Single-color print showing three-quarter figure in SFC uniform with Enterprise and starfield backdrop. 11" x 14".

(A) Plain **5 5 7**
(B) Matted **15 15 18**

Kirk Portrait: Solar Winds, 1988. Black and white bust portrait, 8" x 10".

(A) Plain. **5 5 7**
(B) Matted. **15 15 17**

"Montage" Portrait Series: Solar Winds, 1988. Eight color prints in the series. Montage format features a large central figure surrounded by that same character in assorted poses from the classic series through the *ST IV* movie. A starfield is used as a common backdrop. Includes Kirk, Spock, Sarek, McCoy, Chekov, Scotty, Uhura, and Sulu. 11" x 14" matted. **30 30 35**

Sarek / "The Ambassador": Solar Winds, 1988. Single-color print, 11" x 14". Three-quarter figure in formal Vulcan robes from Trek movies with Star Fleet wall shield emblem as backdrop.

(A) Plain **5 5 7**
(B) Matted **15 15 17**

Sarek Portrait: Solar Winds, 1988. Black and white bust portrait, 8" x 10".

(A) Plain **5 5 7**
(B) Matted **15 15 17**

Seven Star Portfolio: Kelly Freas, 1976. Seven specially commissioned paintings reproduced in full color on 12½" x 19" heavy textured, white paper.

Note: The original paintings were on tour with the Strekcons during 1976-1977. Later, this portfolio of artwork was reprinted in book format as the small press title *Officers of the Bridge*.

➤ S-1, Kirk against star map.
➤ S-2, Spock in environsuit at transporter controls.
➤ S-3, Scotty in kilt, wearing a mustache.

	Issue	*Fair*	*Min*

➤ S-4, McCoy smiling.
➤ S-5, Sulu without shirt and with fencing foil.
➤ S-6, Uhura sitting at communications station.
➤ S-7, Chekov against starfield.

(A) Individual print, unsigned. **1.50 2**
(B) Individual print, signed by Freas. **3 4**
(C) Set of seven, unsigned. **9.95 12 2**
(D) Set of seven, signed. **19.95 25 3**

Spock Portrait: Solar Winds, 1988. Single-colo prints, 11" x 14".

➤ "Future From the Past." Spock in *ST IV* uniform with whales George and Gracie swimming behin him. Oval.
➤ "Legends." Fantasyscape with Spock and unicorn against sunset on planet Vulcan.

(A) Plain **5 5**
(B) Matted **15 15 1**

Star Trek — A Portfolio: Artist Jack Abel, 197(Set of seven black and white pencil drawings on gloss paper. 8½" x 11" in pocket folder. Includes Kirk Spock, McCoy, Scotty, Uhura, Sulu, and Chapel. **2 15 2(**

Star Trek Art Cards: Artist Gail Bennet, 1983 Photo paper reprints of color portrait artwork reproduced in 4" x 6" enlargements. Feature classi Trek character busts, sold individually.

➤ Kirk
➤ Spock
➤ McCoy
➤ Scotty
➤ Sulu
➤ Chekov
➤ Uhura

Price for each. **1.25 1 ?**
Price for set of seven. **10 7 1?**

Star Trek Crew — Future Fantasy: Artist Ker Barr, Cousins Publishing, 1977. Full-color drawing on coated artist's board. Wispy montage of Kirk i foreground holding phaser and communicator with Spock, McCoy, Sulu, Uhura, and Scotty in back ground. Enterprise above firing phasers an planetscape below. Mailed flat, 11" x 14" art boarc format.

Note: This drawing was also released as a 20" x 28 poster. **1.50 10 15**

Star Trek Folio: #P2140, artist Doug Little, Lincoln Enterprises, 1983. Eleven 11" x 14" color portraits featuring *STTMP* stars: Nimoy, Kelley, Doohan Takei, Nichols, Majel Barrett-Roddenberry, Mark Lenard (as a Klingon), Persis Khambatta (Ilia)

	Issue	Fair	Mint

Stephen Collins (Decker), and *ST II* Kirstie Alley (Saavik). **9.95 10 15**

Star Trek Humorous Cards: Vision Aeries, 1988. Humorous art cards in 5½" x 8½" format from original artwork.

➤ #7PSSC008, "Gorn in the U.S.A." — clever Gorn posed as the "Boss," Bruce Springsteen, with guitar and American flag backdrop. Green drawing on white paperstock.

➤ #07PSC009, "Spock Around the Clock" — clock faceplate with Spock heads poised at 12, 3, 6, and 9 o'clock positions. Blue drawing on white paper stock.

➤ #07PSC010, "Toupee Or Not Toupee. That is the Question. To Baldly Go Where No Man Has Gone

Before." Yes, that's right. Profile of Picard holding hairpiece.

Price for each. **1.25 2 3**

Star Trek Portfolios: Gary Hawfitch, 1974. Black and white portrait studies of the Trek characters. Pen and ink on heavy paper. Sets packaged in 9" x 12" heavy paper envelope with 8½" x 11" prints. Sets are captioned.

(A) Set I. "THE STARS OF STAR TREK" with black and white portrait of the Enterprise on the envelope. Includes bust portraits of Captain Kirk, Mr. Spock, Dr. McCoy, Scotty, Sulu, Uhura, Chekov, Nurse Chapel, and Yeoman Rand. **12 20 25**

(B) Set II. "THE STARS OF STAR TREK SET II ALIENS" with portrait of Klingon Battle Cruiser on

Star Trek Folio art print set: Uhura and Saavik, Doug Little, 1983.

27

	Issue	*Fair*	*Mint*

envelope. Includes Salt Monster (MT), alien from (Em), T'Pring (AT), Amanda and Sarek (JB), Talosian (Me), Gorn (Ar), Andorian Ambassador Shras (JB), female Romulan commander (EI), and Klingon Kor (EM). Set of ten prints. **6.50   20   25**

Star Trek Portraits: Star Trek/Lincoln Enterprises.

(A) Artist Criss, 1968. Art folio containing nine black and white prints from charcoal artworks. Head portraits of Kirk, Spock, McCoy, Scotty, Uhura, Sulu, Chekov, Nurse Chapel, and Gene Roddenberry. Ready to frame, medium-weight paper, 8½" x 11". The Spock portrait in this set appeared in *Sixteen* magazine in 1967. **2   15   20**

(B) #2141, Artist Probert, 1970. Art folio with eight color prints from oil paintings. Includes bust portraits

Star Trek Portfolios art print set, Gary Hawfitch, 1974.

of TV Kirk, Spock, McCoy, Uhura, Chekov, an Chapel. Thin glossy paper stock, 8½" x 11".

3.50   8   1

(C) #2200. This set of eight prints, same as (I above, was re-released by Lincoln Enterprises in 198 with the addition of a special print of the starsh Enterprise. **3.95   10   1**

Star Trek Ships: M-5 Productions, 1974. Collectio of glossy prints from original drawing and photo over lays. Set of 30 prints in either art or photo style were sold in assorted formats as individual prints. In cluded renderings of the Enterprise, the Klingon Ba tle Cruiser, and the Romulan Bird of Prey fror different perspectives as seen on classic Trek. Thes works were untitled.

(A) 3½" x 5"	1	3
(B) 5" x 7"	3	4
(C) 8" x 10"	5	6

Star Trek Spaceship Folder: #2190, Lincol Enterprises, 1976. Full-color art prints of the si spaceships used in Star Trek classic and animate series. Includes the Federation Grain Cargo Shi Klingon Battle Cruiser "Devisor," Romulan Raide (Bird of Prey), alien vessel from cartoon episod "Beyond the Farthest Star," Galileo Shuttlecraft, an the Enterprise. Format is 12" x 12". Set of six.

3   4

Star Trek Studies: Artist Bruce Burr, Visio Aeries, 1988. Black and white pen and ink studie Limited edition art prints are studies of the Star Tre novels and the movies. Large 12" x 15½" size.

➢ #06ART001, Kal'th, Klingon warrior
➢ #06ART002, Valkris, female Klingon from *STTM.*
➢ #06ART003, Mhre'karth
➢ #06ART004, Korth
➢ #06ART005, Sulu reclining
➢ #06ART006, Salek from the novel *Strangers Fror the Sky*

(A) Individual prints, unsigned	15	15	1
(B) Individual prints, signed	25	25	3
(C) Set of six, unsigned	80	80	9
(D) Set of six, signed	135	130	13

Star Trek — "Teddy Bears in Space": Sola Winds, 1988. Humorous prints from black and whit pen and ink drawings focusing on cross-over bear an Trek enthusiasts. Format is 8" x 10" with title works.

➢ #TS1, "Our Hero" — TV Spock on bridge sur rounded by autograph-seeking teddy bears.

	Issue	Fair	Mint

#TS2, "Beyond Antares" — Uhura in a group of musical teddy bears.

#TS3, "Made in Moscow" — dancing Russian bears accompanied on the balalaika by Chekov.

#TS4, "Edinburgh Revue" — Scotty with bears in kilts and claymores.

#TS5, "Swordplay" — Sulu with sword surrounded by bears with same.

#TS6, "For This I Went to Med School" — Dr. McCoy sewing up a toy bear, various Teddies looking on.

#TS7, "Space — The Final Frontier" — Captain Kirk with Teddies wearing naval uniforms from throughout the ages.

	Issue	Fair	Mint
) Plain print	**5**	**5**	**7**
) Matted	**15**	**15**	**17**

ar Trek Universe: Artist Rivoche, Destination nterprises, Canada, 1976. Special art portfolio featuring nine black and white prints with 2" white frame borders. Studies are detailed technical drawings of vessels and planetscapes, plus portraits. Titles appear along the bottom. 11" x 14" packaged in a clasp envelope with a portion of the "Nova Rescue" illustrated.

➤ "Tholian Web" — Enterprise in energy field.

➤ "Stratos City" — the cloud city from Cms episode.

➤ "Amok Time" — portrait of Spock.

➤ "First Contact" — early style Enterprise.

➤ "Starship Command" — Kirk with UFP banner.

➤ "Where No Man Has Gone Before."

➤ "Doomsday Machine" — the planet eating weapon.

➤ "Nova Rescue" — front view of the Enterprise.

➤ "Aftermath" — downed Klingon Battle Cruiser on moonscape.

	Issue	Fair	Mint
Set of nine prints.	**5**	**25**	**35**

udio Cassettes

cademy Awards: Startone Recordings, New York, 80. Excerpts of William Shatner and Persis Khamtta (Ilia), plus information on the nomination of *TMP* in three award categories. Eleven minutes.

	Issue	Fair	Mint
	3	**3**	**5**

ll Talks: Startone Recordings, 1983. A collection talk show interviews with William Shatner.

) Number 1, 1977-1983, 183 minutes. Includes:

vo interviews from *Mike Douglas*, 1977
1e *Tonight Show*, 1980
1e *Merv Griffin*, 1980
1e *Toni Tenille*, 1980
1e *Over Easy*, 1980
vo *John Davidson*, 1981
1e *Hour Magazine*, 1981
vo *Tonight Show*, 1982
1e *Good Morning America*, 1982
1e *Merv Griffin*, 1982
1e *Madame's Place*, 1982
1e *Merv Griffin*, 1983

so contains ads for Commodore, Kerosun, the movie *siting Hours*, and *ST II*.

	Issue	Fair	Mint
	10	**10**	**15**

) Number 2, 1982-1983, 81 minutes. Includes:

1e *Good Morning America*, 1982
vo *Tonight Show*, 1982
1e *Merv Griffin*, 1982
1e *Madame's Place*, 1982
1e *Merv Griffin*, 1983

so contains ads for Commodore, Kerosun, *Visiting* ours, and *ST II*.

	Issue	Fair	Mint
	6.50	**7**	**10**

Contamination: #0-671-74045-8, Simon & Schuster Audioworks, 1991. Dramatic reading of the novel written by John Vornholt, with enhanced sound effects and original TV theme music. Two cassettes, 180 minutes.

	Issue	Fair	Mint
	10.95	**11**	**12**

Enterprise: The First Adventure: #0-671-62951-4, Simon & Schuster Audioworks, 1988. Dramatic reading of the novel written by Vonda N. McIntyre. Includes enhanced sound effects and original TV series theme music. The abridged novel is read by Leonard Nimoy and George Takei. One cassette, 90 minutes.

	Issue	Fair	Mint
	9.95	**10**	**12**

Entropy Effect: #0-671-66864-1, Simon & Schuster Audioworks, 1988. Abridged version of the novel written by Vonda N. McIntyre. Contains enhanced sound effects and original TV theme music. Read by Leonard Nimoy and George Takei. One cassette, 90 minutes.

	Issue	Fair	Mint
	9.95	**10**	**12**

Final Frontier: #0-671-67016-6, Simon and Schuster Audioworks, 1989. Dramatic reading of the Pocket Books novel written by Diane Carey, with enhanced sound effects and original TV theme music. Read by Leonard Nimoy and James Doohan. One cassette, 90 minutes.

	Issue	Fair	Mint
	9.95	**10**	**12**

Genesis Project: #101, Sonic Atmo Spheres. This cassette contains new and longer versions of the original *ST II* and *ST III* soundtracks which are composed and performed by Craig Huxley.

	Issue	Fair	Mint
	10.95	**10**	**15**

Issue Fair Mint

Golden Throats: #70187, The Great Celebrity Sing-Off, Rhino Release, 1988. An assortment of celebrity songs which include William Shatner and Leonard Nimoy. Shatner sings "Lucy In The Sky With Diamonds" and "Mister Tambourine Man." Nimoy sings "Proud Mary" and "If I Had A Hammer."

9.95 10 12

Greatest Sci-Fi Hits: Crescendo Records, 1985. A collection of famous science fiction themes played by Neil Norman and His Cosmic Orchestra.
(A) Volume I, GNPS 2138, contains sixteen themes including the music from the classic *Star Trek*.

9.50 10 12

(B) Volume II, GNPS 2133, contains sixteen movie themes including the music from the score of *STTMP*.

9.50 10 12

Green Hills of Earth: #CP 1526, Caedmon Records, 1979. The Robert Heinlein story as read by Leonard Nimoy. Boxed with futuristic artwork cover featuring spaceman and alien planetscape. One cassette, 45 minutes.

8 8 12

Gulliver's Fugitives: #0-671-72319-7, Simon & Schuster Audioworks, 1990. Dramatic reading of the novel written by Keith Sharee, as read by Jonathan Frakes. Contains enhanced sound effects and original *Star Trek* score. One cassette, 90 minutes.

Halley's Comet: Once In A Lifetime: #S1788, Caedmon Records, Geodesium, 1986. Original music and sound effects, plus notes by Dr. William Gutsch, Chairman of the American Museum — Hayden Planetarium. History and diagrams on viewing the comet. Narrated by Leonard Nimoy. One cassette, 45 minutes.

7.95 8 10

Illustrated Man: #CP 1479, Caedmon Records, 1979. Stories from the novel written by Ray Bradbury, as read by Leonard Nimoy. Includes "Illustrated Man," "The Veldt," and "Marionettes, Inc." Box has futuristic alien artwork cover. One cassette, 46 minutes.

8 8 12

Inside Star Trek: Startone Recordings, 1976. This tape contains the same information as is on the LP by Columbia Records. Gene Roddenberry discusses various aspects of Star Trek and science fiction. One cassette, 56 minutes.

4.75 5 8

John Davidson: Startone Recordings, 1982. The entire original cast of *ST II*, plus Bibi Besch (Dr. Carol Marcus), are assembled in a tribute to the new picture. One cassette, 42 minutes.

4 4 8

The Kobayashi Maru: #0-671-70895-3, Simon & Schuster Audioworks, 1990. Dramatic reading of the Pocket novel written by Julia Ecklar, with enhanced

Issue Fair Mint

sound effects and original TV music. Read by James Doohan. One cassette, 90 minutes.

9.95 10 12

Leonard Nimoy Micro-Cassette: Apex DT 2777 Dot Records, circa 1970s. Mini preview of Nimoy's first album on a micro-cassette. Includes four songs, "Theme from *Star Trek*," "Visit To A Sad Planet," "Highly Illogical," and "The Ballad Of Bilbo Baggins." Attached to 5" x 8½" cardstock backing with blister wrap. One cassette.

11.98 12 15

Leonard Nimoy Presents Mr. Spock's Music From Outer Space: Starsounds, 1983. Audio-cassette of the 1968 classic album of music and narratives. Stereo, one cassette, 23 minutes.

8 8 10

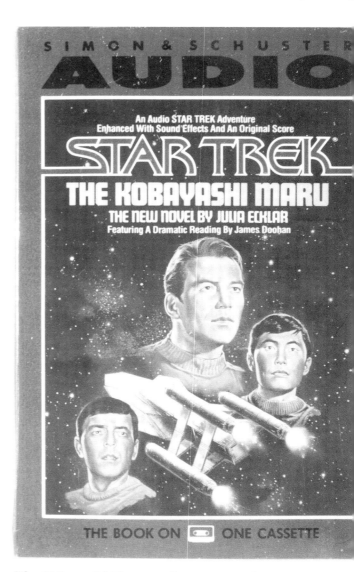

The Kobayashi Maru audio cassette, Simon & Schuster Audioworks, 1990.

Star Trek V: The Final Frontier audio cassette; Leonard Nimoy Micro-Cassette; *TekWar* audio cassette.

	Issue	Fair	Mint

.onard Nimoy Special: #44, Star Tech, 1988. .moy talks about his favorite episode and elements the ST series, *STTMP*, and *ST II*. Also includes e complete "Space Seed" episode.

8 8 10

.onard Talks: Startone Recordings, 1983. A col-ction of talk show interviews with Nimoy.

) Number 1, 1976-1982, 92 minutes. Includes:

.ke Douglas, 1976

.t Hero Sandwich, 1980

.rv Griffin, 1980

.ke Douglas, 1980

.hn Davidson, 1981

.ni Tenille, 1981

.tertainment Tonight, 1982

.day, 1982

.od Morning America, 1982

.so contains ads for *ST II* and Magnavox, 1982.

7.25 7 10

) Number 2, 1982 recordings, 16 minutes, shorter .pe with more recent shows. **3.50 3 6**

.ghts, Camera, Action — *ST III* Special: #46, .ar Tech, 1988. Nimoy hosts and talks about *ST III*.

Includes interview with George Takei and *Starlog* editor Howard Zimmerman, plus some non-Trek. One cassette, 60 minutes. **5 5 7**

Lost Years: #0-671-68632-1, Simon & Schuster Audioworks, 1989. Dramatic reading of the novel by J. M. Dillard with enhanced sound effects and original TV music theme. Read by James Doohan. Two cassettes, 180 minutes. **14.95 15 17**

Man Who Trained Meteors: #C627, Peter Pan Records, 1979. Four exciting stories for children which include "Man Who Trained Meteors," "Robot Masters," "Dinosaur Planet," and "Human Factor." Cassette comes blister-packed on a 7" x 9" cardstock back. Package has a blue header with the same Kirk, Spock, and McCoy *STTMP* bridge scene as the #PR26 *Crier In Emptiness* book and record set.

2.99 10 15

Martian Chronicles: #CP 1466, Caedmon Records, 1979. Single cassette narration of Ray Bradbury's classic sci-fi story. Also includes "There Will Come Soft Rains" and "Usher II." Boxed. Dolby stereo, 49 minutes. **8.98 10 15**

31

	Issue	Fair	Mint

Merv Griffin: Startone Recordings, 1982. A salute to *ST II*. Includes guests Shatner, Nimoy, Kelley, and Bibi Besch. One cassette, 45 minutes.
　4　4　6

Midday Live: Startone Recordings, 1979. William Shatner reveals his thoughts on *Star Trek*, Kirk, and more, plus an in-depth discussion of *STTMP*. One cassette, 35 minutes.
　4　4　6

Music From Return of the Jedi and Other Space Hits: #79065, Odyssey Orchestra, 1983. Sine Qua Non production which includes the *Star Trek* TV theme among its collection of hits. One cassette.
　4.75　5　7

Mysterious Golem: Tara Publications, 1976. Leonard Nimoy reads the story that inspired the writing of *Frankenstein*. A supernatural creature is created with the secrets of the Kabalah. One cassette.
　7　7　10

Passage To Moauv: #C625, Peter Pan Records, 1979. Single-cassette collection containing three children's stories: "Passage To Moauv," "In Vino Veritas," and "Crier In Emptiness." Packaged on cardstock back with green header and *STTMP* bridge scene with Kirk, Sulu, and Uhura.
　2.99　10　15

Prime Directive: #0-671-72631-5, Simon & Schuster Audioworks, 1990. Dramatic reading of the Pocket novel by Judith and Garfield Reeves-Stevens, as read by James Doohan. Includes enhanced sound effects and TV series music. Two cassettes, 180 minutes.
　14.95　15　17

Probe: #0-671-73727-9, Simon & Schuster Audioworks, 1991. Dramatic reading of the novel written by Margaret Bonanno, with enhanced sound effects and original TV theme music. Two cassettes, 180 minutes.
　15.95　16　17

Saturday Night Live: Startone Recordings, 1975. Recording of the Trek spoof with John Belushi as Kirk, Chevy Chase as Spock, and Dan Ackroyd as McCoy and Scotty. One cassette, 12 minutes.
　3　3　6

Sci-Fi Cut-Ups: JPM Studios, 1988. A collection of rib-ticklers which includes the *Star Trek* Bloopers, *Forbidden Planet*, and *Cat People* Trailers, plus more. Originally titled *Jeepers Creepers, Fractured Flickers*. One cassette, 60 minutes.
　9　9　12

Sci-Fi Spectacular: Stage & Screen Productions, 1983. Movie music from *E.T.*, *Close Encounters*, *Star Trek*, and more as performed by Cinema Sound Stage Orchestra. One cassette.
　2.98　3　6

Science Fiction Soundbook: #SBC 104, Caedmon Records, 1977. Packaged set of four cassette tapes plus a program booklet. A 7" x 10" library slipcase includes *Foundation-Mimsy Were The Borogroves* (Shatner), and *Green Hills of Earth-Martian Chronicles* (Nimoy).
　15　20　2

Space Movies: #SSCX716, Stage & Screen Productions, 1986. Cassette featuring famous movie themes. Includes *E.T.*, *Tron*, *Star Wars*, *Planet of the Apes*, and *STTMP*. Dolby stereo.
　2.99　3

Spock's World: #0-671-67917-1, Simon & Schuster Audioworks, 1989. The Pocket novel by Diane Duane as read by Leonard Nimoy and George Takei. Enhanced with sound effects and original TV *ST* music. Two cassettes, 180 minutes.
　14.95　15　1

Star Trek: #GNPS 8006, Crescendo Records, 198. Original television soundtrack, music from the pilot episodes "The Cage" and "Where No Man Has Gone Before" which was reproduced from master tapes stored at Paramount. Music is composed and conducted by Alexander Courage. One cassette.
　9.95　10　1

Star Trek: Fifth Continent Music Corporation, 198. Symphonic suites arranged from the original television scores as produced by Clyde Allen and John Lasher.
(A) #LXDC-703, Volume I, "Is There In Truth N Beauty? / Paradise Syndrome," 40 minutes.
　7.95　8　1
(B) #LXDC-704, Volume 2, "I Mudd," "The Enemy Within," "Spectre of the Gun," and "Conscience of the King," 40 minutes.
　7.95　8　1

Star Trek: Varese Sarabande Records, Inc., 198. Digital cassette recordings of music from selected episodes of *ST*. Scores are played by the Royal Philharmonic Orchestra as arranged by Fred Steiner.
➤ #C704-27, "The Corbomite Maneuver," "Charlie X," "Mudd's Women," and "The Doomsday Machine," 40 minutes.
➤ #C704-30, "Mirror, Mirror," "By Any Other Name," "The Trouble With Tribbles," and "The Empath," 40 minutes.
Price for each.　7.95　8　1

Star Trek Animated: Star Tech, 1988. Set of five cassettes featuring animated Trek episodes. Recorded on TDK tape from a Hi-Fi VCR and equalizer and Dolby C.
➤ #SA-1, "Yesteryear," "The Lorelei Signal," "More Troubles, More Tribbles," "The Survivor," and "Mudd's Passion"

Issue   Fair   Mint

#SA-2, "Once Upon A Planet," "The Terratin Incident," "The Time Trap," and "The Slaver Weapon"

#SA-3, "Beyond The Farthest Star," "Eye Of The Beholder," "The Jihad," and "BEM"

#SA-4, "Albatross," "The Counterclock Incident," "One Of Our Planets Is Missing," and "The Practical Joker"

#SA-5, "Majicks Of Megus-Tu," "Ambergris Element," "The Infinite Vulcan," "Pirates Of Orion," and "How Much Sharper Than A Serpent's Tooth?"

Price for each.   **8   8   10**

Star Trek Animated: Startone Recordings, 1983. Single cassette containing either a 24-minute animated Trek episode or a double recording.

#A-1, "Yesteryear"
#A-2, "One Of Our Planets Is Missing"
#A-3, "The Lorelei Signal"
#A-4, "The Survivor"
#A-5, "Mudd's Passion"
#A-6, "The Ambergris Element"
#A-7, "The Slaver Weapon"
#A-8, "Beyond The Farthest Star"
#A-9, "BEM"
#A-10, "Albatross"

Price for each single episode.   **3.50   4   5**
Price for each double episode.   **4.75   5   6**

Star Trek Bloopers: Startone Recordings, 1979. Independent recording exactly the same as the LP by Blue Pear Records. One cassette, 55 minutes.
                                                 4.75   5   6

Star Trek Bloopers: JPM Studios, 1984. Rare third season out-takes from the series. One cassette, 55 minutes.   **7.98   8   10**

Star Trek Comedy, The Unofficial Album: #VE-2, Vince Emery Presents, 1988. A collection of comedy routines and jokes by comedians about Star Trek. Ten comedy skits including: "ST V — In Search of Cash" by Kevin Pollack, "Star Drek" by Bobby Pickett, "Star Bits" by Rick Warren, and "The Captain's Answering Machine." One cassette.
                                                 9.95   10   12

Star Trek Dream: Star Sounds, 1983. William Shatner talks about Star Trek. One cassette.
                                                 3.50   4   6

Star Trek Episode Tapes: Star Tech, 1988. A new fan-produced collection of the classic series as unedited, hi-fi copies. Each tape contains two episodes per tape. Running time 100 minutes.

#1nx, "The Man Trap" and "Charlie X"
#2nx, "Where No Man Has Gone Before" and "Naked Time"
#3nx, "The Enemy Within" and "Mudd's Women"
#4nx, "What Are Little Girls Made Of?" and "Miri"
#5nx, "Dagger Of The Mind" and "The Corbomite Maneuver"
#6nx, "The Menagerie," Parts I and II
#7nx, "The Conscience Of The King" and "Balance Of Terror"
#8nx, "Shore Leave" and "The Galileo Seven"
#9nx, "Squire Of Gothos" and "Arena"
#10nx, "Tomorrow Is Yesterday" and "Court-Martial"
#11nx, "A Taste Of Armageddon" and "This Side Of Paradise"
#12nx, "The Devil In The Dark" and "Errand Of Mercy"
#13nx, "The Return Of The Archons" and "Space Seed"
#14nx, "The Alternative Factor" and "The City On The Edge Of Forever"
#15nx, "Operation: Annihilate!" and "The Cage"
#16nx, "Amok Time" and "Who Mourns For Adonis?"
#17nx, "The Changeling" and "Mirror, Mirror"
#18nx, "The Apple" and "The Doomsday Machine"
#19nx, "Catspaw" and "I, Mudd"
#20nx, "Metamorphosis" and "Journey To Babel"
#21nx, "Friday's Child" and "The Deadly Years"
#22nx, "Obsession" and "Wolf In The Fold"
#23nx, "The Trouble With Tribbles" and "The Gamesters Of Triskelion"
#24nx, "A Piece Of The Action" and "The Immunity Syndrome"
#25nx, "A Private Little War" and "Return To Tomorrow"
#26nx, "Patterns Of Force" and "By Any Other Name"
#27nx, "The Omega Glory" and "The Ultimate Computer"
#28nx, "Bread And Circuses" and "Assignment: Earth"
#29nx, "Spock's Brain" and "The Enterprise Incident"
#30nx, "The Paradise Syndrome" and "And The Children Shall Lead"
#31nx, "Is There In Truth No Beauty?" and "Spectre Of The Gun"
#32nx, "Day Of The Dove" and "For The World Is Hollow..."
#33nx, "The Tholian Web" and "Plato's Stepchildren"

	Issue	Fair	Mint

➤ #34nx, "Wink Of An Eye" and "The Empath"
➤ #35nx, "Elaan Of Troyius" and "Whom Gods Destroy"
➤ #36nx, "That Which Survives" and "The Lights Of Zetar"
➤ #37nx, "Let That Be Your Last Battlefield" and "The Mark Of Gideon"
➤ #38nx, "Requiem For Methuselah" and "The Way To Eden"
➤ #39nx, "The Cloud Minders" and "The Savage Curtain"
➤ #40nx, "All Our Yesterdays" and "Turnabout Intruder"

Price for each.   **8   8   10**

Star Trek Episode Tapes: Startone Recordings, 1983. All episodes from the television series are available as either edited 45-minute episodes or unedited 50-minute versions. Edited double-episode recordings of your choice are also possible on one cassette.

➤ #ST-1, "The Man Trap"
➤ #ST-2, "Charlie X"
➤ #ST-3, "Where No Man Has Gone Before"
➤ #ST-4, "The Naked Time"
➤ #ST-5, "The Enemy Within"
➤ #ST-6, "Mudd's Women"
➤ #ST-7, "What Are Little Girls Made Of?"
➤ #ST-8, "Miri"
➤ #ST-9, "Dagger Of The Mind"
➤ #ST-10, "The Corbomite Maneuver"
➤ #ST-11, "The Menagerie," Part I
➤ #ST-12, "The Menagerie," Part II
➤ #ST-13, "The Conscience Of The King"
➤ #ST-14, "Balance Of Terror"
➤ #ST-15, "Shore Leave"
➤ #ST-16, "The Galileo Seven"
➤ #ST-17, "The Squire Of Gothos"
➤ #ST-18, "Arena"
➤ #ST-19, "Tomorrow Is Yesterday"
➤ #ST-20, "Court-Martial"
➤ #ST-21, "The Return Of The Archons"
➤ #ST-22, "Space Seed"
➤ #ST-23, "A Taste Of Armageddon"
➤ #ST-24, "This Side Of Paradise"
➤ #ST-25, "The Devil In The Dark"
➤ #ST-26, "Errand Of Mercy"
➤ #ST-27, "The Alternative Factor"
➤ #ST-28, "The City On The Edge Of Forever"
➤ #ST-29, "Operation: Annihilate!"
➤ #ST-30, "Amok Time"
➤ #ST-31, "Who Mourns For Adonis?"

➤ #ST-32, "The Changeling"
➤ #ST-33, "Mirror, Mirror"
➤ #ST-34, "The Apple"
➤ #ST-35, "The Doomsday Machine"
➤ #ST-36, "Catspaw"
➤ #ST-37, "I, Mudd"
➤ #ST-38, "Metamorphosis"
➤ #ST-39, "Journey To Babel"
➤ #ST-40, "Friday's Child"
➤ #ST-41, "The Deadly Years"
➤ #ST-42, "Obsession"
➤ #ST-43, "Wolf In The Fold"
➤ #ST-44, "The Trouble With Tribbles"
➤ #ST-45, "The Gamesters Of Triskelion"
➤ #ST-46, "A Piece Of The Action"
➤ #ST-47, "The Immunity Syndrome"
➤ #ST-48, "A Private Little War"
➤ #ST-49, "Return To Tomorrow"
➤ #ST-50, "Patterns Of Force"
➤ #ST-51, "By Any Other Name"
➤ #ST-52, "The Omega Glory"
➤ #ST-53, "The Ultimate Computer"
➤ #ST-54, "Bread And Circuses"
➤ #ST-55, "Assignment: Earth"
➤ #ST-56, "Spock's Brain"
➤ #ST-57, "The Enterprise Incident"
➤ #ST-58, "The Paradise Syndrome"
➤ #ST-59, "And The Children Shall Lead"
➤ #ST-60, "Is There In Truth No Beauty?"
➤ #ST-61, "Spectre Of The Gun"
➤ #ST-62, "Day Of The Dove"
➤ #ST-63, "For The World Is Hollow..."
➤ #ST-64, "The Tholian Web"
➤ #ST-65, "Plato's Stepchildren"
➤ #ST-66, "Wink Of An Eye"
➤ #ST-67, "The Empath"
➤ #ST-68, "Elaan Of Troyius"
➤ #ST-69, "Whom Gods Destroy"
➤ #ST-70, "That Which Survives"
➤ #ST-71, "The Lights Of Zetar"
➤ #ST-72, "Let That Be Your Last Battlefield"
➤ #ST-73, "The Mark Of Gideon"
➤ #ST-74, "Requiem For Methuselah"
➤ #ST-75, "The Way To Eden"
➤ #ST-76, "The Cloud Minders"
➤ #ST-77, "The Savage Curtain"
➤ #ST-78, "All Our Yesterdays"
➤ #ST-79, "Turnabout Intruder"

	Issue	Fair	Mint
rice for each 45-minute single episode.	4	4	6
rice for each 50-minute single episode.	4.75	5	7
rice for each double-episode cassette.	7.25	8	12

tar Trek Filk Songs: Off Centaur, circa 1980s. ssorted fan-produced cassettes featuring filk songs bout Star Trek themes. One cassette each, which nclude:
- Genesis, by Julia Ecklar.
- Skybound, by Leslie Fish.
- Space Heroes and Other Fools.
- Where No Man, OCP-85.

rice for each. **7.95 8 12**

tar Trek Movies: Star Tech, 1988. Unedited ecordings of the first Star Trek movies. One cas- tte.
- #41nx, *Star Trek: The Motion Picture*
- #42nx, *Star Trek II: The Wrath of Khan*
- #43nx, *Star Trek III: The Search for Spock*

rice for each. **12 12 14**

tar Trek Sound Effects: Crescendo Records, 1988. nice collection of original TV *ST* sound effects. In- udes bridge sounds, transporter, phasers, purring ibbles, and more. One cassette.
- #GNP5-8010 **9.95 10 12**
- #301531, Science Fiction Book Club **9.98 10 12**

tar Trek Special: #45, Star Tech, 1988. The story * Star Trek with cast interviews, the complete *Today how* special, plus Tom Cottle's "Up-Close" edition ith the actors. One cassette, 60 minutes. **5 5 7**

tar Trek Tapes: Startone Recordings, 1978. Same s the LP recording by Sell Enterprises. Includes ex- rpts from old convention appearances by Shatner, imoy, and other members of the *Star Trek* cast. One ssette, 30 minutes. **3.50 4 6**

tar Trek: The Motion Picture: Startone Record- gs, 1979. One cassette featuring the movie, 132 inutes. **8 8 10**

tar Trek: The Motion Picture Read-Along Ad- nture: #161DC, Buena Vista Records, 1983. hildren's book and tape set containing a 24-page ooklet with story and photos from *STTMP*, plus one ory tape cassette with dialogue, sound effects, and usic. Identical recordings are featured on both sides the cassette. The book and cassette are mounted

	Issue	Fair	Mint
on a 7¼" x 11½" cardboard back sealed inside a plastic pouch. The book is 7" x 7".	3.96	10	15

Star Trek II Interviews: Startone Recordings, 1982. *ST II* is discussed with Ricardo Montalban (Khan) on *Merv Griffin* and the *Tonight Show*, plus Kirstie Alley (Saavik) talks with Merv. One cassette, 34 minutes.
4 4 6

Star Trek II Radio Special: Startone Recordings, 1982. The voyage of Star Trek is chronicled as a detailed history of the TV series phenomenon up to and including *ST II*. Includes comments on all major characters, plus Roddenberry interview. One cas- sette, 51 minutes. **4.75 5 8**

Star Trek II: The Wrath of Khan: Startone Recordings, 1982. One cassette featuring the story from the movie, 113 minutes. **7.50 8 10**

Star Trek II: The Wrath of Khan Read-Along Adventure: #162DC, Buena Vista, Records, 1983. Children's book and photos from *ST II* in a 24-page booklet with cassette. Cassette features dialogue, sound effects, and music. Identical recordings are fea-

Star Trek III: The Search for Spock audio cassette, Capital Records, 1984.

	Issue	Fair	Mint

tured on both sides of the cassette. Cardboard mount sealed plastic pouch. The book is 7" x 7".

3.96   5   10

Star Trek III: The Search for Spock: #4XKK-12360, Capital Records, 1984. The complete soundtrack for the movie as composed and conducted by James Horner. Expanded Dynamic range on high quality XDR tape. One cassette, 41 minutes.

8.98   9   12

Star Trek III: The Search for Spock Read-Along Adventure: #163DC, Buena Vista Records, 1983. Story, photos, and tape from *ST III*. Includes 24-page booklet and cassette with character dialogue, sound effects, and music. Identical recordings are featured on both sides of the cassette. Comes attached to cardboard mount and sealed in a plastic pouch. The book is 7" x 7".

2.97   5   10

Star Trek IV Special: #47n, Star Tech, 1988. Interviews with the stars and its creators, plus *Entertainment Tonight*'s coverage of the Star Trek 20th Anniversary celebration. Also features other show interviews and special *ST IV* reviews. One cassette, 120 minutes.

8   8   10

Star Trek IV: The Voyage Home: #6195, MCA Records, 1986. The original motion picture soundtrack with music composed and conducted by Leonard Rosenman. One cassette, 45 minutes.

10.98   12   15

Star Trek IV: The Voyage Home: #0-671-64629-X, Simon & Schuster Audioworks, 1986. Dramatic reading of the Pocket novel written by Vonda N. McIntyre, read by Leonard Nimoy and George Takei, with enhanced sound effects and original TV series music. One cassette, 90 minutes.   **8.95   9   12**

Star Trek IV: The Voyage Home Read-Along Adventure: #171DC, Buena Vista Records, 1986. Children's book and tape set featuring the story from the movie. Booklet with photos from *ST IV*, dialogue, sound effects, and music. Identical recordings are featured on both sides of the cassette. The set is attached to a cardboard back and sealed inside a plastic pouch. The book is 7" x 7".   **4.87   5   10**

Star Trek V: The Final Frontier: #45267, Epic Records, 1989. The original motion picture soundtrack. One cassette.   **10.98   11   13**

Star Trek V: The Final Frontier: #0-671-68507-4, Simon & Schuster Audioworks, 1989. Dramatic reading of the Pocket novel written by J. M. Dillard, read by Leonard Nimoy, with enhanced sound effects and original TV series music. One cassette, 90 minutes.

7.95   8   10

	Issue	Fair	Mint

Star Trek: The Next Generation: #GNP5-8012 Crescendo Records, 1989. The original soundtrack fo the *STTNG* two-hour pilot "Encounter At Farpoint" as composed and conducted by Dennis McCarthy One cassette.   **10.95   11   1**

Star Trek: The Next Generation Episodes: Sta Tech, 1988. A collection of recordings which contai TV shows from *STTNG*. Each cassette contains tw shows except for the pilot movie and the "Star Tre Saga."   100 minutes.

➤ SG-1n, "Encounter At Farpoint"
➤ SG-2n, "The Naked Now" and "Code Of Honor"
➤ SG-3n, "The Last Outpost" and "Where No On Has Gone Before"
➤ SG-4n, "Lonely Among Us" and "Justice"
➤ SG-5n, "The Battle" and "Hide And Q"
➤ SG-6n, "Haven" and "The Big Goodbye"
➤ SG-7n, "Too Short A Season" and "Data Lore"
➤ SG-8n, "Angel One" and "11001001"
➤ SG-9n, "When The Bough Breaks" and "Home Soil"
➤ SG-10n, "Coming Of Age" and "Heart Of Glory"
➤ SG-11n, "The Arsenal Of Freedom" and "Sym biosis"
➤ SG-12n, "Skin Of Evil" and "We'll Always Hav Paris"
➤ SG-13n, "Conspiracy" and "The Neutral Zone"
➤ SG-14n, "The Child" and "Where Silence Ha Lease"
➤ SG-15n, "Elementary, Dear Data" and "The Out rageous Okona"
➤ SG-16n, "Loud As A Whisper" and "The Schizoi Man"
➤ SG-17n, "Unnatural Selection" and "A Matter O Honor"
➤ SG-18n, "The Measure Of A Man" and "Th Daughin"
➤ SG-19n, "Contagion" and "The Royale"
➤ SG-20n, "Time Squared" and "The Icarus Factor"
➤ SG-21n, "Pen Pals" and "Q Who"
➤ SG-22n, "Samaritan Snare" and "Up The Lon Ladder"
➤ SG-23n, "Manhunt" and "The Emissary"
➤ SG-24n, "Peak Performance" and "Shades Of Gray"
➤ SG-25n, "Star Trek Saga: From One Generatio To Another"
➤ SG-26n, "Evolution" and "Ensigns Of Command"
➤ SG-27n, "Survivors" and "Who Watches Th Watchers?"
➤ SG-28n, "The Bonding" and "Boobytrap"
➤ SG-29n, "The Price" and "The Vengeance Factor"

	Issue	*Fair*	*Mint*

➤ SG-30n, "The Defector" and "The Hunted"
➤ SG-31n, "The High Ground" and "Deja Q"
➤ SG-32n, "The Enemy" and "A Matter Of Perspective"
➤ SG-33n, "Yesterday's Enterprise" and "The Offspring"
➤ SG-34n, "Sins Of The Father" and "Allegiance"
➤ SG-35n, "Captain's Holiday" and "Tin Man"
➤ SG-36n, "The Most Toys" and "Sarek"
➤ SG-37n, "Menage A Troi" and "Transfigurations"
➤ SG-38n, "Hollow Pursuits" and "The Best Of Both Worlds"

Price for each. **8** **8** **10**

Star Trek Twin Pack: Peter Pan Records, 1979. Unusual items featuring one cassette with two different children's story books as one set. In this case, one of the two stories in each set is a Trek recording from Peter Pan's earlier LP selections for kids.
➤ #C-102, Captain America and Star Trek Volume I.
➤ #C-103, Star Trek Volume II and Batman Volume I.

Price for each. **—** **15** **20**

Star Trick — The Motion Sickness Picture: JMP Studios, 1988. A collection of edited cut and splice dialogue from *STTMP* used to create a satire. One cassette, 15 minutes. **5** **5** **8**

Star Wreck: #6150, At the Sound of the Beep, Volume IV, Great American Audio Corp., 1986. A collection of telephone answering machine messages done as Trek satires. Includes fifteen messages in musical format. One cassette, 8 minutes.
6.95 **7** **12**

Star Wreck Gift Set: #1-55569-411-X, At The Sound Of The Beep, #7166, Great American Audio, 1990. Special dual audio package featuring two types of telephone answering machine tapes containing a total of 32 humorous messages. Includes "Telephone Comedy & TV Classics" tape #7194 and "Star Wreck" tape #7195. Packaged in pink slipcover case. 1½" x 2½" x 4". **19.95** **20** **21**

Strangers From The Sky: #0-671-64718-0, Simon & Schuster Audioworks, 1987. Dramatic reading of the Pocket novel written by Margaret Wander Bonanno, read by Leonard Nimoy and George Takei. Contains enhanced sound effects and the original TV series music. One cassette, 90 minutes.
8.95 **9** **11**

TekWar: Simon & Schuster Audioworks, 1989. Dramatic reading by William Shatner of his first sci-fi novel, published by Ace-Putnam. Features the story of a 22nd century former Los Angeles cop in Mexico

fighting against the spread of an illegal drug. Two cassettes, 180 minutes.
(A) #0-671-68931-0. **14.95** **15** **17**
(B) #314211, Science Fiction Book Club.
12.95 **13** **17**

Telephone Message Tape: #43-418, Radio Shack, 1988. A collection of novelty answering machine messages, one of which features a parody of Mr. Scott. One cassette. **3.95** **4** **6**

Themes from E.T. The Extraterrestrial And More: #MCAC-6114, MCA Records, Inc., 1982. Theme songs arranged and conducted by Walter Murphey, including the theme from *Star Trek*. One cassette. **2.99** **3** **6**

Time For Yesterday: Simon & Schuster Audioworks, 1989. Dramatic reading of the Pocket novel written by A. C. Crispin, read by Leonard Nimoy and

Star Wreck, #6150, Great American Audio Corporation, 1986.

	Issue	Fair	Mint

George Takei. Contains enhanced sound effects and the original TV series music. One cassette, 90 minutes.

	Issue	Fair	Mint
(A) #0-671-67017-4.	9.95	10	12
(B) #308478, Science Fiction Book Club.	8.95	9	12

Time Stealer: #C626, Peter Pan Records, 1979. A collection of four children's stories on cassette. Includes "Time Stealer," "To Starve A Fleaver," "The Logistics of Stampede," and "A Mirror For Futility." Cassette is blister-packed on 7" x 9" cardstock back with pink header. Cut-out photos of Kirk and Spock with *STTMP* background on top.

	2.99	10	15

Today Show: Startone Recordings, 1982. Preview of *ST II* with Shatner, Montalban, Nicholas Meyer, Bob Sallin, and Ken Ralston of Industrial Light and Magic. One cassette, sixteen minutes.

	4.75	5	7

Transformed Man: Starsounds, 1983. Fan recording of the Shatner LP by Decca Records. Includes Shakespearean narratives, chorales, and instrumentals. One cassette, 34 minutes.

	—	5	7

T.V. Themes: #C64166, Stage & Screen Productions, 1983. Instrumentals and vocal re-creations of favorite television theme songs. Includes *Star Trek*, *M*A*S*H*, *Mission: Impossible*, and *Hill Street Blues*, plus eighteen more as performed by the Video Theatre Orchestra. One cassette.

	2.98	3	5

20/20: Startone Recordings, 1979. An in-depth look at Trek fandom with Roddenberry, Shatner, Nimoy, Kelley, Doohan, Nichols, Joan Winston, Bjo Trimble, Lee Cole, and more. One cassette, 15 minutes.

	3	3	5

Uhura Sings: aR-Way Productions, 1986. Old and new songs by Nichelle Nichols. Includes a new version of the *Star Trek* theme, plus "Space Rock," "Ode to the Space Shuttle," and "Beyond Antares." One cassette.

	8.50	9	12

War of the Worlds: Caedmon Records, 1979. Reading of the H. G. Wells classic by Leonard Nimoy. One cassette, 50 minutes.

	8.98	9	12

Web of the Romulans: #0-671-64719-9, Simon & Schuster Audioworks, 1988. Dramatic reading of the Pocket novel written by M. S. Murdock, read by Leonard Nimoy and George Takei. Also contains special sound effects and music from the original TV series. One cassette, 90 minutes.

	9.95	10	12

Whales Alive: #LC 0013, Living Music, 1987. Leonard Nimoy narrates this special tape about humpback whales. Includes the voices of George and

Gracie from *ST IV*, plus many others. One cassette

	9.95	10	12

William Shatner Specials: Star Tech, 1988. Set o special fan tapings from various TV shows featuring William Shatner. One cassette each, 90-100 minutes

➤ 1n, Shatner in *Big Valley* and *Hawaii Five-0* episodes.

➤ 2n, Shatner in *Outer Limits* and two *Twilight Zone* episodes.

➤ 3n, Shatner in *Twelve O'Clock High* and *Man From U.N.C.L.E.* episodes.

➤ 4n, Bill Talks tape, 90 minutes of interviews with Shatner and his wife Marcy Lafferty.

➤ 5n, Shatner in two unnamed thriller episodes.

Price for each.	8	8	10

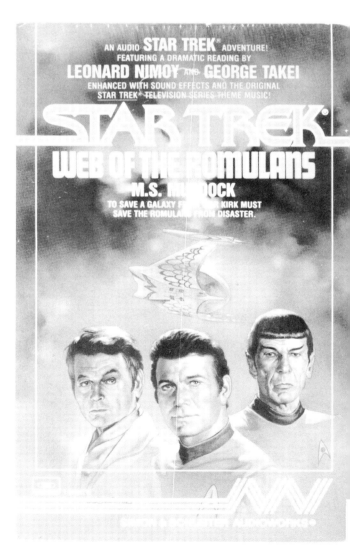

Web of the Romulans audio cassette, Simon & Schuster Audioworks, 1988.

	Issue	Fair	Mint

Yesterday's Son: Simon & Schuster Audioworks, 1988. Dramatic reading of the Pocket novel written by A. C. Crispin, read by Leonard Nimoy and George Takei. Includes sound and music from the TV series. One cassette, 90 minutes.

➤ #0-671-66865-1   **9.95**   **10**   **12**

➤ #308460, Science Fiction Book Club   **8.95**   **9**   **12**

	Issue	Fair	Mint

You And I: Petunia Productions, 1978. Leonard Nimoy speaking the words of love from his book by Celestial Arts. One cassette.   **5**   **5**   **10**

You Are Not Alone: #MCAC-20409, MCA Records, Inc., 1987. A re-issue of Leonard Nimoy's *Mr. Spock's Music From Outer Space* in cassette format. Includes "Alien," "You Are Not Alone," "Where No Man Has Gone Before," the theme from *Star Trek*, and "Where Is Love?" One cassette.   **9.95**   **10**   **12**

B

Badges And I.D. Cards

	Issue	Fair	Mint

Computer Identification Cards: April Publications. Set of eight 2½" x 3" wallet-sized cards designed to resemble computer-generated I.D. cards. Black on white cardstock.

➤ Command Center
➤ Data, #912
➤ Main Mission, #010
➤ Medical, #714
➤ Security, #586
➤ Technical, #254
➤ Visitor, #351

Price for set of eight cards.	6.50	7	10

Price for any of the above, personalized with photo and laminated as an authentic-looking military I.D. card with name, rank, and reserve status, badge with spring-clip.

	5	5	6

Identification Badges: April Publications, 1984. Assorted 2½" x 3" cardstock badges in plastic badge holder with security lock pin back.

➤ Enterprise Boarding Pass
➤ Radiation Detector / Engineering Dept.
➤ Regula I Boarding Pass
➤ Regula I Computer Access Pass
➤ Starfleet Cadet I.D.
➤ Starfleet Command Security Pass
➤ Starfleet Division First Aid Certificate
➤ Starfleet Divisional I.D.
➤ Starfleet Headquarters Access Pass
➤ United Federation of Planets
➤ U.S.S. Reliant Planet Exploration
➤ Vulcan Science Academy

Price for each.	1	1	2

Starfleet Divisional I.D. Cards: April Publications, 1984. Cardstock badges which included a space for photo, name, rank, and status. Badges read "Starfleet Divisional I.D." and the appropriate printed insignia for the proper job description. Also have UFP Janus head emblem in bottom corner. Insignia divisions include:

➤ Command
➤ Engineering
➤ Medical
➤ Science
➤ Ship Personnel
➤ Star Base

Price for set of six cards.	5.50	6	

Price for any of the above, personalized with photo and laminated as a badge holder with spring clip back. Includes name, rank, and reserve status.

	5	5	

Star Fleet Laminated I.D. Badges: New Eye Studios, 1984. Same as the laminated computer identification cards and the Starfleet Divisional I.D. Buyers send in an original photo to be placed on a laminated badge made to be an authentic-looking military I.D. with name, rank, and reserve status in a plastic badge holder with a pin clip back.

➤ Star Fleet Headquarters Access Pass
➤ Vulcan Science Academy Visitor's Pass

Price for each.	5	5	

Star Trek Identification Badges: T-K Graphics, 1984. Various 2¾" x 3½" I.D. cards on colored cardstock and displayed in plastic holders with a pin clip back.

➤ Enterprise Shuttle Pilot
➤ Imperial Klingon Navy

	Issue	*Fair*	*Mint*

➤ Klingon Diplomatic Corps
➤ Star Fleet Academy, with UFP Janus head emblem
➤ Star Fleet Command Security Pass
➤ Star Fleet Drydock Security Pass
➤ Star Fleet Headquarters Access Pass
➤ Star Fleet Intelligence Division
➤ Star Fleet Recruiting Office, with UFP pennant
➤ Star Fleet Transporter Technician
➤ Tribble Inspector
➤ UFP Diplomatic Service, with UFP Janus head emblem
➤ U.S.S. Enterprise Boarding Pass
➤ U.S.S. Enterprise Computer Section
➤ U.S.S. Enterprise Medical Sections
➤ Vulcan Science Academy Visitor's Pass

Price for each.	1.25	1	2

Star Trek Identification Card Assortments: April Publications, 1983. Specific I.D. card sets with raised lettering on wallet-sized 2½" x 3" cards of assorted colors, with a space for the addition of name and photo. Available in twelve sets of five cards each.

(A) Set No. 2.
➤ Klingon Identification
➤ Galactic Transport
➤ Phaser License
➤ Starship Captain
➤ Vulcan Academy Membership

(B) Set No. 2.
➤ Air Team Pass
➤ Deltan Identification
➤ Starfleet Admiral
➤ Vulcan Kolinahr Card
➤ Vulcan Master

(C) Set No. 3.
➤ Enterprise Boarding Pass
➤ Library Card — Memory Alpha
  Starfleet Security Card
➤ Tribble License
➤ Vulcan Identification

(D) Set No. 4.
➤ Enterprise Crew Identification
➤ Envoy — Babel Conference
➤ Science Officer
➤ Starfleet Command Identification
➤ Vulcan Blood Donor Card

(E) Set No. 5.
➤ Federation Immunization Card
➤ Phaser Marksmanship Card
➤ Starfleet Draft Card
➤ Starfleet Officer's Club
➤ Vulcan Space Central

(F) Set No. 6.
➤ Communication's Officer
➤ Federation Ambassador
➤ Import License — Saurian Brandy
➤ Membership — Tribble Society
➤ Starfleet Academy I.D.

(G) Set No. 7.
➤ Cabaret Card — Rigel IV
➤ Federation Social Security Card
➤ Medical Officer I.D.
➤ Space Trader License
➤ Sub-Space Radio Operator License

(H) Set No. 8.
➤ Horta Mining License
➤ Klingon War Academy
➤ Starship Engineering License
➤ Shuttlecraft Operator's License
➤ Vulcan Officer's Club

(I) Set No. 9.
➤ Class A-7 Computer Expert
➤ Federation Diplomatic Courier
➤ Starfleet Commodore
➤ Tribble Breeder's Association
➤ Vulcan Ambassador

(J) Set No. 10.
➤ Orion Slave Trader
➤ Sehlat Kennel Club
➤ Starfleet Academy Honor Society
➤ Starship First Officer
➤ Vulcan Passport

(K) Set No. 11.
➤ Klingon War Crimes Tribunal
➤ Mugato Hunting License
➤ Starfleet Medical I.D.
➤ Starship Passenger's Association
➤ Vulcan Academy Honor Society

(L) Set No. 12.
➤ Enterprise 3-D Chess Club
➤ Federation Diplomatic Corps
➤ Phaser Sharpshooter's Team
➤ Restricted Area Pass
➤ Vulcan Space Trader

Price for each set.	1	1	2

Wallet I.D. Cards: T-K Graphics, 1984. Assorted 2" x 3" I.D.s printed on color stock.
➤ Imperial Klingon Navy Intelligence
➤ Intergalactic Union of Transporter Operators & Technicians Member
➤ North American Tribble Breeder's Association
➤ Phaser Permit
➤ Starbase 13 PX Card

The one-of-a-kind Kirk and Spock banks, Play Pal Incorporated, 1975.

	Issue	Fair	Mint
➤ Star Fleet Command Intelligence Division			
➤ Star Fleet Library			
➤ Star Fleet Medical Association			
➤ Star Fleet Officer's Association			
➤ Star Fleet Security			
➤ Star Fleet Three-Dimensional Chess Club			
➤ Tribble License			

	Issue	Fair	Min
➤ UFP Diplomatic Service			
➤ UFP Intelligence			
➤ UFP Voter Registration			
➤ Vulcan Diplomatic Service			
➤ Vulcan Science Academy I.D.			
Price for each.	.25	.50	

Banks

Star Trek Banks: Play Pal Incorporated, 1975. Standing figures of Kirk or Spock in front of bridge command chair. Made from molded plastic. 11½" high.

(A) Kirk holding communicator.

(B) Spock.

	Issue	Fair	Min
Price for each.	3	20	3

Star Trek bed linens by Stephens: sheet (top) and spread (bottom).

Bed Linens

	Issue	Fair	Mint

Star Trek Action Scene Linens: Stephens. Muslin linens with repeating artwork of large running figure of TV Kirk (wearing red tunic) and Spock in action scene, plus a nice starboard profile of the TV Enterprise. Backdrop fabric is a pastel blue starfield with dark blue, yellow, and red planets and white stars. Plastic-bagged.

Note: This linen set also had matching window drapes. See section listing **Curtains**.

	Issue	Fair	Mint
(A) Twin fitted bottom sheet.	—	25	45
(B) Twin flat top sheet.	—	25	45
(C) Standard pillow case.	—	25	30

Star Trek Classic Linens: Pacific Mills. Dark royal and navy blue background fabric featuring Kirk and Spock figures over starry backdrop with TV Enterprise.

Note: This bed assemble has matching window treatments (see **Curtains**).

	Issue	Fair	Mint
(A) Twin sheet.	—	25	45
(B) Twin bedspread — thin throw.	—	50	85
(C) Standard pillow cases.	—	25	45

ST-20 Coordinates: Aberdeen Mfg., 1987. Complete set of matching bed linens set in Trek motif. 50% Kodel polyester and cotton. Pieces sold separately.

Note: This coordinate set also had matching window drapes. See section listing **Curtains**.

(A) Bed ruffle with box pleat at two corners. Plain navy with constellation starfield print and no lettering.

	Issue	Fair	Min
➤ Style A5794-A twin, 39" x 76".	26.95	20	3
➤ Style A5794-B full, 54" x 76".	28.95	25	3

(B) Comforter. Quilted, with double, repeating pattern artwork of black and white busts of TV Spock, Kirk, McCoy, Uhura, Sulu, Scotty, and Chekov in upswept semi-circle around full-color TV Enterprise in starboard profile over planet. (This pattern in orange, red, yellow, white, brown, and blues is a rendered version of the art illustration on Ernst Enterprise Plate.) Also shown on bedspread is a surrealistic beam-down scene, spacedock, and planet with rear view of miniature Enterprise. Lettering in classic yellow block reads "Twenty Years of Star Trek/To Boldly Go Where No Man Has Gone Before." Character names are printed beneath busts. Packaged in zippered vinyl bag.

	Issue	Fair	Min
➤ Style A5794-T twin, 65" x 86".	35.95	100	12
➤ Style A5794-F full, 76" x 86".	42.95	120	15

(C) Pillow sham. Unquilted and hemmed pillow covers. Art design shows planets "Klinzhai" and "Koblek" with green *ST III* movie Klingon Bird of Prey and two small insets of TV and *STTMP* Enterprise. Yellow letters read "Klingon Empire." Sham is packaged in poly bag. Style A5794 (20" x 26").

	Issue	Fair	Min
	16.95	20	2

Belt Buckles

Classic Design Buckles

Crew Buckle: Antique-finished rectangle with indented sides and bowed top. Bottom shows front profiles of Kirk and Spock in relief inside a circle border. Lettered "Star Trek" above.

	Fair	Mint
	7	9

Crew / Enterprise Buckle: #2440, Lincoln Enterprises, 1976. Antique bronze-toned rectangular buckle with square corners and lettered "Star Trek." Features two right-side Kirk and Spock face profiles in relief below starboard TV ship. 2" x 3".

	Fair	Mint
5	6	8

Enterprise Design Buckles:

(A) TV starship. Navy enamel background with red lettering and white ship, lettered "Star Trek." 2" x 3".

	Fair	Mint
—	8	12

(B) TV Starship / "NCC-1701." Lee, 1976. Bronze metal with scrolled edge. 3¼" x 1⅝" rectangle with starboard classic ship lettered "Star Trek" above with ship's call letters printed below. Red-enameled border.

—	8	1

(C) TV Starship with legend. Bronze-toned oval with ship/legend on reverse, lettered "These Are The Voyages...."

4.95	7	9

(D) TV starship and Saturn. Indiana Metal Company, 1982. Round brass-toned buckle with TV ship below ringed planet and its moons. Green enamel with Froz-n'-color trademark. Lettered "Space the Final Frontier." Reverse has legend "Space, the final frontier..." 2½" in diameter.

10	12	1

Top row: Classic Enterprise on Wave, 1990; classic Spock (in red), 1976; Classic Crew / Enterprise, 1976; Classic Crew. Row 2: Classic Enterprise / NCC-1701, 1976; Classic Spock (in blue), 1976; Classic Enterprise Over Globe; *STTMP* Crew / Insignia, 1979. Row 3: Classic Enterprise on Triangle; Classic Enterprise on Insignia; Classic Enterprise with Legend; *ST II* Insignia, 1984. Bottom row: *STTMP* Enterprise, 1982; ST-20 Pilot Episode Anniversary, 1986; *ST III* Enterprise, 1984.

	Issue	*Fair*	*Mint*

E) TV starship and Saturn. Oval, bronze-toned buckle with very tiny left-side ringed planet and center starboard TV ship. Split lettering above and below. Lettered "Star Trek/U.S.S. Enterprise."

| | — | 8 | 12 |

F) TV starship over globe. Pewter. Starboard ship centered over a stylized globe. Lettered "Star Trek lives/U.S.S. Enterprise" in relief letters. 3" x 1¾".

| | 4 | 9 | 12 |

G) TV starship on insignia base. Tiffany Studios. Bronze-toned base in command insignia shape, 3⅞" x ¼".

| | — | 10 | 15 |

	Issue	*Fair*	*Mint*

(H) TV Starship on triangle. #419, Indiana Metal Company. Brass-toned or silver-toned ship mounted on triangular base. No legend, 4⅛".

| | 2.99 | 4 | 6 |

(I) TV starship over wave. Buckles & Belts Company, 1990. Limited edition buckle, 3¼" x 2½", oval with "wave"-style background and ship. Lettered "Star Trek." Numbered editions.

| | 29.95 | 30 | 32 |

Kirk Buckles:

(A) Lee, 1976. Round bronze-toned buckle, 2" diameter, blue or red enamel with relief profile.

| | — | 5 | 8 |

	Issue	*Fair*	*Mint*

(B) Tiffany Studios. Oval brass-toned buckle with bust of TV Captain Kirk. 2½" in diameter.
4.95 9 12

Spock Buckle: Lee, 1976. Bronze, round buckle with relief head of Spock. Lettered "Star Trek / Mr. Spock" with "Star Trek Lives!" over head. Name caption on right side on blue- or red-enameled background. 2" diameter. **2.95 5 7**

Commemorative Buckles

200th Anniversary of Man's Flight:
(A) *Starlog Magazine*, distributor, 1983. *STTMP* Enterprise and lettered "Star Trek." Ad read "200th Anniversary of Man's Flight Commemorative." This buckle is a reissue of #2444 *STTMP* Enterprise buckle found below, done in silver-plating with 25K gold-plated highlights. Size 3" x 4". Includes certificate of ownership and an engraved issue number on the reverse. Packaged plastic box.
19.95 25 30
(B) Sunday Comics Promotions, Inc., 1983. *STTMP* Enterprise. Lettered "Star Trek." Reissue of #2443 *STTMP* Enterprise buckle found below in brass tone and advertised as 200th Anniversary of Man's Flight Commemorative. Ad is 2" x 6" newspaper ad with illustration of buckle and coupon. Special price includes $1.75 postage. **8.63 8 10**

ST-20 Pilot Episode Commemorative: Lincoln Enterprises. STTMP Enterprise. Detailed scroll-edge with corner-cut rectangle. Shows deep relief portside movie ship in starfield below large poxed moon on the right. Lettered "Star Trek/The Final Frontier" on banners floating above/below. Registered and numbered with certificate of authenticity.
(A) #J2446, 1986, brass. **24.95 25 30**
(B) #J2447, 1986, polished with 24K gold trim on black enamel with red highlights.
59.95 60 70
(C) #J2579, 1987, color enamel edition. Ship in gold

	Issue	*Fair*	*Mint*

beneath white planet, blue background with red scrolls. **5.95 6 8**

Movie Design Buckles

STTMP — Crew / Insignia Buckles: Lee, 1979. Three designs of this buckle featuring relief busts of Kirk, Spock and flanking Insignias on both sides, 2 x 3", cut-off corners.
Note: Lee also made a similar belt.
➤ Bronze tone, solid.
➤ Bronze tone with red enamel insignias.
➤ Bronze tone with white and green insignias.
Price for each. **2.95 5 8**

STTMP **Enterprise Buckles:** Olde New England Mint, engravers, Lincoln Enterprises, distributor, 1982. *STTMP* Enterprise. Registered, numbered with mint certificate of authenticity. Lettered "Star Trek/U.S.S. Enterprise." Shows movie ship in port profile over starfield.
(A) #2443, bronze. **20 25 30**
(B) #2444, sterling silver with 24K gold.
180 200 275

ST II **Insignia Design Official Uniform Buckles**
(A) #2445, Lincoln Enterprises, 1984. Bronzed metal-finished buckle cast from the same mold used to design the uniform buckles seen in the movies *ST II*, *ST III*, and *ST IV*. Tubular encircled command insignia has cut-out center star. 2⅝" in diameter. **14.95 16 20**
(B) Later version, same as above, but polished gold toned finish. **— 12 15**

ST III — **Enterprise Buckle:** #P2445, Lincoln Enterprises, 1984. Official movie commemorative shows *ST III* movie ship in starboard profile between flying banners and triple large planets. Pewter alloy base, rectangle has deeply etched design. Reverse has synopsis of "The Saga Continues ...," an 82-word summary of the third movie. 2½" x 3½". Numbered, registered with certificate. Package includes an original drawing. **19.95 20 25**

Belt Pouches

Star Trek Belt Pouches: T-K Graphics, 1987. Belts in various shades of tan and brown with attached hand-sewn and polyester-lined pouches for carrying valuables. These are water-resistant and come in assorted textures with snap closures. Silk-screened designs on the front.
➤ Imperial Klingon Fleet with Klingon cruiser.
➤ Star Fleet Academy with Janus head design.

➤ Star Fleet Command Intelligence Division.
➤ Star Fleet HQ Tactical Operations Center with UFP pennant.
➤ UFP Diplomatic Service with Janus head.
➤ U.S.S. Enterprise with schematic Enterprise.
➤ U.S.S. Enterprise/NCC-1701.
Price for each. **4.50 4 8**

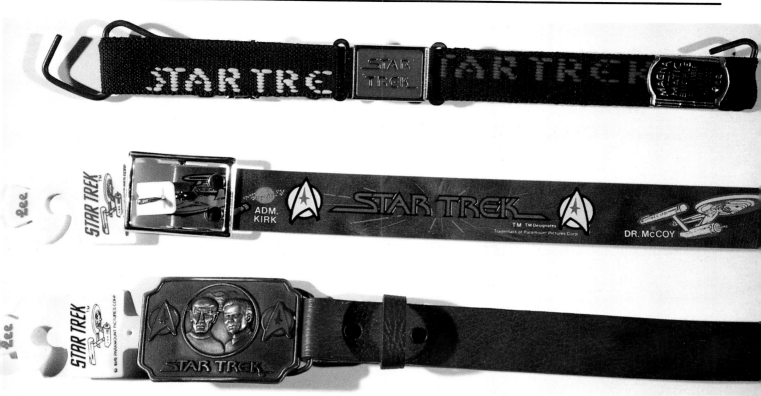

Belts by Lee (top to bottom): *STTMP* Movie Title Logo design (1978), *ST II* Ships design (1982), *STTMP* Crew/Insignia design (1979).

Belts

	Issue	Fair	Mint

This section lists dress apparel belts where either the belt fabric or its attached buckle sports a Trek motif, and toy equipment belts fashioned after the classic Star Fleet utility belts.

Dress Belts

Star Trek Enterprise Design Belts:

A) Lee Belts, 1976. Child's elastic stretch belt. Fabric belt has repeating TV Enterprise and "Star Trek" lettering. Colors: red with gray and white design, navy with blue and red design, brown with orange design. — 8 12

Note: Belts are designed to match Lee Boy's ties. See section listing for **Neckties**.

B) Rarities Mint, 1989. Adult leather reversible belt with coin buckle. Belt features a ¾"-diameter minted .999 silver coin executed in gold-plating on brass, mounted on a 3" x 2¼" rectangular buckle. Obverse shows starboard TV Enterprise with lettering "Where No Man Has Gone Before." Belt reverses to black or brown; sized up to 42-inch waist. 42 40 45

	Issue	Fair	Mint

(C) Lee Belts, 1976. Child's vinyl belt. Traditional belt in brown or black. Buckle is brass-toned oval with TV Enterprise in relief. No legend. 2.99 12 15

STTMP **Crew/Insignia Design Belt:** Lee, 1979. Child's vinyl belt with brass buckle featuring relief busts of Kirk, Spock, and red encircled insignias flanking both sides. Buckle is a rectangle with cut corners. Lettered "Star Trek" below. 3.50 10 12

STTMP **Movie Title Logo Belts:** Elastic stretch belts.

(A) Lee Belts, 1978. Logo Belt. Magna-Matic buckle is unornamented and made of red and silver metal. Cloth belt fabric has "Star Trek" in white and red lettering sewn over a basic navy background. — 10 12

(B) Lee Belts, 1979. Logo Belt Buckle. Child's traditional cloth belt in assorted colors. Logo buckle reads "Star Trek" in the movie title style. 3 10 12

ST II **Ships Design Belt:** Lee, 1982. Unusual leatherette belt has red movie title logo, white encircled insignias, and blue and white Enterprise with

Remco's Utility Belt packaged in two box styles: 1976 release (left) and 1978 (right).

	Issue	Fair	Mint

gold Reliant sewn repeating pattern. Buckle is a traditional, non-ornamented open buckle.

| | 4.25 | 14 | 16 |

Utility Belts

Star Trek Classic Utility Belts: Remco Industries. Plastic play set replicas of the TV equipment belts. Includes small child-size plastic toys: tricorder, communicator, and type II TV phaser (that shoots plastic

	Issue	Fair	Min

tracer discs — eight included). Equipment attache to a black plastic waist belt. Two different package releases.

(A) 1976, #203. Navy window box shows toy phase and color photo inset of Kirk and Spock, 8" x 14½" 2¼".

| | 5 | 60 | 75 |

(B) 1978, also #203. Light blue window box il lustrates a cartoon Kirk and measures larger size 10 x 14" x 2".

| | 5 | 45 | 55 |

Binoculars

Star Trek Binoculars: #9239, Larami Corporation, 1968. White plastic binoculars with orange eyepieces, lens rim, and focal adjuster. 5½" x 5½". Words "Star Trek" appear across both barrels in black decals. In-

cludes black plastic neck strap in a 7½" x 10¾" blister pack. Photo scenes from "Shore Leave" and the famous Spock holding the Enterprise poster boasts a NBC affiliation.

| | 1 | 10 | 15 |

Blueprints

Animated Freighter: Geoffrey Mandel, Interstellar Associates. Blueprints of the Trek robot cargo ship from the animated cartoon episode "More Tribbles, More Trouble." Includes exteriors plus drawings for model builders. Set of three sheets.

| | 4.95 | 5 | 6 |

Assorted Great Ship Profiles: L. Allen Everhart, Starcraft Productions. Exterior views of four famous spacecraft. Includes U.S.S. Enterprise, Valley Forge (*Silent Running*), Battlestar Galactica, and the Orion shuttle (*2001*). Set of four sheets, 8½" x 22".

| | 5.95 | 6 | 8 |

Assorted Ship Profiles: Todd Guenther, Starstation Aurora. Sideviews of various ships which include the U.S.S. Enterprise. Set of two sheets, 11" x 17".

| | 2 | 2 | 5 |

Blueprinting The Science Fiction Universe Shane Johnson, The Noron Group. A collection of sci-fi blueprints of ships, weapons, and equipment from *Star Trek*, *Star Wars*, *Battlestar Galactica*, and other future worlds. Available in four individual golden art folios. Each folio contains a set of six 18" x 24" sheets

➤ Volume I, one sheet with hand phaser (*ST III*).

➤ Volume II, one sheet with tricorder (*ST III*).

	Issue	Fair	Mint

➤ Volume III, one sheet with Klingon communicator (*ST III*).

➤ Volume IV.

Price for each. **12 12 15**

Dreadnought Comparison Chart: Todd Guenther, Starstation Aurora. External and cut-away views of the Dreadnought Class ships. Set of five sheets, 8" x 17". **3 3 5**

Drone Spy Reconnaissance Ship: Marc E. Shammai. Set of four sheets. **3 3 5**

DY Series Comparison Chart: Michael Morrissette, Starstation Aurora. Blueprint of the Botany Bay Sleeper Ship from "Space Seed." One sheet. **3.95 4 5**

Enterprise Legacy Comparison Chart: Six Centuries of Bold Adventure. A recognition guide including twelve historical ships bearing the name "Enterprise" from the years 1755-2303. One sheet, 20" x 25". **5 5 6**

Enterprise Soundstage Blueprints: #P-2191, Lincoln Enterprises, 1984. Reproductions of the actual blueprints used on the sets on Paramount stages #9 and #10. Interior and exterior details on Trek set positions in relation to the building itself and landscape positions. **3 6 10**

Federation Size Comparison Charts: Starstation Aurora. A group of blueprint sets featuring side views of the various starships of the Star Trek universe.

(A) Chart I, Todd Guenther and Michael Morrissette. Shows exteriors of Federation cruisers, heavy cruisers, tugs, freighters, and scouts. Twelve ships on two 20" x 28" sheets. **4.95 5 6**

(B) Chart II, Todd Guenther. A supplement showing the Enterprise, Belknap, Avenger, Knox, Federation, Ascension, and K'Teremny Class vessels. Set of two 21" x 26" sheets. **5.95 6 7**

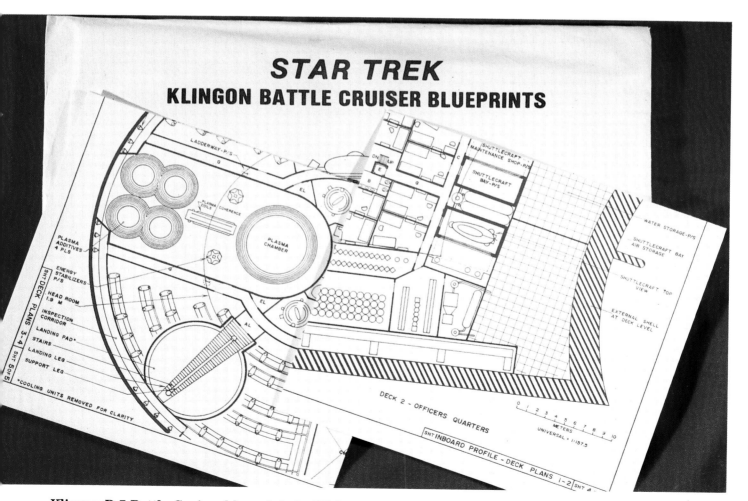

Klingon D-7 Battle Cruiser blueprints by Michael McMaster, Galactic Designs & Productions.

	Issue	Fair	Mint

Galileo Shuttlecraft: L. Allen Everhart, Starcraft Designs. Shows exterior and cut-away views of the Galileo. Set of two 18" x 24" sheets.
3 3 5

Galileo Shuttlecraft Class F: 1988. Special model builder's blueprints. Includes exteriors, interiors, and control details in three-quarter view, plus a text with photos and painting details. Set of six 11" x 17" sheets. 4.95 5 6

Gorn Defense Force Battlecruiser: Allen C. Peed III, Starcraft Productions. Exteriors of previously unknown Gorn ships from the episode "Arena." Set of two 8½" x 14" sheets. 3.50 3 5

Joshua Class Starship: Specs of this Federation Command Cruiser, plus the Joshua and Jerico Class Warpshuttles. Includes SSD gaming sheet. Set of seven blueprints. 9.95 10 11

K-7 Space Station: Two sets of blueprints for the famous space station from the episode "The Trouble With Tribbles."

(A) First edition, Geoffrey Mandel and Kenneth Altman, Pan Galactic Press. Exterior designs only. Set of four 15½" x 22½" sheets. 3 3 5

(B) Revised edition, Geoffrey Mandel and Kenneth Altman, Pan Galactic Press. Extended plans for the Class K Rest & Recreation Facility with exterior and interior designs. Set of five 17" x 22" sheets.
4.95 5 6

Klingon Bird of Prey Scout Vessel: From *ST III*, Kruge's Klingon-Romulan hybrid craft built as a result of a Klingon exchange trade with the Romulans for their cloaking device.

(A) Lawrence Miller, Lawrence Miller Design. Exterior and interior layouts, plus the bridge and cloaking device technology. Set of six 18" x 24" sheets.
10.95 10 11

(B) Lincoln Enterprise. Assorted profiles include outboard and inboard designs, top views, and deck elevations #1-10. Set of eight 12" x 28" sheets.
4.95 5 7

Klingon D-7 Battlecruiser: Michael McMaster, Galactic Designs & Productions. From the TV series. Exterior and interior designs. Set of eight 13½" x 29" sheets. 7.95 8 9

Klingon D-7 Battle Cruiser Chart: Geoffrey Mandel, Interstellar Associates, 1977. Single blueprint showing a three-view cross-section of the TV Klingon vessel. Special thanks given to Michael McMaster. One 23" x 35" sheet. 2.95 10 15

	Issue	Fair	Min

Klingon K'T'Orr Class Destroyer: Marc E. Shammai. Full blueprint specs, plus interior and exterior designs. Set of nine 11" x 16" sheets.
8.95 9 1

Klingon Katanga Class Vessel: L. Allen Everhart, Starcraft Designs. Giant size sheet of the D-7/5 Class vessel from *STTMP*. Exterior profiles only. 24" x 60"
6 6 1

Kobayashi Maru Neutronic Fuel Carrier: Roger Sorenson, Starstation Aurora. Details this unseen ship from *ST II* with exteriors only. Set of four 14" x 17" sheets. 4.95 5

Major Deep Space Craft Size Comparison Chart: Michael McMaster, Galactic Designs & Productions. Special edition poster chart. A large comparison chart featuring 45 starships in side profile. Includes the Klingon D-7, Romulan D-6, the Enterprise, K-7 Space Station, a Tholian Flagship, and the Flagship Fesarius. One sheet.

Merchantman Federation Class J Ships: L. Allen Everhart, Starcraft Productions. From *ST III*. Set of five sheets. 6.95 7

Olympus Class Dreadnought: Specs on this three engine vessel (from *STTNG*) similar to the Alaska Class ships, plus a descriptive text. One 20" x 25" sheet. 5 5

Paladin Class Scout / Destroyer: Temporal Graphics, 1990. From *STTNG*. Blueprints feature profile cut-aways, forward, top aft and port views, plus shuttlecraft specs. Information includes Deflector Grid and Planetary Landing Systems material as well. There is also a role-playing supplement. Set of four sheets. 5.96 6

Regula One Orbital Station Deckplans: FASA, 1990. See **Role Playing Games**.

Regula One Space Laboratory: Lawrence Miller, Lawrence Miller Designs. From *ST II*. Full interior layouts plus exploded views, outboard, and cut-away. Set of five 9" x 16" sheets. 8.95 9 1

Romulan Bird of Prey Cruiser: Michael McMaster, Galactic Designs & Productions. Interior and exterior designs plus specs on the plasma weapon. Set of five 18" x 24" sheets. 6.95 7 8

Romulan L-85 Battleship: From *STTNG*. Ship recognition chart with exterior angles and specs. Comes rolled as one 20" x 25" sheet.
5 5

Science Fiction Letterheads: Lawrence Miller Design, 1987. Contains materials to help create your own personalized stationary with 22 famous sci-fi letterheads with the use of a photo copier. Includes Trek

Romulan Bird of Prey Cruiser blueprints, Galactic Designs & Productions, Michael McMaster renderings.

	Issue	Fair	Mint

etterheads: Enterprise, Klingon Command, Regula
)ne, Science Academy, and Star Fleet Command.
8.95   9   10

ielayana Class Starship Corellian Freighter:
ihane Johnson & D. Holt, The Noron Group. Inte-
iors and exteriors included. Set of four 18" x 24"
iheets.   **6.95   7   8**

iherman Class Cargo Drone: Todd Guenther,
itarstation Aurora. Interiors and exteriors of this
essel from the animated cartoon series. Set of ten
3½" x 17" sheets.   **5.95   6   7**

ihips of the Star Fleet: Volume #1, 2290-91, by
:alon Riel, Mastercom Data Center. State of the
'leet blueprints in tradepaper format. Includes
•lueprints on ten classes of cruisers, seven classes of
rigates, eleven fold-out glossies, an appendix, and a
;lossary. Some ships covered include Constitution,
:oronado, Achernar, Enterprise, Belknap, Tikopai,
iurya, Avenger, Knox, Endurance, Cyane, and Strike
:ruiser. 126 pages, 9" x 12". **24.95   25   26**

	Issue	Fair	Mint

S.S. Aurora Class Space Cruiser: Todd Guenther,
Starstation Aurora. This Tholian vessel, designed to
travel between the Sol and Eridani star systems, appeared in the classic TV episode "The Way To Eden."
Exteriors plus small drawings for model builders. Set
of two 16" x 2" sheets.   **2.95   3   4**

S.S. Kobayashi Maru Neutronic Fuel Carrier:
David Neilson. From *ST II*. Set of four 14" x 17"
sheets.   **4.95   4   5**

S.S. Vadenda Class Star Freighter: Allen C. Peed
III, Starcraft Productions. A giant nonbased cargo
ship which does not carry a planetary designation letter. Set of twelve 14" x 22" sheets.
9.95   10   11

Starbase 79: Lawrence Miller, Lawrence Miller
Design, 1991. Interior and exterior views for this
Flagship UFP starbase, plus supplement. Set of six
11" x 22" sheets.   **12.95   13   14**

	Issue	Fair	Mint

Star Fleet Cargoshuttle: 1990. Exterior and interior details of the new Enterprise 1701-A shuttle. Six sheets. **10.95 11 12**

Star Fleet Communicator: Nova Productions, 1986. Specs on the working of one of Star Trek's most valuable pieces of equipment. Eight views. **3 3 5**

Starship Blueprints: #P2183, Lincoln Enterprises, 1984. Imaginative vessel of the future as envisioned by Gene Roddenberry and possibly the starship of a new TV series. Includes the torus-like ship, Metatransit system, and Metaflier section of this luxury cruiser. Companion set to P2182, full-color 2" x 3" poster. Set of three 11" x 17" sheets. **2.50 5 10**

Starship Fleet Blueprints: Allen H. Fishbeck, Fishbeck Designs, 1987. Set of twelve sheets. **— 7 8**

Star Trek Blueprints: One of the first mass-produced blueprints featuring the Enterprise. Includes every foot of the vessel to scale: bridge, sick bay, photon torpedo banks, crew's quarters, shuttlecraft bay, science labs, etc.

(A) Franz Joseph, Franz Joseph Designs. Blueprint sheets produced for limited distribution and never mass-marketed. Sheets come as rolled copies. Set of twelve sheets. **— 75 150**

(B) Franz Joseph, Ballantine Books, 1975. Original mass-produced package in brown plastic/vinyl pocket with snap closure. Set of twelve 9" x 30" sheets. **5 50 75**

Star Trek III **Blueprints:** Starstation Aurora. Advance print showing preview designs for the spacecraft to appear in the movie. One 24" x 36" sheet. **5 5 10**

Star Trek Hand Phaser: Details and specs on the phaser from the "Menagerie" episode. One 11" x 17" sheet. **1 1 2**

Star Trek Modeler's Blueprints: Set One, 1990. Set of new blueprints featuring several Trek vessels which may be constructed to scale using available ERTL Star Trek model kits. Includes animated Robot Cargo ship, armored warp shuttle, DY-100 "Space Seed" ship, the Galileo, and K-7 Space Station. Set of twelve sheets. **4.95 5 6**

Star Trek: The Motion Picture **Official Blueprints:** Assorted ship profiles from the movie. Includes new Katanga Klingon vessel, new Enterprise, Vulcan Shuttle, Work Bee, and more.

	Issue	Fair	Mint

(A) David Kimble, Wallaby Books, 1979. Packaged in vinyl plastic pocket with snap closure. Set of fourteen 13½" x 19" sheets. **6.95 20 30**

(B) David Kimble. Reprints of the original blueprint set marketed as *Star Trek: The Motion Picture* Blueprints. Contains fourteen 11" x 17" sheets in paper pocket. **9.95 9 10**

U.S.S. Almeida Class Heavy Cruiser Freighter Michael Morrissette, Starstation Aurora. Set of five 18" x 22" sheets. **— 5 6**

U.S.S. Avenger Class Heavy Frigate: David John Neilson. Specs on the vessel from *ST II* which features the Reliant, plus plans for the Surya Frigate and the Killer Bee Assault Pod. Set of six 14" x 18" sheets. **7.95 8 9**

U.S.S. Caracal Class Command Cruiser: Todd Guenther, Starstation Aurora. Designs for the ship that precedes the Reliant in construction. Set of twelve 8½" x 28" sheets. **7.50 7 8**

U.S.S. Decatur Prototype Test Starship: Todd Guenther, Starstation Aurora. Specs printed on heavy gold paper. One 23" x 29" sheet. **3.95 4 6**

U.S.S. Detroyat Class Heavy Cruiser: Michael Morrissette, Starstation Aurora. General plans and specs. Set of six 10½" x 25" sheets. **6.50 7 8**

U.S.S. Durance Cargo / Tug Class Starship: Todd Guenther, Starstation Aurora. External and cut-away views of the UFP tug. Set of five 8" x 17" sheets. **4 4 6**

U.S.S. Enterprise: Franz Joseph, Pan Galactic Press. Reproductions of Joseph's famous blueprint packet published by Ballantine in 1975. Exterior and interior profiles folded inside a white paper pocket. Set of twelve 9" x 29" sheets. **7.95 8 9**

U.S.S. Enterprise Alaska Class Battle Cruiser Designs for the N.C.C. 1701-C Enterprise, the last before the *STTNG* ship. One rolled 20" x 25" sheet. **5 5 6**

U.S.S. Enterprise and Shuttlecraft Galileo: Matt Jeffries, Star Trek Enterprises, 1968. The official plans from the drawing board of Matt Jeffries, Art Director for the *Star Trek* series. Details focus only upon weaponry, structural dimensions, and multi angle perspectives. These were very simple blueprints, but the first of what would become an entire genre of blueprints devoted to the Star Trek universe. These pen and ink illustrations also appeared in the Roddenberry/Whitfield paperback *The*

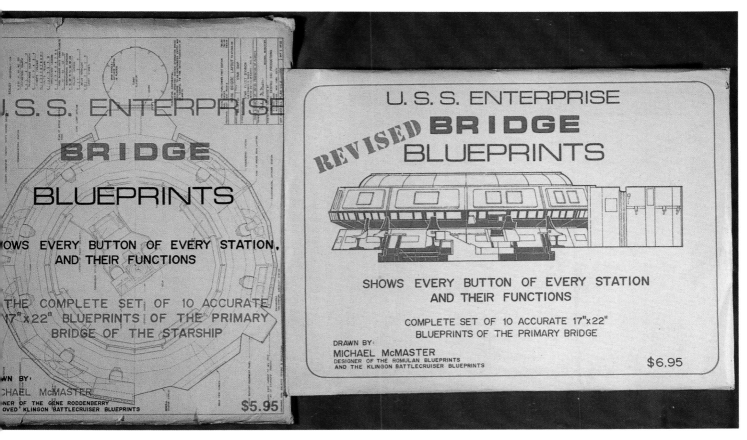

.S. Enterprise bridge blueprints, the rare first edition with top view cover and the second edition, Galactic Designs & Productions.

	Issue	Fair	Mint

Making of Star Trek published by Ballantine in 1968. Set of six drawings on 8½" x 11" white bond paper.

- Starship Enterprise with size comparison to the CVA-65 Enterprise aircraft carrier.
- U.S.S. Enterprise (top, front, and side schematics), one sheet.
- Galileo 1707'7 shuttlecraft, exterior and interior seating plans, two sheets.
- Hangar deck, bay, and aft sections, two sheets.

Price for each. .50 10 20

U.S.S. Enterprise Bridge: Contains all the bridge stations, switches, and functions.

A) Michael McMaster, Galactic Designs & Productions. TV Enterprise. Blue design cover. Set of ten 17" x 22" sheets. 5.95 6 10

B) Michael McMaster, Galactic Designs & Productions. *STTMP* Enterprise. Revised edition with this legend stamped in black on red and blue cover. Set of ten 17" x 22" sheets. 6.95 7 8

C) Michael McMaster, Galactic Designs & Productions. Revised again with black design cover. Set of ten 12" x 36" sheets. 9.95 10 11

	Issue	Fair	Mint

(D) Lawrence Miller, Lawrence Miller Design, 1991. All new blueprints for the U.S.S. Enterprise 1701 bridge. Includes the refit of 7912.07, and the redesign changes of 8101.03 plus comparison to the original bridge of 0965.03. Set of ten 17" x 22" sheets. 14.95 15 16

U.S.S. Enterprise Construction Plans: L. Allen Everhart, Starcraft Productions. Shows the various design stages the Enterprise went through before attaining its TV look. Set of four 11" x 17" sheets. 6.95 7 9

U.S.S. Enterprise Deck Plan: FASA, 1983. See **Role Playing Games**.

U.S.S. Enterprise Heavy Cruiser Evolution: Shows the Enterprise from its early designs and into the future. Text included. Set of three 24" x 36" sheets. 9.95 10 11

U.S.S. Enterprise Giant Blueprints: Two sheets with a large format, showing designs for two Enterprise vessels.

	Issue	Fair	Mint

(A) TV Enterprise, one 24" x 60" sheet.

        6.95   **6**   **7**

(B) *STTMP* Enterprise, one 24" x 60" sheet.

        6.95   **6**   **7**

U.S.S. Enterprise / Klingon Cruiser Reversible Blueprint Poster: Star Trek Con, 1972. See **Posters**.

U.S.S. Enterprise NCC-1701D Centurian Series Battlecruiser: Designs for the *STTNG* ship N.C.C. 1701-D. Set of four blueprint sheets with a fifth information sheet included. **6.95** **6** **7**

U.S.S. Enterprise NCC-1701D, Galaxy Class: 1988. Set of four sheets. **4.95** **5** **6**

U.S.S. Enterprise NCC-1701D, *Star Trek: The Next Generation* Blueprints: FASA, 1989. See **Role Playing Games**.

U.S.S. Enterprise TV Profiles: Compares two TV designs as seen from the pilot episode "The Cage" and the regular series.

➤ Type I, "The Cage" Enterprise.

➤ Type II, Enterprise as seen on the classic series. Price for each. **6.95** **7** **8**

U.S.S. Excelsior Warp Drive: Todd Guenther & Jason Genser, Starstation Aurora. From *ST III*. Official SFC Datapack designs of this Ingram Class starship. Shows exterior and cut-away specs with a comparison chart. Special collector's edition in a vinyl plastic pocket. Set of eight 12½" x 29" sheets.

        9.95   **10**   **12**

U.S.S. Federation Class Dreadnought: Allen C. Peed, Starcraft Productions. Designs for this largest Starfleet starship. Exterior and interior specs, which include inboard desk plans, sick bay, engineering, hangar decks, deflector shields, and cloaking device. Set of ten 9" x 27" sheets. **9.95** **10** **11**

U.S.S. Flagstaff Drone Spy Reconnaissance Ship: Marc E. Shammai. Blueprints of this Federation sensor-carrying drone used to explore dangerous phenomenon. Set of four 11" x 17" sheets.

        4.95   **5**   **6**

U.S.S. Grissom, Glenn Class Fleet Survey Ship: L. Allen Everhart, Starcraft Productions. From *ST III*. Outboard and cut-away views. Set of four 16" x 22" sheets. **5.95** **6** **7**

U.S.S. Hornet Class Starship: Lawrence Miller, Lawrence Miller Design. Specs on this SFC, which was designed to pursue Orion fast attack craft. Inboard and outboard profiles, plus a special information supplement. Set of seven 18" x 23" sheets.

        10.95   **11**   **12**

	Issue	Fair	Mint

U.S.S. Ianar Fast Frigate: Exterior views and specs. Includes print of Renner Corvette Class vessel. Set of six 11" x 17" sheets. **5.95** **6**

U.S.S. Independence Class Freighter: Geoffrey Mandel, Interstellar Associates. Interior and exterior plans. Set of eleven 8½" x 14" sheets.

        4.95   **5**

U.S.S. Lynx Timeship Prototype: Lawrence Miller, Lawrence Miller Design, 1991. Wall charts of the Federation top secret research time ship. Set of five 18" x 24" sheets. **12.95** **13**

U.S.S. Menahga Battlecruiser Prototype: Michael Morrissette, Starstation Aurora. One 24" x 36" sheet. **3.50** **4**

U.S.S. Reliant: Popular Avenger Class ship from *ST II*.

(A) Todd Guenther, Starstation Aurora. Interiors and exteriors of this ship in a vinyl plastic pouch with snap closures. Set of ten 16" x 28" sheets.

        9.95   **10**   **11**

(B) Todd Guenther, Starstation Aurora. Includes the Coventry, Detroyat, Surya, and Ptolemy Class vessels and histories. One 24" x 36" sheet.

        3.50   **3**

U.S.S. Reliant Deck Plans: FASA, 1983. See **Role Playing Games**.

U.S.S. Renner Class Escort Destroyer: Rafael Gonzalez, Miami Naval Yards. Specs of this Federation destroyer. Set of four 11" x 17" sheets.

        4.95   **5**

U.S.S. Saladin Class Destroyer/Scout: L. Allen Everhart, Starcraft Productions. Exterior and interior specs deck by deck. Set of nine 16" x 19" sheets. **7.95** **8** **9**

Weapons and Field Equipment: Shane Johnson, Noron Group. Individually packaged blueprint sets which cover a broad science fiction media range. Set of five 17" x 22" sheets each.

➤ Volume 1, details on Jupiter II laser pistol, Sandman gun, light sabers, and phaser rifles.

➤ Volume 2, details on Star Trek phasers III and IV, Jupiter II laser rifle, Sandman follower types I and II, and Alpha Stungun.

➤ Volume 3, details on phasers and communicators. Includes Starfleet phaser Mark II, Klingon hand weapon, and Star Trek phaser II, Mark II.

Price for each. **7.95** **8** **10**

The colorful Star Trek Game by Palitoy, 1975, packaged in England.

	Issue	Fair	Mint

Vulcan Harp: 1990. Detailed construction plans to make an actual musical instrument known as a Vulcan harp as first seen on the TV series. Includes one-to-one templates, plus electronic schematics. Set of twelve 24" x 48" sheets. **7.95 8 9**

Weapons of the Eugenics: 1990. Declassified blueprints of the technical plans on late 1990s eugenics wars. Precedes the stardate of the TV series. Text includes Politics of the Eugenics, tales, biographies, vehicles, and weapons. 24 pages of blueprints. **5.95 6 7**

Board Games

Star Trek Action and Adventure in Outer Space: #2676-3, Hasbro, 1974. Children's fold-out board game with four playing pieces, pair of dice, two spinners, and a peg-hole board. Animation-style box lid illustrates TV Enterprise from the cartoon series Promo Cel — Running McCoy, Kirk, Spock, and Sulu. Also has three action scene insets. **5 25 30**

Star Trek Game: #2293-9, Ideal Toy Corp, 1966. Fold-out board game for 2-4 players. Object is to race in space from Earth to designated planet and back, keeping your fuel ships within reach. 19" square board shows Earth ringed by six alien planets. Includes one six-sided die, four tokens, four cardboard mission cards, 36 fuel packs, and color fuel discs. Boxed 10½" x 19¼". Cover is realistic art rendering

of TV Spock, Kirk, and Uhura with bridge viewscreen action scene. **2.50 45 60**

Star Trek Game: #20015, Palitoy (Bradgate Wholesale Div.), England, 1975. Children's fold-out board game. Includes six cardboard stand-up crew figures (four Klingon, Kirk, Spock) and two plastic monsters. Board shows the Mego artwork heads from the TV eight-inch doll cardstocks, plus colorful action scenes. Box art is TV Enterprise, Kirk, and Spock. **3.50 40 50**

Star Trek 3-D Game: #802, Dimensional Ind. Corporation, 1968. Unusual heavy cardstock 8½" x 11" playing board. Game is to flip coins on outlines drawn on the backside. The front of the playing board is a 3-D "holographic" photo of portside classic Enterprise

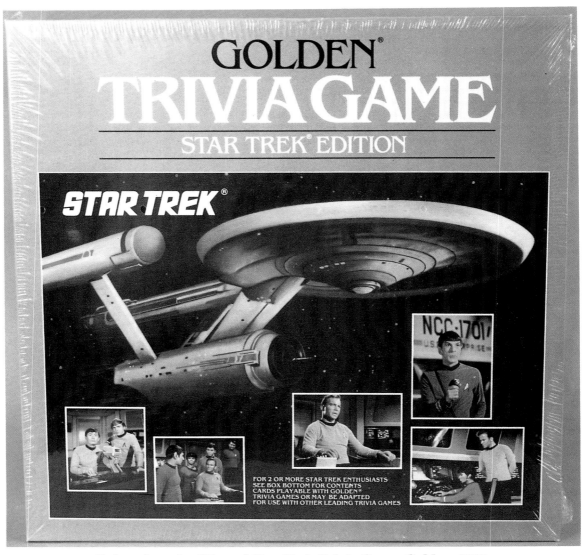

Deluxe boxed edition of Star Trek Trivia Game, Golden, 1985.

	Issue	Fair	Mint

over two red planets with "Star Trek" lettering. Game is similar to tiddlywinks. **1 20 30**

***Star Trek The Motion Picture* Game:** Milton Bradley, 1979. For 2-4 players. Object is to travel the galaxy seeking out alien phenomenon, complete three missions, and return home. Oversize 26½" x 27" game board features six individual triangular Space Sector punch-ons. Central panorama is Enterprise in pursuit of Klingon Cruisers. Includes two six-sided dice, four miniature plastic starship pawns, 24 mission cards, 32 star cards, six clips, and 60 control markers. Boxed 14" x 19" with cover art

of Kirk, Spock, Uhura, McCoy, Scotty, Ilia, and the *STTMP* Enterprise. **9 25 35**

***Star Trek* Trivia Game:** #4161, Golden Trivia Game, Star Trek Edition, Western Publishing Company, Inc., 1985. Card and plastic board tray set for two or more players. Quiz categories are Aliens, Trek Trivia, Science Fiction, Alien Worlds, Quotes, and the Ship's Crew. Includes 216 printed cards (1,296 questions), one die, four-point value cards and instructions. 12½" x 12" box shows photo of TV Enterprise.

(A) Deluxe box. **11 20 30**
(B) Card box only. **7 10 15**

Book Cover

***Star Trek: The Next Generation* Bookcover:** KITN-TV, Minneapolis/St. Paul, 1988. Unusual

promo item produced by Pepsi, True Value Hardware Stores, and Gardner Brothers Homes. Distributed by

	Issue	Fair	Mint

KITN-TV. Standard paperstock book cover for school-books featuring color photo of the *STTNG* Enterprise on the front and an anti-smoking ad on the reverse.

These were handed out free at locations throughout Minneapolis. Folding instructions along front right-hand side. 11½" x 14½". **N/A 2 4**

Bookmarks

Beam Me Up Scotty Bookmark: #H-847, Groan-Ups, Antioch Publishing Company, 1985. Red lettering says "Beam Me Up Scotty, There's No Intelligent Life Down Here" on yellow and blue planetscape. Choice of purple or blue tassel. **.99 1 2**

Star Trek Character Bookmarks: Michael Verina, 1979. Fan-produced bookmarks in beige or aqua.
➤ "Live long and prosper," with Spock
➤ "Part of Me," with Spock
   "Perhaps they were right," with Kirk
➤ "To boldly go," with Kirk
Price for each. **1 2 3**

Star Trek Bookmarks: T-K Graphics, 1987. Black lettering or design on colored cardstock strips. 2" x ¾".
➤ "Beam Me Up Scotty!"
➤ "Star Fleet Command Intelligence Division"
➤ "Tribble Breeding is a Hairy Experience"
   "Star Trek Forever" with Janus head
➤ "Star Fleet Tactical Operations Center" with UFP emblem

➤ "U.S.S. Enterprise" with schematic
Price for each. **.25 .50 1**

Star Trek The Motion Picture Bookmark: Pocket Books, 1979. Special give-away promo advertising the *STTMP* novel. Reads "The Human Adventure is Just Beginning." **Free 2 3**

Star Trek: The Next Generation Bookmark: #0-681-550-368, One Stop Posters, 1987. 2" x 7¼" cardstock bookmark with *STTNG* Enterprise on top and "Explore New Worlds With Books" on the bottom. The reverse features a 6" ruler scale. **1.25 1 2**

Strangers From The Sky Bookmark: Pocket Books, 1987. Special cardstock cut-out featuring the TV Enterprise on the front and an advertisement for *Strangers From The Sky* Trek novel by Margaret Wander Bonanno on the reverse. This was a promo item given away over the counter to people purchasing the book. **Free 1 2**

Bookplates

Star Trek Theme: T-K Graphics. Self-sticking plates with space for personalization. Reads "from the library of," 2" x 4" format. Fifteen plates per packet.
A) 1984, Khan design, drawing by Bob Suh. **1.75 3 4**
B) 1984, "Star Fleet Academy Library." **1.75 3 4**

(C) 1990, Starship Enterprise silhouette. **4 4 5**

STTNG Title Logo: #0-929477-95-2, O.S.P. Publishing, 1989. 24 nameplate stickers with front view of *STTNG* ship and Title Logo beneath. 3" x 4", plastic-bagged. **3 3 4**

Books

A Call To Darkness: Star Trek: The Next Generation #9, #0-671-68708-5, Pocket Books, November 1989, paperback, 274 pages, novel by Michael Jan Friedman. **3.95 3 4**

Abode of Life: Star Trek #6, paperback except where noted, 207 pages, novel by Lee Corey.
A) #0-8398-2931, Gregg Press, 1986, hardcover. **11.95 12 15**
B) #0-671-83297-2, Pocket Books, May 1982, Timescape edition. **2.50 5 8**

(C) #0-671-47719-6, Pocket Books. **2.95 4 5**
(D) #0-671-62746-5, Pocket Books, Gertrude logo. **3.50 4 5**
(E) #0-671-66149-3, Pocket Books, sixth printing. **3.95 4 5**
(F) #0-671-70596, Pocket Books. **4.50 4 5**

A Flag Full of Stars: Star Trek #54, #0-671-73918-2, Pocket Books, paperback, April 1991, 241 pages,

The Best of Trek with Eddie Jones artwork
cover, 1974.

The Best of Trek 16, Roc Science Fiction, 1991.

	Issue	Fair	Mint

novel by Brad Ferguson. Second book in the Lost Years saga.

	Issue	Fair	Mint
	4.95	5	6

***Battlestations!*:** Star Trek #31, Pocket Books, November 1986, paperback, 275 pages, novel by Diane Carey. Sequel to *Dreadnought!*

	Issue	Fair	Mint
(A) #0-671-63267-1.	3.50	4	5
(B) #0-671-66201-2.	3.95	4	5
(C) #0-671-70183.	4.50	4	5

***The Best of Trek*:** Signet, paperback, 239 pages, by Walter Irwin and G. B. Love. Nonfiction articles and stories taken from *Trek Magazine*. The *Best of Trek* #1-5 and #7 have cover art by Eddie Jones; #6, #8, #9, and #10 have art by Paul Alexander. To date, fifteen volumes edited by Irwin and Love have appeared under the Signet imprint. The premiere of *Best of Trek #1* heralded the debut of the first Trek anthology of original literature in paperback format.

	Issue	Fair	Min

All of the volumes' covers display some of the most surreal spaceships ever produced in association with the Trek universe as depicted on TV.

	Issue	Fair	Min
(A) #0-451-11682-8, 1974.	1.75	2	
(B) #0-451-11682-8.	2.50	2	
(C) #0-451-14311-6.	2.95	2	

***The Best of Trek* #2:** Signet, paperback, 196 pages, by Walter Irwin and G. B. Love.

	Issue	Fair	Min
(A) First edition, 1977.	1.95	2	
(B) #0-451-09836-6.	2.50	2	
(C) #0-451-12368-9.	2.75	2	
(D) #0-451-12368-9.	2.95	2	
(E) #0-451-13466-4.	2.95	2	
(F) #0-451-12368-9.	3.50	3	

***The Best of Trek* #3:** Signet, paperback, 196 pages, by Walter Irwin and G. B. Love.

	Issue	Fair	Min
(A) #0-451-09582-0, 1979.	1.95	2	

	Issue	Fair	Mint
(B) #0-451-11807-3.	2.50	2	3
(C) #0-451-13092-8.	2.95	2	3

The Best of Trek #4: Signet, paperback, 214 pages, by Walter Irwin and G. B. Love.

(A) #0-451-11221-0, 1981.	2.25	2	4
(B) #0-451-12356-5.	2.75	2	4
(C) #0-451-13465-6.	2.95	2	4
(D) #0-451-15176-3.	2.95	2	(4)
(E) #0-451-13465-6.	3.50	3	4

The Best of Trek #5: Signet, paperback, 201 pages, by Walter Irwin and G. B. Love.

(A) #0-451-11751-4, 1982.	2.50	2	4
(B) #0-451-11751-4.	2.75	2	(4)
(C) #0-451-12947-4.	2.95	2	4
(D) #0-451-12947-4.	3.50	3	4

The Best of Trek #6: Signet, paperback, 191 pages, by Walter Irwin and G. B. Love.

(A) #0-451-12493-6, 1983.	2.25	3	(4)
(B) #0-451-12493-6.	2.75	3	4
(C) #0-451-15177-1.	2.95	3	4

The Best of Trek #7: Signet, paperback, 201 pages, by Walter Irwin and G. B. Love.

(A) #0-451-12977-6, 1984.	2.75	3	4
(B) #0-451-14204-7.	2.95	3	(4)
(C) #0-451-14204-7.	3.25	3	4

The Best of Trek #8: Signet, paperback, 221 pages, by Walter Irwin and G. B. Love.

(A) #0-451-13488-5, February 1985.	2.95	3	(4)
(B) #0-451-13488-5.	3.50	3	4

The Best of Trek #9: #0-451-13816-3, Signet, September 1985, paperback, 207 pages, by Walter Irwin and G. B. Love. 2.95 / 3 / (4)

The Best of Trek #10: #0-451-13816-3, Signet, June 1986, paperback, 204 pages, by Walter Irwin and G. Love. 2.95 / 3 / (4)

The Best of Trek #11: #0-451-12368-9, Signet, November 1986, paperback, 204 pages, by Walter Irwin and G. B. Love. 2.95 / 3 / (4)

The Best of Trek #12: #0-451-14925-3, Signet, paperback, 206 pages, by Walter Irwin and G. B. Love. 2.95 / 3 / (4)

The Best of Trek #13: #0-451-15325-3, Signet, May 1988, paperback, 204 pages, by Walter Irwin and G. B. Love. 3.50 / 3 / (4)

The Best of Trek #14: #0-451-15614-5, Signet, November 1988, paperback, 220 pages, by Walter Irwin and G. B. Love. 3.50 / 3 / (4)

The Best of Trek #15: #0-451-45015-9, Penguin Books (with Roc logo), June 1990, paperback, 207 pages, by Walter Irwin and G. B. Love. 3.95 / 3 / (4)

The Best of Trek #16: #0-451-45047-9, Roc Science Fiction (New American Library), March 1991, paperback, 208 pages, by Walter Irwin and G. B. Love. 3.99 / 4 / (5)

Best of the Best of Trek: The First Mega Collection, #0-451-45017-5, Penguin Books, July 1990 (with Roc logo), tradepaper, 370 pages, by Walter Irwin and G. B. Love. 9.95 / 10 / 11

Black Fire: Star Trek #8, 220 pages, novel by Sonni Cooper.

(A) #0-8398-2935-3, Gregg Press, hardcover, 1986.	11.95	12	15

(B) #0-671-83632-3, Pocket Books paperback, Timescape imprint on center cover, January 1983. 2.95 / (5) / 10

(C) #0-671-83632-3, Pocket Books paperback, numbered cover.	2.95	5	8
(D) #0-671-61758-3, Pocket Books paperback, Gertrude logo.	3.50	4	5
(E) #0-671-65747-X, Pocket Books paperback, seventh printing.	3.95	4	5
(F) #0-671-70548.	4.50	4	5

Blast of Activities: #1310, Merrigold Press, 1979, softcover, 32 pages. Children's coloring book. Full-color cover with Spock holding phaser. 8½" x 11". .59 / 1 / 5

Bloodthirst: Star Trek #37, Pocket books, paperback, 264 pages, novel by J. M. Dillard.

(A) #0-671-64489-0.	3.95	4	5
(B) #0-671-70876.	4.50	4	(5)

Boogeymen: Star Trek: The Next Generation #17, #0-671-70970-4, Pocket Books, paperback, novel by Mel Gilden. 4.95 / 5 / 6

✔ ***Buck Alice and the Actor Robot***: Gap Books, 1988, 245 pages, by Walter Koenig. Original fiction.

(A) Gap Books, hardcover.	17.95	20	25
(B) Gap Books, hardcover, special autographed edition.	35	35	45
(C) #1-55547-240-0, Guild Press, paperback.	3.95	3	(8)
(D) #1-55547-240-0, Critic's Choice, paperback.	3.50	3	6

Captain's Honor: Star Trek: The Next Generation #8, #0-671-68487-6, Pocket Books, September 1989, 255 pages, novel by David and Daniel Dvorkin. 3.95 / 3 / 4

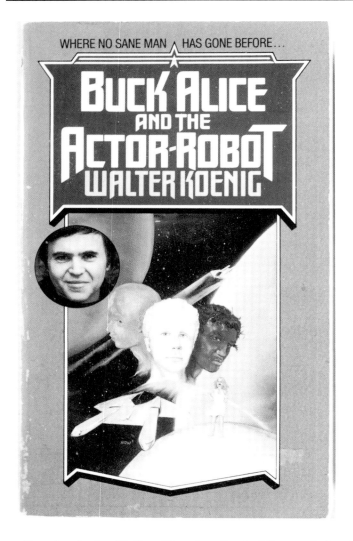

Two books by Walter Koenig: *Buck Alice and the Actor Robot,* Guild Press edition, 1985 and *Chekov's Enterp* Pocket Books, 1980.

	Issue	*Fair*	*Mint*

Captain's Log: #0-671-68652-6, Pocket Books, July 1989, tradepaper, 224 pages, by Lisabeth Shatner. William Shatner's personal account of the making of *ST V*. **9.95 10 (11)**

Chain of Attack: Star Trek #32, Pocket Books, paperback, 251 pages, novel by Gene Deweese.

(A) #0-671-63269-8, February 1987.
3.50 3 (4)

(B) #0-671-66658-4. **3.95 3 4**

Chekov's Enterprise: #0-671-83286-7, Pocket Books, 1980, paperback, 222 pages, by Walter Koenig. Autobiographical account on the making of *STTMP*. This is an unusual movie tie-in book associated with *STTMP* and a nice collectible. It is the only nonfiction paperback on Trek for adults that Pocket has published. **2.25 20 30**

	Issue	*Fair*	*Min*

Children of Hamlin: Star Trek: The Next Genera tion #3, #0-671-67319-X, Pocket Books, Novembe 1988, paperback, 252 pages, novel by Carmen Carter **3.95 3**

Come Be with Me: #0-833-96033-8, Blue Mountair Arts, September 1978, tradepaper, 60 pages, b Leonard Nimoy. Original poetry.
4.95 15 2.

Contamination: Star Trek: The Next Generatio #16, #0-671-70561-X, Pocket Books, March 199 paperback, 273 pages, novel by John Vornholt. **4.95 5**

Corona: Star Trek #15, 192 pages, novel by Gre Bear.
(A) #0-8398-2889-6, Gregg Press, hardcover, 1985. **11.95 12 1**
(B) #0-671-47390-5, Pocket Books, April 1984, pape back. **2.95 (4)**

he tradepaper *Cyperpunk Trek!*, Topper Books, 1990.

	Issue	Fair	Mint
C) #0-671-62749-X, Pocket Books, paperback, ertrude logo.	3.50	4	5
D) #0-671-66341-0, Pocket Books, paperback.	3.95	4	5
E) #0-671-70798, Pocket Books, April 1984, paper-ack.	4.50	4	5

Covenant of the Crown: Star Trek #4, 191 pages, ovel by Howard Weinstein.

	Issue	Fair	Mint
A) Gregg Press, 1985, hardcover.	11.95	12	15
B) Literary Guild, 1981, hardcover.	9.99	10	12
C) #04082, Science Fiction Book Club edition, 1981, ardcover.	4.98	4	6
D) #04082, same as above.	5.98	5	6
E) #0-671-83307-3, Pocket Books, December 1981, aperback, Timescape.	2.50	(5)	10
F) #0-671-83307-3.	2.95	5	8
G) #0-671-67072.	3.95	4	5
H) #0-671-70078.	4.50	4	5

Crisis on Centaurus: Star Trek #28, Pocket Books, 54 pages, novel by Brad Ferguson.

	Issue	Fair	Mint
A) #2436, Science Fiction Book Club, 1986, ardcover.	4.98	5	6
B) #0-671-61115-1, March 1986, paperback.	3.50	4	5
C) #0-671-65753-4.	3.95	4	5
D) #0-671-70799.	4.50	4	5

British edition, *Deep Domain*, Star Trek novel 2 (U.S. Pocket Books #33).

	Issue	Fair	Mint

Cry of the Onlies: Star Trek #46, #0-671-68167-2, Pocket Books, October 1989, paperback, 255 pages, novel by Judy Klass. 4.50 4 (5)

Cyberpunk Trek!: #0-88687-485-8, Topper Books (Pharos Books), 1990, tradepaper, 110 pages, by Jim Meddick. Black and white ink cartoons first published as *Robotman Comic Strips* by United Feature Syndicate, Inc. in 1987. Includes introduction by Mr. Spock with cartoons on movies, aliens, science television, and Star Trek. Cover has small photo insert of Spock. 6.95 7 9

Day of the Dove: See *Star Trek 11*.

Death's Angel: Bantam Books, paperback, 213 pages, novel by Kathleen Sky.

	Issue	Fair	Mint
(A) #0-553-14703-X, April 1981.	2.25	(15)	20
(B) #0-553-14703-X, June 1981.	2.25	5	10

61

	Issue	Fair	Mint

(C) #0-553-24637-2, April 1984.

| | 2.95 | 5 | 8 |

(D) #0-553-24637-2, fourth printing.

| | 2.95 | 4 | 6 |

(E) #0-553-24983-5, July 1985, Spectra logo with second edition cover art.

| | 2.95 | 3 | (4) |

Deep Domain: Star Trek #33, Pocket Books, paperback, 275 pages, novel by Howard Weinstein.

(A) #0-671-63329-5, April 1987.

| | 3.50 | 4 | (5) |

(B) #0-671-67077.

| | 3.95 | 4 | 5 |

(C) #0-671-70549.

| | 4.50 | 4 | 5 |

Demons: Star Trek #30, Pocket Books, paperback, 271 pages, novel by J. M. Dillard.

(A) #0-671-62524-1, July 1986.

| | 3.50 | 4 | (5) |

(B) #0-671-66150-7.

| | 3.95 | 4 | 5 |

(C) #0-671-70877.

| | 4.50 | 4 | 5 |

Devil World: Bantam Books, paperback, 153 pages, novel by Gordon Eklund.

(A) #0-553-13297-0, November 1979.

| | 1.75 | 10 | (15) |

(B) #0-553-24577-1, January 1985.

| | 2.95 | 3 | (5) |

Doctor's Orders: Star Trek #50, #0-671-66189-2, Pocket Books, June 1990, paperback, 291 pages, novel by Diane Duane.

| | 4.50 | 5 | (5) |

Doomsday World: Star Trek: The Next Generation #12, #0-671-70237-8, Pocket Books, July 1990, paperback, novel by Carter.

| | 4.50 | 4 | 5 |

Double, Double: Star Trek #45, #0-671-66130-2, Pocket Books, April 1989, paperback, 308 pages, novel by Michael Jan Friedman.

| | 3.95 | 4 | (5) |

Dreadnought!: Star Trek #29, Pocket Books, paperback, novel by Diane Carey. Prequel to *Battlestations!*

(A) #0-671-61873-3.

| | 3.50 | 4 | (5) |

(B) #0-671-66500-6.

| | 3.95 | 4 | 5 |

(C) #0-671-72567.

| | 4.50 | 4 | 5 |

Dreams of Raven: Star Trek #34, Pocket Books, paperback, 255 pages, novel by Carmen Carter.

(A) #0-671-64500-5, May 1987.

| | 3.50 | 4 | (5) |

(B) #0-671-67794.

| | 3.95 | 4 | 5 |

(C) #0-671-70281.

| | 4.50 | 4 | 5 |

Dwellers in the Crucible: Star Trek #25, Pocket Books, paperback, 308 pages, novel by Margaret Wander.

(A) #0-671-60373-6, September 1985.

| | 3.50 | 4 | 5 |

(B) #0-671-60373-6, third printing.

| | 3.50 | 4 | 5 |

(C) #0-671-60373-6, fifth printing, with red lettering on spine.

| | 3.50 | 4 | 5 |

	Issue	Fair	Min

(D) #0-671-66088-8, sixth printing.

| | 3.95 | 4 | |

Encounter at Farpoint: Star Trek: The Nex Generation #1, #0-671-65241-9, Pocket Books, October 1987, paperback, 192 pages, by David Gerrold Novelization of the first episode of *STTNG*.

| | 3.95 | 4 | |

Encyclopedia of Trekkie Memorabilia: #0-89689 066-X, Books Americana, 1988, tradepaper, 269 page by Christine Gentry and Sally Gibson-Downs. Pric guide to Star Trek collectibles.

| | 16.95 | 17 | 2 |

Enemy Unseen: Star Trek #51, #0-671-68403-8 Pocket Books, October 1990, paperback, 279 page novel by V. E. Mitchell.

| | 4.50 | 4 | |

Enterprise: The First Adventure: Pocket Book 371 pages, novel by Vonda N. McIntyre. The cover this book represents another step by Pocket Books t increase their literary repertoire of gimmick cover The use of a cut-away, cover in the front upper righ hand corner, which reveals an artwork picture of th Enterprise from the underlying page is a first.

(A) #104471, Science Fiction Book Club edition, 198 hardcover.

| | 5.98 | 6 | |

(B) #104471.

| | 6.98 | 6 | |

(C) #0-671-62581-0, September 1986, paperback.

| | 3.95 | (4) | |

(D) #0-671-62581-0, third printing, without corne cut-out on cover.

| | 3.95 | 4 | |

(E) #0-671-65912.

| | 4.50 | 4 | |

Entropy Effect: Star Trek #2, 224 pages, novel b Vonda McIntyre. This was the first book in a con tinuing line of original Star Trek novels for adul audiences and the first of the now defunct **Timescap** imprints. It was followed sporadically by seven mor books under the same imprint up until March 198 the last book being *The Wounded Sky*.

(A) #0-8398-2831-4, Gregg Press, 1981, hardcover.

| | 10.95 | 10 | 1 |

(B) #0-671-83692-7, Pocket Books, June 1981, paper back, Timescape logo with white cover.

| | 2.50 | 5 | 1 |

(C) #0-671-49300-0, Pocket Books, April 1984, paper back with blue cover.

| | 2.95 | 5 | |

(D) #0-671-62229-3, Pocket Books, paperback wit blue cover and yellow title.

| | 3.50 | 4 | |

(E) #0-671-66499, Pocket Books, paperback.

| | 3.95 | 4 | |

(F) #0-671-72416, Pocket Books, paperback.

| | 4.50 | 4 | |

	Issue	Fair	Mint

Exiles: Star Trek: The Next Generation #14, #0-671-0560-1, Pocket Books, November 1990, paperback, 71 pages, novel by Howard Weinstein.

	4.50	4	5

Eyes of The Beholders: Star Trek: The Next Generation #13, #0-671-70010-3, Pocket Books, September 1990, paperback, 243 pages, novel by A. C. Crispin.

	4.50	4	5

Far-Out Fun: #1309, Merrigold Press, 1979, softcover, 32 pages, 8½" x 11". Children's color and activity book. Artwork cover with Enterprise over sunburst and *STTMP* theme.

	.50	3	5

Fate of the Phoenix: Bantam Books, paperback, 262 pages, novel by Sondra Marshak and M. Culbreath. ③

(A) #0-553-12779-9, May 1979. **1.95** ⑤ **10**
(B) October 1979. **1.95** 4 5
(C) October 1981. **1.95** 4 5
(D) #0-553-24638-0, April 1984.
2.95 4 5
(E) #0-553-24638-0, May 1985, second edition artwork cover. **2.95** 4 5
(F) #0-553-27932-7, August 1989, eighth printing.
3.95 4 5

Final Frontier: Pocket Books, 434 pages, novel by Diane Carey.

(A) #135400, Science Fiction Book Club, hardcover.
6.98 6 7
(B) #0-671-64752-0, January 1988, paperback, with cut-out corner on cover. **4.50** 4 ⑤
(C) #671-69655, paperback. **4.95** 4 5

Final Nexus: Star Trek #43, #0-671-66018-7, Pocket Books, December 1988, paperback, 282 pages, novel by Gene DeWeese. **3.95** 4 ⑤

Final Reflection: Star Trek #16, 253 pages, novel by John M. Ford.

(A) #0-8398-2885-3, Gregg Press, 1985, hardcover.
11.95 12 15
(B) #0-671-473-3, Pocket Books, May 1984, paperback. **2.95** ④ 5
(C) #0-671-62230-7, Pocket Books, paperback, Gertrude logo. **3.50** 4 5
(D) #0-671-67075, Pocket Books, paperback.
3.95 4 5
(E) #0-671-70764, Pocket Books, paperback.
4.50 4 5

Fortune's Light: Star Trek: The Next Generation #15, #0-671-70836-8, Pocket Books, January 1991, paperback, 278 pages, novel by Michael Jan Friedman. Originally *Spartacus* was slated to be *STTNG* #15. **4.50** 5 6

	Issue	Fair	Mint

Futuristic Fun: Softcover, 60 pages, 8" x 11". Children's color and activity book. Cartoon-style artwork cover with Enterprise over photo insets of Kirk and Spock.

(A) #1257-1, Whitman, 1979. **.40** 3 5
(B) #1308, Merrigold, 1979. **.50** 3 5

Galactic Whirlpool: Bantam Books, paperback, 223 pages, novel by David Gerrold.

(A) #0-553-124242-9, October 1980.
2.25 5 ⑩
(B) Second printing, May 1981.
2.25 5 8
(C) Third printing, October 1981.
2.25 4 5
(D) #0-553-24170-2, July 1984, second edition artwork cover. **2.95** 4 5
(E) #0-553-24170-2, August 1989.
3.95 ④ 5

Ghostwalker: Star Trek #53, #0-671-64398-3, Pocket Books, February 1991, paperback, 273 pages, novel by Barbara Hambly. **4.95** 5 ⑥

Giants In The Universe: #0-394-83558-1, Random House, 1977, hardcover, eight pages, by Kay Wood. Children's pop-up book with three-dimensional cut-outs. A good collectible because of its relative rarity. Only about 11,597 copies were sold by retail outlets.
4.95 25 50

Gulliver's Fugitives: Star Trek: The Next Generation #11, #0-671-70130-4, Pocket Books, May 1990, paperback, 282 pages, novel by Keith Sharee.
4.50 4 5

Home Is The Hunter: Star Trek #52, 0-671-66662-2, Pocket Books, December 1990, paperback, 278 pages, novel by Dana Kramer-Rolls. **4.50** 4 ⑤

How Much For Just The Planet?: Star Trek #36, Pocket Books, 185 pages, novel by John M. Ford.

(A) #107714, Science Fiction Book Club, hardcover.
4.98 4 5
(B) #0-671-62998, Pocket Books, paperback.
3.95 ④ 5
(C) #0-671-72214, Pocket Books, paperback.
4.50 4 5

I am not Spock: Celestial Arts, 135 pages, by Leonard Nimoy. Autobiography with photos. Celestial Arts originated out of Millbrae, California, and printed this one Trek book in 1975. This book is both rare and original. It is the first Trek nonfiction tradepaper ever produced.

(A) #0-890-87717-5, November 1975, tradepaper.
4.95 ㉟ **50**

 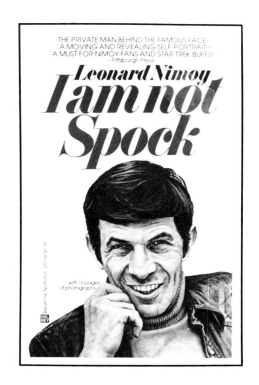

I am not Spock, **Celestial Arts, 1975 and the rare Del Rey paperback edition, 1977.**

	Issue	Fair	Mint
(B) #0-345-25719-7, Del Rey, May 1977, paperback.	1.75	30	40

Idic Epidemic: Star Trek #38, Pocket Books, paperback, 278 pages, novel by Jean Lorrah.

	Issue	Fair	Mint
(A) #0-671-63574-3, February 1988.	3.95	4	(5)
(B) #0-671-70768.	4.50	4	5

Ishmael: Star Trek #23, Pocket Books, paperback, 255 pages, novel by Barbara Hambly.

	Issue	Fair	Mint
(A) #0-671-55427-1, May 1985.	3.50	(4)	5
(B) #0-671-55427-1, second printing.	3.50	4	5
(C) #0-671-66089-6, fourth printing.	3.95	4	5

Jeopardy At Jutterdon / In Sticker Pictures: #2169-2, Whitman Publishing, 1979, softcover, sixteen pages, 8½" x 12". Children's story and activity book with stickers.

	Issue	Fair	Mint
	.79	5	10

Killing Time: Star Trek #24, Pocket Books, paperback, 311 pages, novel by Della Van Hise.

(A) #0-671-52488-7, July 1985. This first edition was recalled by Paramount when it was discovered that an early, unrevised manuscript had been printed in error.

	Issue	Fair	Mint
	3.50	10	(15)
(B) #0-671-52488-7, reissue without embossed title.	3.50	4	(5)

	Issue	Fair	Min
(C) #0-671-52488-7, Gertrude logo.	3.50	4	
(D) #0-671-65921-9, fifth printing.	3.95	4	
(E) #0-671-70597.	4.50	4	

Klingon Dictionary: Pocket Books, paperback, 17 pages, by Mark Okrand. Guide to Klingon vocabulary.

	Issue	Fair	Min
(A) #0-671-54349-0, December 1985.	3.95	4	
(B) #0-671-54349-0, second printing.	3.95	4	
(C) #0-671-66648-7, third printing.	3.95	4	
(D) #0-671-66648-7.	4.95	4	(?)

Klingon Gambit: Star Trek #3, 158 pages, novel by Robert E. Vardeman.

	Issue	Fair	Min
(A) #0-8398-2834-9, Gregg Press, 1981, hardcover.	10.95	10	1?
(B) #0-671-47720-X, October 1981, paperback, Timescape imprint.	2.95	5	8
(C) #0-671-47720-X, Timescape on cover corner.	2.95	4	(5)
(D) #0-671-47720-X, no Timescape on cover.	2.95	4	

	Issue	Fair	Mint

E) #0-671-62231-5, Gertrude logo.

    3.50   4   5

F) #0-671-66342.   3.95   4   5

G) #0-671-70767.   4.50   4   5

Kobayashi Maru: Star Trek #47, #0-671-65817-4, Pocket Books, December 1989, paperback, 254 pages, novel by Julia Ecklar.   4.50   4   (5)

Launch Into Fun: #1311, Merrigold Press, 1979, softcover, 32 pages, 8" x 11". Children's color and activity book. Red cover with color photo insets of Kirk, Spock, and McCoy in *STTMP* uniforms.

    .59   3   5

Leonard Nimoy, A Star's Trek: A Taking Part series book, #0-875-18376-X, Dillon Press, 1988, hardcover, 63 pages, by John Mickles Jr. Children's biography about the life and career of Leonard Nimoy with color and black and white photos.

    9.95   10   12

Letters To Star Trek: #0-345-25522-4, Ballantine Books, 1977, paperback, by Susan Sackett. Compilation of letters written to the *Star Trek* cast.

    1.95   10   (15)

Lost Years: Pocket Books, 307 pages, novel by J. M. Dillard.

A) #0-671-68293-8, October 1989, hardcover, 215 pages.   17.95   18   20

B) #157834, Science Fiction Book Club, 1989, hardcover, 215 pages.   8.98   9   10

C) #0-671-70795-7, August 1990, paperback, 440 pages.   4.95   (5)   6

Make-A-Game Book: #0-671-95552-7, Wanderer Books (Simon & Schuster), November 1979, tradepaper, nine pages, by Bruce and Greg Nash. A punch-out board game with *STTMP* theme. Contains official, single-sheet letter from Star Fleet Command assigning your mission, a 20" x 32" gaming sheet, and playing pieces. This is the most unique of the Trek books issued by Simon & Schuster over the years.

    6.95   10   15

Make-Your-Own-Costume Book: 188 pages, by Lyn Edelman Schurnberger. Children's costume patterns and designs of clothing from *STTMP* with color illustrations.

A) #0-671-25180-5, Simon & Schuster, 1979, hardcover.   12   15   20

B) #0-671-79109-X, Wallaby Books, 1979, tradepaper.   6.95   10   15

Making of Star Trek: Ballantine Books, paperback, 414 pages, by Stephen Whitfield and Gene Roddenberry. Interesting events behind the creation of the *Star Trek* TV series. This book is the first adult non-fiction paperback on Trek ever produced and the first promo tie-in book associated with TV Trek. The typographic cover style also makes it a good collectible. This book has had 22 separate printings. Assorted prices and editions follow.

(A) #73004, September 1968, first printing.   (15)   .95   10   25

(B) #0-345-01621-0, July 1970, sixth printing.   .95   5   10

(C) #0-345-24691-8, January 1975, fourteenth printing with silver cover.   1.50   5   6

(D) #0-345-34019-1, September 1986, 22nd printing.   4.95   4   5

(E) #0-345-34019-1, December 1989, 25th printing.   4.95   4   5

Making of Star Trek: The Motion Picture: #0-671-79109-5, Wallaby, 1982, tradepaper, 221 pages, by Susan Sackett and Gene Roddenberry. Behind-the-scenes on the making of the first Star Trek movie.

    7.95   15   25

Making of Star Trek II: The Wrath of Khan: #0-671-46182-6, Pocket Books, 1982, tradepaper, 223 pages, by Allan Asherman. Behind-the-scenes on the filming of the second Star Trek movie.

    7.95   15   25

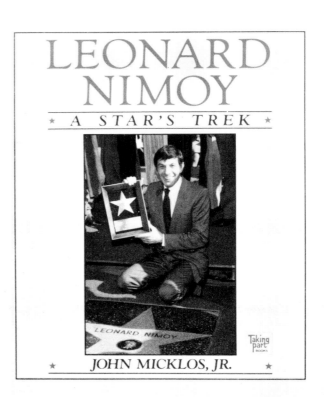

Leonard Nimoy, A Star's Trek, **Dillon Press, 1988.**

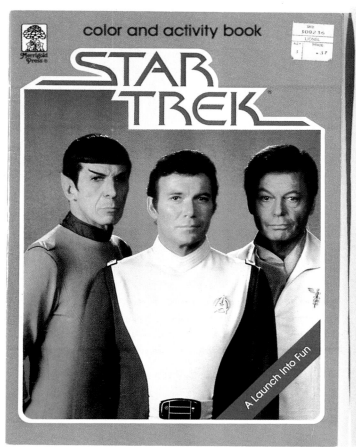 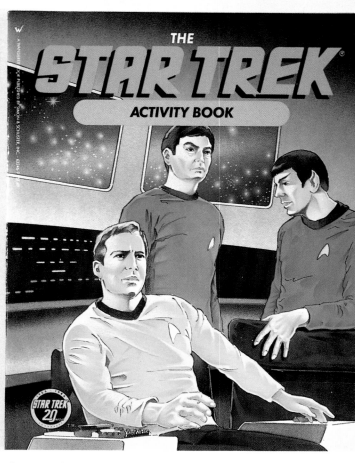

A Launch Into Fun, Merrigold Press, 1979; *The Star Trek Activity Book*, Wanderer Books, 1986.

	Issue	Fair	Mint

Making of the Trek Conventions: By Joan Winston. Autobiography on the joys of Star Trek convention going. It chronicles the planning, coordinating, and tribulations associated with the production of Trek cons of the early 1970s and makes interesting reading. This book is hard to find in hardcover.

(A) #0-385-13112-7, Doubleday, 1977, hardcover, 252 pages. **7.95 15 25**

(B) #0-872-16573-6, Playboy Press, November 1979, paperback, 254 pages. **2.25 5 15**

Masks: Star Trek: The Next Generation #7, Pocket Books, paperback, 277 pages, novel by John Vornholt.

(A) #0-671-67980-5, July 1989. **3.95 4 5**

(B) #0-671-70878-3. **4.50 4 5**

Meaning In Star Trek: 208 pages, by Karin Blair. An examination of social philosophy and psychology within the Star Trek universe. A narrative cover makes this book a good collectible.

(A) #0-89012-010-2, Anima Publications, 1979, hardcover. **9.95 15 20**

	Issue	Fair	Min

(B) #0-872-16573-6, Warner Books, 1979, paperback **2.25 5 1**

Memory Prime: Star Trek #42, Pocket Books, paperback, 309 pages, novel by Gar and Judith Reeves Stevens.

(A) #0-671-65813-1, October 1988. **3.95 ④**

(B) #0-671-70550. **4.50 4**

Metamorphosis: #0-671-68402-7, Pocket Books, March 1990, paperback, 371 pages, novel by Jean Lorrah. First giant novel about *STTNG*. **4.95 4**

Mindshadow: Star Trek #27, Pocket Books, paperback, 252 pages, novel by J. M. Dillard.

(A) #0-671-60756-1, January 1986. **3.50 ④**

	Issue	Fair	Mint
B) #0-671-66090-X, third printing.			
	3.95	4	5
C) #0-671-70420.	4.50	4	5

Mirror Friend, Mirror Foe: Paperback, 223 pages, novel co-authored by George Takei and Robert Asprin. When first released in the Playboy Press edition, this book did better sales with young readers than it did adult sci-fi fans. Playboy originally planned to issue two more paperback sequels to this one, the second to be entitled *Stellar Flower, Savage Flower*. Despite claims of their appearance in 1982, the sequels were never released. There was even some talk of releasing all three novels in a special hardcover trilogy called *Star Stalker*, which never materialized. Many collectors may be unaware of the fact that there was a concious effort by Playboy to attract sales through the clever manipulation of Trek themes. This included the main character's sword battles and the book title, which alluded to Trek episodes "The Naked Time" and "Mirror, Mirror."

	Issue	Fair	Mint
(A) #0-87216-581-7, Playboy Press, 1979.			
	1.95	5	(10)
(B) #0-441-55380-9, Ace, December 1985.			
	2.75	3	5

(2)

Mission To Horatius: Whitman Publishing, 1968, hardcover, 210 pages, children's novel by Mack Reynolds. This was the first *authorized* Star Trek novel ever produced. Very important collectible as it was sanctioned by Desilu Studios and because of the author's untimely death in 1983. .79 (20) 40

Mr. Scott's Guide to the Enterprise: Pocket Books, 128 pages, by Shane Johnson.

	Issue	Fair	Mint
(A) #113472, Book Club Edition, 1987, oversized hardcover.	9.98	10	12
(B) #0-671-63576-X, July 1987, tradepaper.			
	10.95	11	12

Monsters of Star Trek: Pocket Books, paperback, 117 pages, by Daniel Cohen. Children's book which includes descriptions of famous Trek aliens and black and white photos. Good collectible because it was the

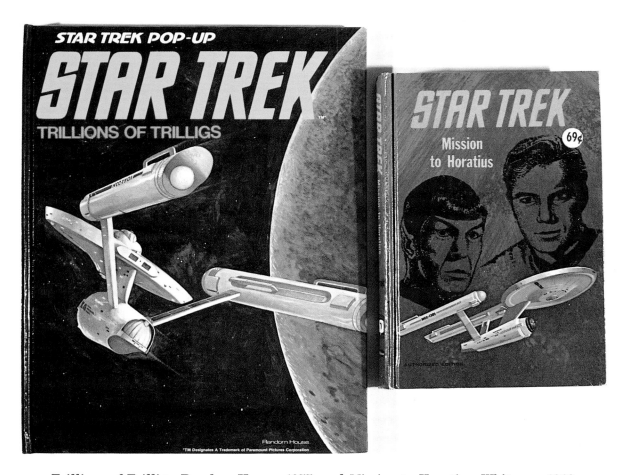

Trillions of Trilligs, Random House, 1977, and *Mission to Horatius*, Whitman, 1968.

	Issue	Fair	Mint

first Trek paperback ever produced for children and young readers.
(A) #0-671-56057-3, January 1980.

	1.75	⑤	8

(B) #0-671-52360-0, January 1980, with Archway logo. **1.95 3 4**
(C) #0-671-63232-9, with second edition artwork cover featuring mugato alien. **2.50 3 4**
(D) #0-671-68549-X, 1989. **2.75 3 ④**

Mudd's Angels: Bantam Books, paperback, 177 pages, novel by J. A. Lawrence. Good example of a symbolic design cover.
(A) #0-553-11802-1, May 1975. **1.75 10 ⑮**
(B) #0-553-24666-6, February 1985.

	2.95	3	5

Mutiny on the Enterprise: Star Trek #12, paperback, 189 pages, novel by Robert E. Vardeman.
(A) #0-8398-2887-X, Gregg Press, 1985, hardcover.

	11.95	12	15

(B) #0-671-46541-4, Pocket Books, October 1983, paperback, Timescape imprint. **2.95 ⑤ 8**
(C) #0-671-46541-4, Pocket Books, paperback.

	2.95	4	5

(D) #0-671-67073, Pocket Books, paperback.

	3.95	4	5

(E) #0-671-70800, Pocket Books, paperback.

	4.50	4	5

My Enemy, My Ally: Star Trek #18, Pocket Books, 309 pages, novel by Diane Duane.
(A) #025908, Literary Guild and Science Fiction Book Club editions, 1984, hardcover. **4.98 5 6**
(B) #025908, hardcover. **5.98 5 6**
(C) #0-671-50285-9, Pocket Books, July 1984, paperback. **2.95 4 5**
(D) #0-671-55446-8, Pocket Books, paperback, fifth printing. **3.50 4 5**
(E) #0-671-65866, Pocket Books, paperback.

	3.95	4	5

(F) #0-671-70421, Pocket Books, paperback.

	4.50	4	5

My Stars!: #0-914350-1, Vulcan Books, 1980, tradepaper, 125 pages, by Michael C. Goodwin. Star Trek humor portrayed through ink cartoons. The cartoons in this book previously appeared in a Salt Lake City newspaper called the *Desert News* and the comics ran from January to September 1977 before being compiled into this anthology. **5.95 10 15**

Official Star Trek Cooking Manual: #0-553-11819-6, Bantam Books, July 1978, paperback, 203 pages, by Mary Ann Picard. Star Trek recipes.

	1.95	25	50

	Issue	Fair	Min

Official Star Trek Quiz Book: #0-671-55652-5 Wallaby, May 1985, tradepaper, 256 pages, b Mitchell Maglio. Star Trek trivia questions, history and photo quizzes. **6.95 7 1**

Official Star Trek Trivia Book: Pocket Books, 20 pages, by Rafe Needleman. Star Trek trivia quizze
(A) #0-671-83090-2, 1980, hardcover.

	6.95	15	2

(B) #3658, Book Club edition, 1980, hardcover.

	3.95	10	1

(C) #0-671-83090-X, January 1980, paperback.

	2.25	5	1

On The Good Ship Enterprise: My 15 Years Wit Star Trek: #0-89865-253-7, Donning Starblaze Ed tions, 1983, tradepaper, 285 pages, autobiography b Bjo Trimble. **5.95 6 1**

Pandora Principle: Star Trek #49, #0-671-65815-8 Pocket Books, April 1990, paperback, 273 pages, nove by Carolyn Clowes. **4.50 4 ⑤**

Pawns and Symbols: Star Trek #26, Pocket Book paperback, 277 pages, novel by Majliss Larson.
(A) #0-671-55425-5, November 1985.

	3.50	④	

(B) #0-671-66497. **3.95 4**

Peacekeepers: Star Trek: The Next Generation #2 #0-671-66929-X, Pocket Books, September 1988 paperback, 310 pages, novel by Gene DeWeese.

	3.95	4	

Perry's Planet: Bantam Books, paperback, 13 pages, novel by Jack C. Haldeman.
(A) #0-553-13580-5, February 1980.

	1.75	5	⑩

(B) #0-553-13580-5, March 1980.

	1.75	5	

(C) #0-553-24193-1, September 1984, second editio cover artwork. **2.95 3**

Pilgrim's Progress: Star Trek: The Next Genera tion #14, #0-671-070560-1, Pocket Books, November 1990, paperback, novel by Howard Weinstein.

	4.50	4	

Planet Ecnal's Dilemma: Softcover, 58 pages, 8" 11". Children's coloring book. This book appeared i three different forms.
(A) #1035-1, Whitman Publishing, 1978, with cartoo cover of TV Enterprise and yeoman.

	.49	3	

(B) #1081, Whitman Publishing, 1978.

	.49	3	

(C) #1306, Merrigold Press, 1978, with color phot from TV Trek. **.59 3 5**

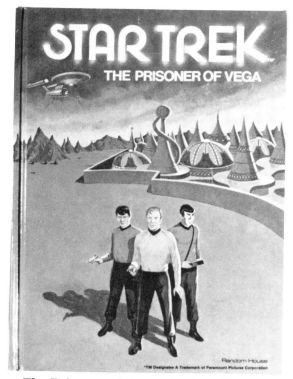

The Prisoner of Vega, Random House, 1977, with a vignette cover.

	Issue	Fair	Mint
Planet of Judgement: Bantam Books, paperback, 151 pages, novel by Joe Haldeman.			
(A) #0-553-11145-0, August 1977.	1.75	5	⑩
(B) Second printing.	1.75	5	8
(C) Third printing.	1.75	4	6
(D) #0-553-24168-0, April 1984, second edition cover artwork.	1.75	3	5

Power Hungry: Star Trek: The Next Generation #6, #0-671-67714-4, Pocket Books, May 1989, 273 pages, novel by Howard Weinstein. **3.95 4 5**

Price of the Phoenix: Bantam Books, paperback, 182 pages, novel by Sondra Marshak and Myrna Culbreath. This is the prequel to *Fate of the Phoenix*. ③

	Issue	Fair	Mint
(A) #0-553-100978-2, July 1977.	1.75	5	⑩
(B) #0-553-100978-2, December 1977.	1.75	5	8
(C) #0-553-100978-2, April 1978.	1.95	4	5
(D) #0-553-24635-6, April 1984.	2.95	4	5
(E) #0-553-24635-6, March 1985, second edition cover artwork.	2.95	4	5
(F) #0-553-24635-6, August 1989.	3.95	4	5

Prime Directive: Hardcover, novel by Judith and Garfield Reeves-Stevens.

	Issue	Fair	Mint
(A) #0-671-70772-8, Pocket Books, September 1990, 406 pages.	18.95	19	20
(B) #177741, Science Fiction Book Club, November 1990, 404 pages.	8.98	9	10

Prisoner of Vega: Random House, hardcover, 45 pages, children's fiction by Christopher Cerf and Sharon Lerner, illustrated by Robert Swanson. This book features the rarest type of Trek cover, the vignette style, Artwork cover stretches from front to back in a continuous scene. This book had a total sales of 16,890 copies in the regular edition. Gibraltar books sales were 6,097 copies.

	Issue	Fair	Mint
(A) #0-399-93576-4, Gibraltar Library binding, 1977.	3.99	5	10
(B) #0-394-83576-X, 1977.	2.95	15	⑳

Probe: #0-671-72420-7, Pocket Books, April 1991, hardcover, novel by Margaret Wander Bonanno. Continues the story after the *ST IV* movie.
18.95 19 ㉑

Prometheus Design: Star Trek #5, 190 pages, novel by Sondra Marshak and Myrna Culbreath.

	Issue	Fair	Mint
(A) #0-8398-2936, Gregg Press, hardcover, 1986.	11.95	12	15
(B) #0-671-83398-7, Pocket Books, March 1982, paperback, Timescape imprint.	2.50	⑤	8
(C) #0-671-49299-3, Pocket Books, paperback.	2.95	4	5
(D) #0-671-62745-7, Pocket Books, paperback, Gertrude logo.	3.50	4	5
(E) #0-671-67435, Pocket Books, paperback,	3.95	4	5

Renegade: Star Trek #55, #0-671-65814-X, Pocket Books, June 1991, paperback, novel by Gene Deweese.
4.95 5 ⑥

Rescue At Raylo: Softcover, 8" x 11". Children's color and activity book. This book appeared in two versions.

	Issue	Fair	Mint
(A) #1261, Whitman Publishing, 1978, with cartoon artwork of TV Enterprise and Mr. Spock. Photo insert of Kirk on bridge.	.49	3	5
(B) #1307, Merrigold Press, 1979, with green cover and Spock on *STTMP* bridge.	.59	3	5

Rock and a Hard Place: Star Trek: The Next Generation #10, #0-671-69364-6, Pocket Books, January 1990, paperback, 244 pages, novel by Peter David. **3.95 4 5**

Romulan Way: Star Trek #35, Pocket Books, paperback, 254 pages, novel by Diane Duane and Peter Morwood.

	Issue	Fair	Mint
(A) #0-671-63498-4.	3.50	④	5
(B) #0-671-68085.	3.95	4	5
(C) #0-671-70169.	4.50	4	5

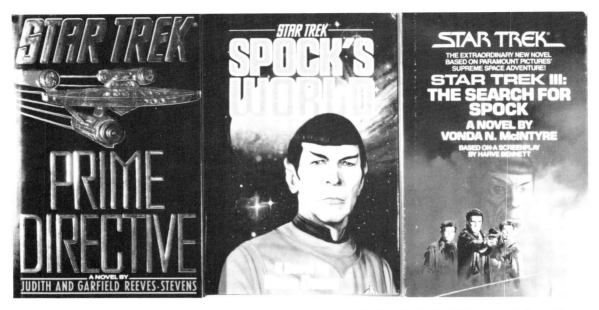

Three hardcover novelizations: *Prime Directive* with Book Club Editions of *Spock's World*; and *Star Trek III: The Search for Spock.*

Star Fleet Medical Reference, first edition fanzine (see Small Press section) and the Ballantine release.

	Issue	Fair	Mint

Rules of Engagement: Star Trek #48, #0-671-66129-9, Pocket Books, February 1990, paperback, 254 pages, novel by Peter Morwood. **4.50** **4** ⑤

Shadow Lord: Star Trek #22, Pocket Books, paperback, 280 pages, novel by Laurence Yep.
(A) #0-671-47392-1, February 1985. **2.95** **4** ⑤
(B) #0-671-66087-X. **3.95** **4** **5**

Shatner: Where No Man...: #0-441-88975-1, Ace Books, Tempo-Star Edition, 1979, paperback, 327 pages, by William Shatner, Sondra Marshak, and Myrna Culbreath. Biography with photos. This paperback received a limited distribution and is a very desirable collectible. **2.25** **50** **75**

Spartacus: Star Trek: The Next Generation #17, Pocket Books, July 1991, paperback, novel by T. L. Mancour. Originally scheduled for release in January 1991. **4.50** **5** **6**

Spock Messiah!: Bantam Books, paperback, 182 pages, novel by Theodore Cogswell and Charles A. Spano Jr. ②
(A) #0-553-10159-5, September 1976. **1.75** **10** ⑮
(B) #0-553-10159-5, October 1976. **1.75** **5** **10**
(C) #0-553-10159-5, June 1977. **1.75** **5** **8**
(D) #0-553-10159-5, February 1978. **1.75** **4** **6**
(E) #0-553-24674-7, October 1984, second edition artwork cover. **2.95** **3** **5**

Spock Must Die!: Bantam Books, paperback, 188 pages, novel by James Blish. This was the first Trek fiction in paperback format for adults. There have been nineteen printings. Assorted copies include:
(A) #0-553-05515-0, February 1970. **.60** ⑤ **10**
(B) #0-553-02245-0. **1.25** **5** **8**
(C) #0-553-10749-0. **1.50** **4** **5**
(D) #0-553-19797-0. **1.50** **4** **5**
(E) #0-553-12589-3, October 1978, second edition artwork cover. **1.75** **4** **5**
(F) #0-553-12591-0. **1.75** **4** **5**
(G) #0-553-24634-8, April 1984. **2.95** **4** **5**
(H) #0-553-24634-8, April 1985. **2.95** **4** **5**
(I) #0-553-24634-8, August 1989. **3.95** **4** **5**

Spock's World: Pocket Books, 388 pages, novel by Diane Duane.
(A) #0-671-66851-X, September 1988, hardcover. **16.95** **17** **18**

	Issue	Fair	Mint

(B) #141705, Science Fiction Book Club, 1988, hardcover. **6.98** **7** **8**
(C) #0-671-66773-4, August 1989, paperback. **4.95** **5** ⑥

Starfleet Medical Reference Manual: Ballantine Books, tradepaper, 160 pages, by Eileen Palestine. Medical blueprints from the Star Trek universe. This book is a must for all collectors. It was originally released as a fan-produced book (see **Small Press**) before being bought by Ballantine.
(A) #0-345-27473-3, October 1977. **6.95** **10** **15**
(B) Second edition, November 1977. **6.95** **7** **10**

Starless World: Bantam Books, paperback, 152 pages, novel by Gordon Eklund.
(A) #0-553-12731-8, November 1978. **1.95** **10** ⑮
(B) Second printing, November 1978. **1.95** **5** **10**
(C) Third printing, August 1979. **1.95** **3** ⑤
(D) #0-553-24675-5, November 1984, second edition artwork cover. **2.95** **3** **4**

Startoons: #0-872-16579-5, Playboy Press, December 1979, paperback, 50 pages, by Joan Winston. Science fiction cartoon strips rendered in pen and ink, which include Star Trek themes. **1.95** **5** **10**

Star Trek: #0-425-0442-4, Berkley, paperback, by Jeff Rovin. No date set for release. **1.95** **N/A** **N/A**

Star Trek: 136 pages, fictional novelizations of the *Star Trek* episodes. Stories include "Charlie's Law," "Dagger Of The Mind," "The Unreal McCoy," "Balance Of Terror," "The Naked Time," "Miri," and "The Conscience Of The King."
(A) #0-8488-0431-7, Amereon Ltd., hardcover. **13.95** **14** **15**
The following are Bantam Books paperbacks. There have been 31 printings. Sample issues include:
(B) #F3459, January 1967. **.50** **5** ⑩
(C) Second through sixteenth printings. **.75** **5** **8**
(D) #0-553-07869, seventeenth printing, 1972. **.75** **4** **5**
(E) #0-553-08589, nineteenth printing, 1972. **.95** **4** **5**
(F) #0-553-02114, May 1975. **1.25** **4** **5**
(G) #0-553-10835, February 1977. **1.50** **3** **4**

The first *Star Trek* novelization by James Blish, featuring a cover with the only NBC series artwork ever produced.

	Issue	Fair	Mint
(H) #0-553-12589, October 1978.	1.75	3	4
(I) #0-553-12591, May 1979.	1.75	3	4
(J) #0-553-13869-3, July 1979.	1.95	2	③
(K) #9857, 31st printing, December 1979, special Book Club edition.	.95	2	3

Star Trek 2: Bantam Books, paperback, 122 pages, by James Blish. Novelizations of "Arena," "A Taste Of Armageddon," "Tomorrow Is Yesterday," "Errand of Mercy," "Court Martial," "Operation: Annihilate," "City On The Edge Of Forever," and "Space Seed." There have been 24 printings. Sample issues include:

	Issue	Fair	Mint
(A) #F3439, February 1968, photo cover.	.50	5	10
(B) #0-553-05559, photo cover.	.60	5	8
(C) #0-553-08066, photo cover.	.95	4	5
(D) #0-553-02171, photo cover.	1.25	④	5
(E) #0-553-10811, photo cover.	1.50	2	3
(F) #0-553-13877-4, second edition artwork cover.	1.95	2	3
(G) #0-553-13877-4, December 1979.	2.50	2	3

Star Trek 3: Bantam Books, paperback, 118 pages, by James Blish. Novelizations of "The Trouble With Tribbles," "The Last Gunfight," "The Doomsday Machine," "Assignment: Earth," "Mirror, Mirror," "Friday's Child," and "Amok Time." There have been 21 printings. Sample issues include:

	Issue	Fair	Mint
(A) #F4371, April 1979, black photo cover.	.50	5	8
(B) #553-08683, black photo cover.	.95	4	5
(C) #553-02253, white photo cover.	1.25	2	3
(D) #553-10818.	1.50	2	3
(E) #553-12312-2, photo cover with rainbow colors.	1.75	2	3
(F) #9068, fourth printing, Book Club edition, photo cover.	.95	2	③
(G) #9068, sixteenth printing, Book Club edition, black photo cover.	1.50	2	3

Star Trek 4: Bantam Books, paperback, 134 pages, by James Blish. Novelizations of "All Our Yesterdays," "The Devil In The Dark," "The Enterprise Incident," "Journey To Babel," "The Menagerie," and "A Piece Of The Action." There have been fourteen printings. Sample issues include:

	Issue	Fair	Mint
(A) #0-553-07009-0, June 1971.	.75	4	⑤
(B) #0-553-08579, photo cover.	.95	4	5
(C) #0-553-2172, photo cover.	1.25	3	4
(D) #0-553-10812, photo cover.	1.50	2	③
(E) #0-553-12311-4, July 1979, second edition artwork cover.	1.75	2	3

Star Trek 5: Bantam Books, paperback, 136 pages, by James Blish. Novelizations of "Let This Be Your Last Battlefield," "Requiem For Methuselah," "The Tholian Web," "The Turnabout Intruder," "The Way To Eden," and "Whom Gods Destroy." There were fifteen printings. Sample issues include:

	Issue	Fair	Mint
(A) #0-553-07300-0, February 1972.	.75	3	④
(B) #0-553-08180, artwork cover.	.95	3	4
(C) #0-553-08180, artwork cover.	1.25	2	3
(D) #0-553-10840, artwork cover.	1.50	2	3

	Issue	*Fair*	*Mint*
E) #0-553-12325.	1.75	2	3
F) #0-553-14383-2, June 1980.	1.95	2	3

Star Trek 6: Bantam Books, paperback, 149 pages, by James Blish. Novelizations of "The Apple," "By Any Other Name," "The Cloud Minders," "The Lights Of Zetar," "The Mark Of Gideon," and "The Savage Curtain." There were fourteen printings. Sample issues include:

A) #0-553-07364-0, April 1972.	.75	4	(5)
B) #0-553-08184-0, artwork cover.			
	.95	4	5
C) #0-553-09154, vertical title.	1.25	2	3
D) #0-553-10815, vertical title.	1.50	2	3
E) #0-553-11697, vertical title.	1.50	2	3
F) #0-553-12911, horizontal title.			
	1.75	2	3
G) #0-553-13874, horizontal title.			
	1.95	2	3
H) #0-553-13874-X, 1979, horizontal title.			
	2.50	2	3

Star Trek 7: Bantam Books, paperback, 155 pages, by James Blish. Novelizations of "The Changeling," "The Deadly Years," "Elaan Of Troyius," "The Paradise Syndrome," and "Who Mourns For Adonis?" There have been twelve printings. Sample issues include:

A) #0-553-07480-0, July 1972.	.75	4	(5)
B) #0-553-08610, vertical title on artwork cover.			
	.95	4	5
C) #0-553-08150, vertical title.	1.25	2	3
D) #0-553-02240, vertical title with white spine.			
	1.25	2	3
E) #0-553-10815, vertical title.	1.50	2	3
F) #0-553-12907-4, horizontal title with second edition artwork cover.	1.75	2	3
G) #0-553-13873, April 1979, horizontal title.			
	1.95	2	3

Star Trek 8: Bantam Books, paperback, 170 pages, by James Blish. Novelizations of "Catspaw," "The Enemy Within," "For The World Is Hollow And I Have Touched The Sky," "Spock's Brain," "Where No Man Has Gone Before," and "Wolf In The Fold." There have been eleven printings.

A) 0-553-07550-0, November 1972.			
	.75	3	(4)
B) #0-553-08170, vertical title.	.95	3	4
C) #0-553-02250, vertical title.	1.25	2	3
D) #0-553-10816, vertical title.	1.50	2	3
E) #0-553-1273-1, horizontal title.			
	1.75	2	3

Star Trek 9: Bantam Books, paperback, 183 pages, by James Blish. Novelizations of "The Immunity Syndrome," "Obsession," "The Return Of The Archons," "Return To Tomorrow," "That Which Survives," and "The Ultimate Computer." Assorted printings:

(A) #0-553-07808-0, August 1973.	.75	3	(4)
(B) #0-553-08628.	.95	3	4
(C) #0-553-02238.	1.25	2	3
(D) #0-553-11285.	1.50	2	3
(E) #0-553-11211.	1.75	2	3

Star Trek 10: Bantam Books, paperback, 164 pages, by James Blish. Novelizations of "The Alternative Factor," "The Empath," "The Galileo Seven," "Is There In Truth No Beauty?," "The Omega Glory," and "A Private Little War." There have been twelve printings.

(A) #0-553-08401, February 1974.			
	.75	3	(4)
(B) #0-553-08611, vertical title.	.95	3	4
(C) #0-553-02241, vertical title.	1.25	2	3
(D) #0-553-10796, vertical title.	1.50	2	3
(E) #0-553-11992.	1.75	2	3
(F) #0-553-13866.	1.95	2	3
(G) #0-553-23235, horizontal title. December 1979.			
	2.50	2	3

Star Trek 11: Bantam Books, paperback, 188 pages, by James Blish. Novelizations of "Bread And Circuses," "Plato's Stepchildren," "The Squire Of Gothos," "What Are Little Girls Made Of?," and "Wink Of An Eye." There have been seven printings.

(A) #0-553-08717, April 1975.	1.25	3	(4)
(B) #0-553-13502-3, horizontal title.			
	1.75	3	4
(C) #0-553-11417.	2.50	2	4
(D) #0-553-25169-4, October 1985, with new Day of the Dove artwork cover.	2.95	3	4

Star Trek 12: Bantam Books, paperback, 177 pages, by James Blish. Novelizations of "And The Children Shall Lead," "The Corbomite Maneuver," "The Gamesters Of Triskelion," "Patterns Of Force," and (4) "Shore Leave."

(A) #0-553-11382-8, November 1977.			
	1.75	5	(10)
(B) #0-553-11382-8, October 1979.			
	1.75	5	8
(C) #0-553-25252-6, November 1985, new artwork cover with Spectra logo.	2.95	3	5

Star Trek Action Toy Book: #0-394-83277-9, Random House, 1976, tradepaper, six pages, by James Razzi. Children's book of paper punch-outs of phaser, tricorder, Klingon cruiser, Enterprise, translator, communicator, Vulcan ears, and a standing figure of Kirk. This was the first juvenile Trek book produced by

Issue   Fair   Mint

Random House and it is one-of-a-kind. Net sales were about 179,406 copies.   **2.95   10   15**

Star Trek Activity Book: #0-671-63246-9, Wanderer Books, 1986, softcover, 32 pages, 8½" x 11", by Peter Lerangis, illustrated by Carlos Garzon. Children's game book with puzzles, mazes, etc. Full-color cover artwork of Kirk, Spock, and McCoy from TV Trek.
    1.49   2   (4)

Star Trek Adventure Coloring Book: 0-671-63244-2, Wanderer, 1986, softcover, 32 pages, 8" x 11", by Ellen Steiber, illustrated by Paul Abrams. Children's story and coloring book. Color artwork cover features Kirk, Spock, Sulu, and Enterprise.
    1.49   2   4

Star Trek Alien Coloring Book: #0-671-63245-0, Wanderer, 1986, softcover, 32 pages, 8" x 11", by Peter Trewin, illustrated by Paul Abrams. Children's story and coloring book. Color artwork cover shows *STTMP* Klingon, Spock, and T'Lar.   **1.49   2   (4)**

Star Trek Catalog: 1979, by Gerry Turnbull. A listing of Trek merchandise and sources for acquisitions.

(A) #0-448-14053-5, Today Press, (Division of Grosset & Dunlap), tradepaper, 240 pages.
    6.95   (10)   12

(B) #0-441-78477-1, Ace reprint, paperback, 140 pages.   **2.50   (5)   10**

Star Trek Coloring Books: Parkers Run Publishing, 1978, by Liza Hamill. Set of two story coloring books, titled "Unchartered World" and "War in Space." Price for each.   **—   5   10**

Star Trek Coloring Book #1: #C1856, Saalfield Publishing Company, 1975, softbound, 64 pages, 8" x 11". Children's cartoon-style coloring book. Kirk and Spock on cover.   **.49   5   8**

Star Trek Coloring Book #2: #C1862, Saalfield Publishing Company, 1975, softbound, 64 pages, 8" x 11". Children's coloring book, mazes, dot-to-dot, etc. Color cover features bust of Spock rendered in oil paint medium.   **.49   5   8**

Star Trek Compendium: Pocket Books, tradepaper, 187 pages, by Allan Asherman. A guide to Star Trek television episodes and movies.

(A) #0-671-79145-1, 1981, Wallaby logo.
    9.95   10   12

(B) #0-671-79145-1, six more printings with the same ISBN.   **9.95   10   12**

(C) #0-671-62726-0, September 1986, second edition red photo cover with *ST IV* update.
    9.95   10   12

Issue   Fair   Mint

(D) #0-671-68440-X, July 1989, black photo cover with *ST V* update.   **10.95   11   12**

Star Trek Concordance: Ballantine Books, tradepaper, 256 pages, by Bjo Trimble. A detailed dictionary of words from the *Star Trek* episodes with a special locator wheel on the front cover. The rotating wheel pinpoints the name of every episode from classic Trek with its respective call letters, air date, and the page where it can be found in the book. This book is a collector classic and has the first cover using gimmick advertising in the history of Trek literature. It is also the first adult tradepaper devoted to Trek topics.

(A) #0-345-25137-7, October 1976.
    6.95   (75)   125

(B) Special Book Club edition, 1976, with yellow sticker seal on front cover.   **3.95   75   100**

Star Trek V: The Final Frontier: Pocket Books, 331 pages, by J. M. Dillard. Movie novelization based on the story by William Shatner, Harve Bennett, and David Loughery.

Bjo Trimble's *Star Trek Concordance*, published by Ballantine, 1976.

	Issue	*Fair*	*Mint*
A) #156000, hardcover, Science Fiction Book Club, 1989.	4.98	4	5
B) #0-671-68008-0, June 1989.	4.50	4	(5)

Star Trek Foto Novel #1, City Of The Edge of Forever: Bantam Books, Mandala Productions, paperback, 150 pages. *Star Trek* episode told through balloon dialogue and color photos. The idea for these books came from Mandala, a California-based company, which offered the photo novel concept to Bantam. This unusual method of story-telling has its origins in European novels of the same sort. Since Bertelsmann Publishing Group of West Germany has owned Bantam since 1968, this idea was not new to them. These are much sought-after collectibles.

A) #0-553-11345-3, 1977.	1.95	15	(20)
B) #0-553-12564.	2.25	10	15
C) #0-553-12564.	2.50	10	15

Star Trek Foto Novel #2, Where No Man Has Gone Before: Bantam Books, Mandala Productions, paperback, 150 pages.

A) #0-553-11346-1, 1977.	1.95	10	(15)
B) #0-553-12526.	2.25	10	12
C) #0-553-12526.	2.50	10	12

Star Trek Foto Novel #3, The Trouble With Tribbles: Bantam Books, Mandala Productions, paperback, 150 pages.

A) #0-553-11347-X, 1977.	1.95	10	(15)
B) #0-553-12689.	2.25	10	12
C) #0-553-12689.	2.50	10	12

Star Trek Foto Novel #4, A Taste Of Armageddon: Bantam Books, Mandala Productions, paperback, 150 pages.

A) #0-553-11348-8, 1978.	1.95	10	(15)
B) #0-553-12744.	2.25	10	12
C) #0-553-12744.	2.50	10	12

Star Trek Foto Novel #5, Metamorphosis: Bantam Books, Mandala Productions, paperback, 150 pages.

A) #0-553-11349-6, 1979.	1.95	10	(15)
B) #0-553-12173.	2.25	10	12

Star Trek Foto Novel #6, All Our Yesterdays: Bantam Books, Mandala Productions, paperback, 150 pages.

A) #0-553-11350-X, 1978.	1.95	15	(20)
B) #0-553-13509.	2.25	10	15
C) #0-553-13509.	2.50	10	15

Star Trek Foto Novel #7, The Galileo Seven: #0-553-12041-7, Bantam Books, Mandala Productions, 1978, paperback, 150 pages. 2.25 15 (20)

Star Trek Foto Novel #8, A Piece Of The Action: #0-553-12022-0, Bantam Books, Mandala Productions, 1978, paperback, 150 pages. 2.25 15 (20)

	Issue	*Fair*	*Mint*

Star Trek Foto Novel #9, The Devil In The Dark: #0-553-12021-2, Bantam Books, Mandala Productions, 1978, paperback, 150 pages. 2.25 15 (20)

Star Trek Foto Novel #10, Day Of The Dove: #0-553-12017-4, Bantam Books, Mandala Productions, 1978, paperback, 150 pages. 2.25 15 (20)

Star Trek Foto Novel #11, The Deadly Years: #0-553-12028-X, Bantam Books, Mandala Productions, 1978, paperback, 150 pages. 2.25 15 (20)

Star Trek Foto Novel #12, Amok Time: #0-553-12012-3, Bantam Books, Mandala Productions, 1978, paperback, 150 pages. 2.25 20 (30)

Star Trek IV: The Voyage Home: #0-671-63243-4, Wanderer, 1986, tradepaper, 92 pages, by Peter Lerangis. Children's novelization of the movie with color photos. 5.95 6 7

Star Trek IV: The Voyage Home: Pocket Books, 274 pages, by Vonda N. McIntyre. Novelization of the movie.

(A) #106302, hardcover, Science Fiction Book Club, 1986.	5.98	6	7
(B) #0-671-63266-3, December 1986, paperback.	3.95	4	(5)
(C) #0-671-70283, fifth printing.	4.50	4	5

Star Trek: Good News In Modern Images: Andrews and McMeel, 1978, 156 pages, by Betsy Caprio. Pop culture study of the original *Star Trek* shows illustrating how the message in the show's episodes was also the message of the world's great religious groups. Contains "Energize" pages at the end of every chapter with questions and exercises. Also includes a fun quiz at the end of the book. Limited edition of 5,000 copies. Cover has white lettering on starfield.

(A) Hardcover.	—	20	30
(B) Paperback.	—	15	20

Star Trek: Good News In Modern Images: #3400-6, Sheed, Andrews and McMeel, 1979, 156 pages, by Betsy Caprio. Nonfiction. — 10 15

Star Trek Guide: Aeonian Press, softcover, 36 pages, by J. Ed Clauss. Children's episode guide to TV Trek.

(A) #0-88411-079-6, 1976, with side view of TV Enterprise on cover.	2.95	5	10
(B) #0-88411-079-6, 1978, side view of Enterprise.	3.95	5	8
(C) #0-88411-079-6, 1988, with top view of Enterprise on cover.	5.95	5	8
(D) #0-88411-079-6, 1990.	7.95	7	8

	Issue	Fair	Mint

Star Trek Interview Book: #0-671-61794-X, Pocket Books, July 1988, tradepaper, 278 pages, by Allan Asherman. Nonfiction interviews with the cast and crew of the *Star Trek* series. **7.95 8 10**

Star Trek Intragalactic Puzzles: #0-553-01083-2, Bantam Books, November 1977, tradepaper, 128 pages, by James Razzi. Puzzles and trivia.
5.95 10 15

Star Trek Lives!: Bantam Books, paperback, 274 pages, by Jacqueline Litchenberg. An auto-biographical journey of personal experiences connected with Star Trek TV.
(A) 0-553-02151-6, July 1975. **1.95 5 10**
(B) 0-553-02151-6, seven more printings with the same ISBN. **1.9 5 8**

Star Trek Log One: 195 pages, by Alan Dean Foster. First of ten books containing novelizations of the Star Trek cartoon series. Buoyed by the success of the *Making of Star Trek* and their movie tie-ins with *Star Wars*, Ballantine began publishing the *Logs* in conjunction with the airing of animated Trek episodes in 1974. In the late 1970s, Ballantine sold out to Lester and Judy Del Rey and this managerial shift is reflected in the publication of the *Logs*. *Logs* #1-8 originally appeared with cartoon covers. After the change of ownership, all *Logs* were reprinted with a Del Rey logo, including the new *Logs* #9 and #10. Editions include:
Amereon Library, hardcover, 1975:
(A) #0-88411-081-8, with green cover.
13.95 14 15
(B) #0-88411-081-8, with purple cover.
17.95 18 20
(C) Aeonian Press, tradepaper, 1974.
7.95 8 10
Ballantine Books, paperback, approximately seventeen printings:
(D) #0-345-24014-6, June 1974, cartoon cover.
.95 5 (8)
(E) #0-345-24014-6, cartoon cover.
1.25 3 5
(F) #0-345-25042-7, cartoon cover.
1.50 3 5
(G) #0-345-25811-8, May 1977, Del Rey logo with second edition yellow artwork cover.
1.50 3 5
(H) #0-345-27601. **1.75 3 5**
(I) #0-345-33349-7, October 1985, Del Rey logo with brown cover. **2.95 3 4**

Star Trek Log Two: 177 pages, by Alan Dean Foster. Editions include:
Amereon Library, hardcover, 1975:

Star Trek Log Three with cartoon cover, Ballantine, 1974.

	Issue	Fair	Mint

(A) #0-88411-082-6, with green cover.
13.95 14 15
(B) #0-88411-082-6, with purple cover.
17.95 18 20
(C) Aeonian Press, tradepaper, 1974.
7.95 8 10
Ballantine Books, paperback, approximately twelve printings:
(D) #0-345-24184-3, September 1974, cartoon cover.
.95 5 (8)
(E) #0-345-24388-9, cartoon cover.
1.25 3 5
(F) #0-345-24435-4, cartoon cover.
1.25 3 5
(G) #0-345-25043, cartoon cover.
1.50 3 5
(H) #0-345-28265-5, December 1979, Del Rey logo with second edition orange artwork cover.
1.75 3 5
(I) #0-345-32646-6, January 1985, Del Rey logo with blue cover. **2.95 3 4**

Star Trek Log Three: 215 pages, by Alan Dean Foster. Editions include:

	Issue	*Fair*	*Mint*

Amereon Library, hardcover, 1975:
A) #0-88411-083-4, with green cover.
13.95   14   15

B) #0-88411-083-4, with purple cover.
17.95   18   20

C) Aeonian Press, tradepaper, 1975.
7.95   8   10

Ballantine Books, paperback, approximately twelve printings:
D) #0-345-24260-2, January 1975, cartoon cover.
1.25   5   (8)

E) #0-345-25044-3, cartoon cover.
1.50   3   5

F) #0-345-25813-4, Del Rey logo with second edition red artwork cover.
1.50   3   5

G) #0-345-31553-7, August 1984.
2.25   3   5

H) #0-345-33318-7, September 1985, Del Rey logo with orange cover.
2.95   3   4

Star Trek Log Four: 215 pages, by Alan Dean Foster. Editions include:
Amereon Library, hardcover, 1975:
A) #0-88411-084-2, with green cover.
13.95   14   15

B) #0-88411-084-2, with purple cover.
17.95   18   20

C) Aeonian Press, tradepaper, 1975.
7.95   8   10

Ballantine Books, paperback, approximately seven printings:
D) #0-345-24435-4, March 1975, cartoon cover.
1.25   5   (8)

E) #0-345-25045, cartoon cover.
1.50   3   5

F) #0-345-25814, Del Rey logo with second edition artwork cover.
1.50   3   5

G) #0-345-27553-5, purple cover with Del Rey logo.
1.75   3   5

H) #0-345-33350-0, October 1985, Del Rey logo with blue cover.
2.95   3   4

Star Trek Log Five: 195 pages, by Alan Dean Foster. Editions include:
Amereon Library, hardcover, 1975:
A) #0-88411-085-0, with green cover.
13.95   14   15

B) #0-88411-085-0, with purple cover.
17.95   18   20

C) Aeonian Press, tradepaper, 1975.
7.95   8   10

Ballantine Books, paperback, approximately seven printings:

(D) #0-345-24532-6, August 1975, cartoon cover.
1.25   5   (8)

(E) #0-345-25046, cartoon cover.
1.50   3   5

(F) #0-345-25815-0, December 1977, Del Rey logo with second edition purple artwork cover.
1.75   3   5

(G) #0-345-33351-9, October 1985, Del Rey logo with aqua cover.
2.95   3   4

Star Trek Log Six: 195 pages, by Alan Dean Foster. Editions include:
Amereon Library, hardcover, 1976:
(A) #0-88411-086-9, with green cover.
13.95   14   15

(B) #0-88411-086-9, with purple cover.
17.95   18   20

(C) Aeonian Press, tradepaper, 1976.
7.95   8   10

Ballantine Books, paperback:
(D) #0-345-25655-1, March 1976, cartoon cover.
1.50   5   (8)

(E) #0-345-25816-9, December 1977, Del Rey logo with second edition blue artwork cover.
1.75   3   5

(F) #0-345-33352-7, October 1985, Del Rey logo with mauve cover.
2.95   3   4

Star Trek Log Seven: 182 pages, by Alan Dean Foster. Editions include:
Amereon Library, hardcover, 1976:
(A) #0-88411-087-7, with green cover.
13.95   14   15

(B) #0-88411-087-7, with purple cover.
17.95   18   20

(C) Aeonian Press, tradepaper, 1976.
7.95   8   10

Ballantine Books, paperback:
(D) #0-345-24965-8, June 1976, cartoon cover.
1.50   10   (15)

(E) #0-345-25817, Del Rey logo with second edition artwork cover.
1.50   3   5

(F) #0-345-27683-7, with Del Rey logo.
1.75   5   8

Star Trek Log Eight: 183 pages, by Alan Dean Foster. Editions include:
Amereon Library, hardcover, 1976:
(A) #0-88411-088-5, with green cover.
13.95   14   15

(B) #0-88411-088-5, with purple cover.
15.95   16   18

(C) Aeonian Press, tradepaper, 1976.
7.95   8   10

	Issue	Fair	Mint

Ballantine Books, paperback:
(D) #0-345-25141-5, August 1976, cartoon cover.

	1.50	15	(20)

(E) #0-345-25818-5, December 1977, Del Rey logo with second edition green artwork cover.

	1.50	10	15

(F) #0-345-27602, with Del Rey logo.

	1.75	10	15

Star Trek Log Nine: 183 pages, by Alan Dean Foster. Editions include:
Amereon Library, hardcover, 1977:
(A) #0-88411-090-7, with green cover.

	13.95	14	15

(B) #0-88411-090-7, with purple cover.

	17.95	18	20

(C) Aeonian Press, tradepaper, 1977.

	7.95	8	10

Ballantine Books, paperback:
(D) #0-345-25557-7, February 1977, Del Rey logo with (2) second edition green artwork cover.

	1.50	(20)	(25)

(E) #0-345-27165, with Del Rey logo.

	1.50	10	15

Star Trek Log Ten: 215 pages, by Alan Dean Foster. Editions include:
Amereon Library, hardcover, 1977:
(A) #0-88411-090-7, with green cover.

	13.95	14	15

(B) #0-88411-090-7, with purple cover.

	17.95	18	20

(C) Aeonian Press, tradepaper, 1977.

	7.95	8	10

Ballantine Books, paperback:
(D) #0-345-27212-9, January 1978, Del Rey logo with (2) artwork cover.

	1.95	(25)	35

Star Trek Maps: #0-553-01202-9, New Eye Photography, Bantam Books, 1980, tradepaper, 32 pages. Includes *Introduction to Navigation* technical manual and four full-color wall maps of the Federation. Klingon and Romulan planetary systems. Packaged in a slipcover jacket. This is undoubtedly Bantam's most memorable nonfiction product and it is hard to classify it as either a poster or a book. It is probably the single most coveted collectible among fans.

	8.95	100	(150)

***Star Trek* Miniature Book**: Amistad Press, publisher Yolanda Carter, circa 1970s. A miniature limited edition hardbound book manufactured by designers of dollhouse mini-furnishings. This rare and unusual collectible is a real book with approximately twenty black and white illustrations on interior pages by *Star Trek Concordance* illustrators

A collector's dream: *Star Trek* Miniature Book, Amistad Press. Bookends from the Star Trek Chess Set, Franklin Mint.

	Issue	Fair	Mint

George Barr, Mattewillis Beard, Tim Courtney, and Don Simpson. Each book measures 1" x 1" and comes numbered and signed. The outside cover has an adhesive sticker with artwork drawing of the Enterprise. Limited to 300 copies.

	—	200	300

Star Trek: Phaser Fight: #0-671-63248-5, Which Way Books #24, Archway (Pocket Books), 1986, paperback, 118 pages, by Barbara and Scott Siegel. Children's adventure game book. As an Ensign aboard the Enterprise, your actions determine your fate.

	2.50	3	

Star Trek Postcard Book: See **Postcards**.

Star Trek Punch Out and Play Album: #C2272, Saalfield Publishing, 1975, softcover. Children's activity book with punch-out play figures to color.

	.89	10	1

Star Trek Puzzle Book: #0-671-63247-7, Wanderer, 1980, softcover, 32 pages, 8" x 11", by Peter Lerangis and illustrated by Carlos Garzon. Children's activity book with mazes, rebus, tracing projects, etc. Color artwork cover shows TV Kirk, Spock, and Uhura on planetscape.

	1.49	3	5

Star Trek Puzzle Manual: Bantam Books, paperback, 126 pages, by James Razzi. Game and puzzle book. Approximately eight printings.
(A) #0-553-01054-9, November 1976, tradepaper.

	5.95	15	20

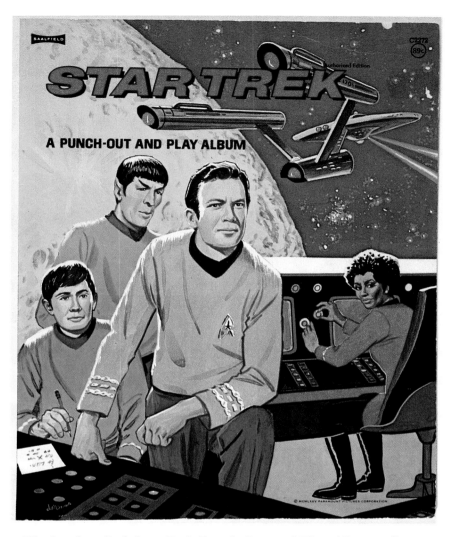

The hard-to-find *Star Trek Punch Out and Play Album*, **#C2272,**
Saalfield Publishing, 1975.

	Issue	Fair	Mint
B) #0-553-11691-6, November 1976.	1.25	5	(10)
C) #0-553-10549, August 1977, abridged edition.	1.25	5	8
D) Second printing, October 1977.	1.25	5	8
E) Third printing, October 1977.	1.25	5	8
F) Fourth printing, October 1977.	1.25	5	8
G) #0-553-16066-1, January 1978, abridged with Scholastic logo.	1.50	4	6
H) Sixth printing, March 1978.	1.50	4	6
I) Seventh printing, March 1978.	1.50	4	6
J) Eighth printing, November 1978.	1.50	4	6

	Issue	Fair	Mint
(K) #0-553-12131-6, 1977, Special Book Club edition.	1.50	4	6

***Star Trek Quiz Book*:** Signet, paperback, 150 pages, by Bart Andrews and Brad Dunning. Star Trek trivia questions. This book was later re-released as the *Trekkie Quiz Book*, which enhances its value tremendously. The name was changed in the hopes of attracting younger readers. About 218,975 *Trekkie Quiz Books* deluged the market after the abrupt name change.

	Issue	Fair	Mint
(A) #0-451-074907-1, June 1977.	1.50	(10)	15
(B) Second printing as *Trekkie Quiz Book*, 1977.	1.50	5	10
(C) Third printing as *Trekkie Quiz Book*, 1977.	1.50	5	8
(D) #0-451-08413-6, fourth printing as *Trekkie Quiz Book*, 1977.	1.50	3	5

	Issue	Fair	Mint

Star Trek Reader: Dutton, hardcover, 422 pages, by James Blish. Reprint compilation of Bantam paperbacks *Star Trek #1-4*. Contained 21 episode stories from *Star Trek*. These were the first adult hardcovers produced in the Star Trek genre. Oddly enough, these hardcovers appeared after the first Blish paperbacks *Star Trek #1-12* were in print, a reversal of the usual progression of hardcovers into paperbacks. Covers on Volumes I-III were drawn by Lou Feck. The cover of Volume IV was drawn by S. Fantoni.
(A) Dutton, original hardcover, 1970.

	5.95	15	25

Assorted Book Club editions:
(B) #031369, 1970. **3.95** 10 15
(C) #031369. **5.50** 8 10
(D) #031369, 1990. **7.98** 8 9

Star Trek Reader II: Dutton, hardcover, 457 pages, by James Blish. Reprint compilation of Bantam paperbacks *Star Trek #5-7*. Contained nineteen TV episode adaptations.
(A) Dutton, original hardcover, 1972. **5.95** 15 25

Assorted Book Club editions:
(B) #023515, 1972. **3.95** 10 15
(C) #023515, 1983. **5.50** 8 10
(D) #023515, 1990. **7.98** 8 9

Star Trek Reader III: Dutton, hardcover, 447 pages, by James Blish. Reprint compilation of Bantam paperbacks *Star Trek #8-10*. Contained nineteen TV episode adaptations.
(A) Dutton, original hardcover, 1973. **5.95** 15 20

Assorted Book Club editions:
(B) #020313, 1973. **3.95** 10 15
(C) #020313, 1983. **5.50** 8 10
(D) #020313, 1990. **7.98** 8 9

Star Trek Reader IV: Dutton, hardcover, 472 pages, by James Blish. Reprint compilation of Bantam paperbacks *Star Trek #11-12*.
(A) Dutton, original hardcover, 1974. **5.95** 15 25

Assorted Book Club editions:
(B) #033191, 1974. **3.95** 10 15
(C) #033191, 1983. **5.50** 8 10
(D) #033191, 1990. **7.98** 8 9

Star Trek Space Flight Chronology: #0-671-79089-7, Wallaby (Pocket Books), January 1980, 192 pages, by Stan Goldstein and Fred Goldstein, and illustrated by Rick Sternbach. Detailed spacecraft chronology within the *Star Trek* TV universe, plus charts and graphs of historical events. **8.95** 35 45

Star Trek Speaks: #0-671-79091-9, Wallaby, 1970 tradepaper, 160 pages, by Susan Sackett, Fred Goldstein, and Stan Goldstein. Analysis of the philosophies inherent in TV Trek. This book is a good collectible because of its narrative cover art, which uses only editorial print to entice Trek readers into buying it simply on the prestige of the authors' names. This style of cover is rare among Star Trek literature. **2.95** 10 1

Star Trek Starfleet Technical Manual: Ballantine, tradepaper, 180 pages, by Franz Joseph. Detailed technical designs, blueprints, and drawings for spacecraft, uniforms, flags, codes, etc. of TV Trek. This tradepaper had the largest, single first printing in the history of science fiction publishing when it was released in 1975. After its third week on the book shelves, it went to #1 on the *New York Times* Best sellers List and remained there for three months.
(A) #0-345-24730-2, 1975, with hardcover vinyl protector and one-page letter to cadets. **6.95** 50 100
(B) #0-345-34074-4, September 1986, special 20th Anniversary edition. **10.95** 10 1

Star Trek Starfleet Technical Manual, **by Franz Joseph, 1975.**

	Issue	Fair	Mint

tar Trek That Never Was: #0-671-61442-8, Pocket Books, scheduled for release in October 1988, tradepaper, by Allan Asherman. This book, although publicized, never made it into print because of contractual problems with Paramount. It contained never-before-released material concerning the second Star Trek series proposed for the 1970s which was to include the original Kirk, McCoy, and Scott characters plus the Vulcan Xon. The series was shelved after many original scripts were already written. Notable contributors were Norman Spinrad, Theodore Sturgeon, John Meredith Lucas, and David Ambrose.

7.95   N/A   N/A

tar Trek: The First 25 Years: Pocket Books, September 1991, hardcover, by Gene Roddenberry and Susan Sackett. Interviews and behind-the-scenes reflections on the history of Trek from its TV inception, its cancellation, its fan network, the movies, and *tar Trek: The Next Generation.* Full-color and black and white photos.

N/A

	Issue	Fair	Mint

Star Trek: The Motion Picture: 252 pages, by Gene Roddenberry. Novelization of the movie.

	Issue	Fair	Mint
(A) #0-686-60888-7, Simon & Schuster, 1980, hardcover.	9.95	15	20
(B) #038307, Science Fiction Book Club, 1979, hardcover.	5.98	5	6

Pocket Books, paperback.

	Issue	Fair	Mint
(C) #0-671-83088-0, December 1979.	2.50	5	6
(D) Second through seventh printings.	2.50	4	6
(E) #0-671-54685-6, eighth printing, 1980, with silver band on cover.	2.95	4	5
(F) #0-671-64654.	3.50	4	5
(G) #0-671-67795-0, tenth printing.	3.95	4	5
(H) #0-671-73200.	4.50	4	5

Star Trek: The Motion Picture Giant Coloring Books: Wanderer, 1979. Oversized hardcover coloring books for children. Contain characters and action scenes from *STTMP.* Set of two.

	Issue	Fair	Mint
(A) Volume I, Kirk, Spock, and Ilia on cover.	2.95	5	10
(B) Volume II, V-Ger cover.	2.95	5	10

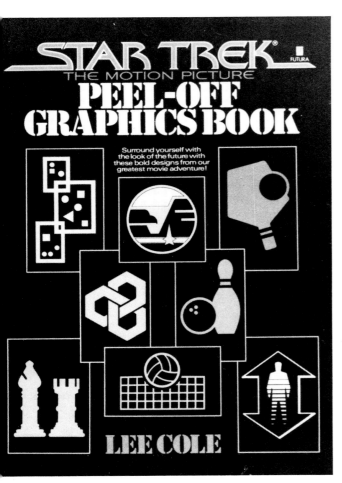

Star Trek: The Motion Picture Peel-Off Graphics Book, Wanderer, 1979.

Star Trek: The Motion Picture Photostory, Pocket Books, 1980.

Star Trek: The Motion Picture Pop-Up Book, Wanderer, 1980.

	Issue	Fair	Mint

Star Trek: The Motion Picture Peel-Off Graphics Book: #0-671-79104-4, Wanderer, 1979, tradepaper, ten pages, by Lee Cole. Children's sticker book containing removable stickers with graphic designs, door signs, and logos from *STTMP*.   6.95   15   20

Star Trek: The Motion Picture Photostory: #0-671-83089-9, Pocket Books, April 1980, paperback, 160 pages, by Richard J. Anobile. *STTMP* told with color stills and dialogue blurbs. This book resulted partly from the retail success of Bantam's Fotonovels and served as a competitive sales item.   2.95   15 ↓   25

	Issue	Fair	Mint

Star Trek: The Motion Picture Pop-Up Book: #0-671-95536-5, Wanderer, 1980, hardcover, by Tor Lokvig and illustrated by Chuck Murphey. Children's version of *STTMP* as told with 3-D cut-outs.   4.95   25   35

Star Trek: The Motion Picture U.S.S. Enterprise Bridge Punch-Out Book: #0-671-95544-6, Wanderer, 1979, tradepaper, 32 pages, by Tor Lokvig and illustrated by Chuck Murphey. Paper cut-outs which assemble to make the *STTMP* bridge.   5.95   15   25

Star Trek: The Motion Picture U.S.S. Enterprise Punch-Out Book: #0-671-95560-8, Wanderer, 1979,

	Issue	Fair	Mint

tradepaper, 32 pages, by Tor Lokvig and illustrated by Chuck Murphey. A series of paper cut-outs designed to be assembled together to make the *STTMP* Enterprise. **5.95 25 35**

Star Trek: The New Voyages: Bantam Books, paperback, 237 pages, by Sondra Marshak and Myrna Culbreath. A compilation of short fictional stories.
A) #0-553-02719-X, March 1976. **1.75 5 8**
B) #0-553-02719-X, second printing, March 1976. **1.75 4 6**
C) #0-553-02719-X, April 1976. **1.75 4 6**
D) #0-553-02719-X, June 1976. **1.75 4 6**
E) #0-553-02719-X, November 1976. **1.75 4 6**
F) #0-553-02719-X, April 1977. **1.75 4 5**
G) #0-553-02719-X, December 1977. **1.75 4 5**
H) #0-553-12753-5, February 1979. **1.95 4 5**
I) #0-553-12753-5, September 1979. **1.95 4 5**
J) #0-553-14323, June 1980. **2.25 4 5**
K) #0-553-24636-4, April 1984. **2.95 4 5**
L) #0-553-24636-4, August 1985, second edition photo cover with Spectra logo. **2.95 4 5**
M) #0-553-28124-0, 1989. **3.95 4 5**

Star Trek: The New Voyages 2: Bantam Books, paperback, 252 pages, by Sondra Marshak and Myrna Culbreath. More short fictional stories.
A) #0-553-11392-5, January 1978. **1.95 5 8**
B) #0-553-11392-5, second printing, March 1978. **1.95 4 6**
C) #0-553-11292-5, July 1978. **1.95 4 6**
D) #0-553-11292-5, September 1978. **1.95 4 6**
E) #0-553-14959-5, January 1981. **2.25 4 5**
F) #0-553-22948-6, June 1982. **2.50 4 5**
G) #0-553-22948-6, March 1983. **2.50 4 5**
H) #0-553-23756-X, April 1984, second edition artwork cover with Spectra logo. **2.95 4 5**
I) #0-553-27933-5, twelfth printing, August 1989. **3.95 4 5**

	Issue	Fair	Mint

Star Trek: The Next Generation Technical Manual: #0-671-70427-3, Pocket Books, July 1991, tradepaper, by Rick Sternbach and Michael Ukuda, with an introduction by Gene Roddenberry. Inside the *STTNG* Enterprise via sketches, blueprints, and line drawings. **12.95 13 15**

Star Trek: The Worlds of the Federation: Pocket Books, 155 pages, by Shane Johnson. Guide to Federation planets from the *STTNG* universe. Star charts and drawings.
(A) #0-671-66989-3, Pocket Books, August 1989, tradepaper. **11.95 11 (12)**
(B) #158774, Science Fiction Book Club, 1989, hardcover, with special full-color insert of exotic aliens painted by Don Ivan Punchatz. **14.98 14 15**

Star Trek III: The Search for Spock: 297 pages, by Vonda McIntyre. Novelization of the movie.
(A) #0-8398-2839-X, Gregg Press (G. K. Hall), 1984, hardcover. **12.95 12 15**
(B) #037226, Science Fiction Book Club, Pocket Books, 1984, hardcover. **5.98 5 6**
Pocket Books, paperback:
(C) #0-671-49500-3, June 1984. **2.95 (3) 4**
(D) #0-671-67198, sixth printing. **3.95 3 4**

Star Trek III: The Search for Spock Postcard Book: See **Postcards**.

Star Trek III: The Search for Spock Movie Trivia: #0-671-50137-2, Wanderer, June 1984, softcover, by William Rotsler. A children's flip-pad-style game book with puzzles, word games, and trivia quizzes about *ST III*. Includes a yellow felt marker inside shrink-wrapped cover. **2.95 5 10**

Star Trek III: The Search for Spock Short Stories: #0-671-50139-9, Wanderer, 1984, tradepaper, 126 pages, by William Rotsler. Children's fiction which includes five original stories: "The Azphari Enigma," "The Jungles of Memory," "A Vulcan, A Klingon and an Angel," "World's End," and "As Old as Forever." **3.95 5 10**

Star Trek III: The Search for Spock Story Book: Simon & Schuster, hardcover, 32 pages, by Lawrence Weinberg. Children's novelization of *ST III* with color photos.
(A) #0-671-47662-9, 1984, blue cover edition. **6.95 10 15**
(B) #4887, Doubleday Book Club and Literary Book Club edition, 1984, with black cover and white spine, five photo inserts of the crew. **5.95 5 8**

	Issue	Fair	Mint

Star Trek III: The Search for Spock, The Vulcan Treasure: #0-671-50138-0, Wanderer, 1984, trade-paper, 117 pages, by William Rotsler. A plot-it-your-self adventure book for children.

| | 3.95 | 5 | 10 |

Star Trek Trivia Mania: #0-8217-1732-4, Zebra Books, September 1985, paperback, 238 pages, by Xavier Einstein. One thousand trivia questions on Trek.

| | 2.50 | 3 | 6 |

Star Trek: TV and Movie Tie-Ins: Creative Education, 1979, 32 pages, by James A. Lely. Children's guide to TV Trek.

| (A) #0-87191-718-1, hardcover. | 7.95 | 8 | 10 |
| (B) Softcover. | 3.95 | 4 | 8 |

Star Trek II Biographies: #0-671-46391-8, Wanderer, 1982, tradepaper, 159 pages, by William Rotsler. Children's book with biographies of Trek characters updated to the *ST II* time frame.

| | 3.95 | 5 | 10 |

Star Trek II Distress Call: #0-671-46389-6, Wanderer, 1982, tradepaper, 126 pages, by William Rotsler. Children's choose-your-own adventure occurring in a Star Trek universe.

| | 3.95 | 5 | 10 |

Star Trek II Short Stories: #0-671-46390-X, Wanderer, 1982, tradepaper, 159 pages, by William Rotsler. Children's stories with characters from *ST II*. This is a nice collectible because of the anomaly on the front cover. The color photo of the movie Enterprise on the cover is upside-down.

| | 2.95 | 5 | 10 |

Star Trek II: The Wrath of Khan: 233 pages, by Vonda N. McIntyre. Novelization of the movie.

| (A) #0-8398-2832-2, Gregg Press (G. K. Hall), hardcover, 1982. | 10.95 | 10 | 15 |
| (B) #031195, Science Fiction Book Club, Pocket Books, 1982, hardcover. | 6.98 | 6 | 7 |

Pocket Books, paperback:

(C) #0-671-45610-5, July 1982.	2.50	3	5
(D) Second printing through fifth printing.	2.50	3	4
(E) #0-671-47232-1, title in yellow.	2.75	3	4
(F) #0-671-55248-1, with silver band on cover.	2.95	3	4
(G) #0-671-63494-1, with white band on cover and new Gertrude logo.	3.50	3	4
(H) #0-671-67426-9.	3.95	3	4

Star Trek II: The Wrath of Khan Photostory: Pocket Books, paperback, 160 pages, by Richard Anobile. Movie adaptation told with black and white photos and dialogue blurbs. The first edition ap-

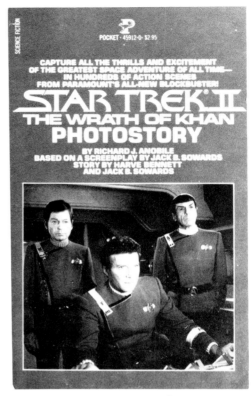

The ill-fated *Star Trek II: The Wrath of Khan Photostory* by Pocket.

	Issue	Fair	Mint

peared with misplaced pages and was pulled from the shelves. The resulting new edition had the corrected pages, but featured the photo of an upside-down Enterprise during a Nebula battle. This second photo book by Pocket was done with black and white pictures instead of color in order to defray printing costs.

| (A) #0-671-45912-0, 1982, with misplaced pages. | 2.95 | 15 | 20 |
| (B) #0-671-45912-0, 1982, with corrected pages, but upside-down photo of Enterprise. | 2.95 | 5 | 10 |

Star Trek Voyage To Adventure: Which Way Books #15, Archway, paperback, 113 pages, by Michael J. Dodge and illustrated by Gordon Tomei. A plot-it-yourself adventure for kids. This was the first Trek adventure fiction title in paperback.

| (A) #0-671-50989-6, 1984, first edition with white cover. | 1.95 | 3 | 5 |
| (B) #0-671-62492-X, with yellow cover. | 2.50 | 2 | 4 |

Star Wreck The Generation Gap: #0-312-92359-7, October 1990, St. Martin's Paperbacks, paperback, 117 pages, by Leah Rewolinski, illustrated by Harry Trumbore. Unauthorized parody with Star Trek and

	Issue	Fair	Mint

STTNG plots. Formally an Excellent Words Editorial Services Edition screenplay (August 1989).

3.50   4   5

Strange & Amazing Facts About Star Trek: #0-671-63014-8, Archway, 1986, paperback, 113 pages, by Daniel Cohen. Children's book of Trek history, trivia, and photos. 2.50   3   4

Strangers From the Sky: 402 pages, by Margaret Wander Bonanno. Star Trek giant novel.
(A) #108829, Science Fiction Book Club, Pocket Books, 1987, hardcover. 5.98   5   (6)
Pocket Books, paperback:
(B) #0-671-64049-6, July 1987, with corner cut-out on cover. 3.95   (4)   5
(C) #0-671-65241-6, without corner cut-out. 3.95   4   5
(D) #0-671-65913. 4.50   4   5

Strike Zone: Star Trek: The Next Generation #5, #0-671-67940-6, Pocket Books, March 1989, paperback, 275 pages, novel by Peter David. 3.95   3   4

Survivors: Star Trek: The Next Generation #4, #0-671-67438-2, Pocket Books, January 1989, paperback, 253 pages, novel by Jean Lorrah. 3.95   3   4

Tears of the Singers: Star Trek #19, 252 pages, novel by Melinda Snodgrass.
(A) #0-8398-2934, Gregg Press, 1986, hardcover. 11.95   12   15
Pocket Books, paperback:
(B) #0-671-50284-0, September 1984. 3.50   (4)   5
(C) #0-671-67076. 3.95   4   5
(D) #0-671-69654. 4.50   4   5

Teklords: #0-399-13495-6, Putnam, April 1991, hardcover, novel by William Shatner. Sequel to *Tek War.* 17.95   18   (20)

Tek War: Ace-Putnam, novel by William Shatner.
(A) Phantasia Press, hardcover, special limited edition signed and numbered, in slipcover case. 75   75   100
(B) #0-399-13495-6, Ace-Putnam, 1990, 216 pages, hardcover. 17.95   18   (20)
(C) #0-441-80208-7, Ace, August 1990, paperback, 307 pages. 4.50   5   6

Thank You For Your Love: #0-88396-114-8, Blue Mountain Arts, 1980, tradepaper, 30 pages, by Leonard Nimoy. Original poetry, 4" x 5½". 2.50   20   30

These Words Are For You: #0-88396-148-2, Blue Mountain Arts, 1981, tradepaper, 64 pages, by Leonard Nimoy. Original poetry. 4.95   20   30

Three Minute Universe: Star Trek #41, #0-671-65816-6, Pocket Books, August 1988, paperback, 264 pages, novel by Barbara Paul. 3.95   (4)   5

Time For Yesterday: Star Trek #39, Pocket Books, paperback, 303 pages, novel by A. C. Crispin. Sequel to *Yesterday's Son.*
(A) #0-671-60371. 3.95   4   (5)
(B) #0-671-70094. 4.50   4   5

Timetrap: Star Trek #40, #0-671-64870-5, Pocket Books, June 1988, paperback, 221 pages, novel by David Dvorkin. 3.95   4   (5)

Trekkie Quiz Book: See *Star Trek Quiz Book.*

Trek or Treat: #0-345-25679-4, Ballantine Books, tradepaper, 96 pages, by Terry Flanagan and Eleanor Ehrhardt. Black and white stills and humorous dialogue designed purely for laughs. This book was Ballantine's competitive move to profit in the wake of the popularity of Bantam's Fotonovels, whose balloon-caption books were well-accepted by the public. 2.95   5   8

Trek To Madworld: Bantam Books, paperback, 177 pages, novel by Stephen Goldin.
(A) #0-553-12618-0, January 1979. 1.95   10   (15)
(B) #0-553-14550, August 1980. 2.25   5   10
(C) #0-553-24676-3, December 1984, with second edition artwork cover. 2.95   4   5
(D) #0-553-24676-3, August 1989. 3.95   4   5

Trellisane Confrontation: Star Trek #14, Pocket Books, paperback, 190 pages, novel by David Dvorkin.
(A) #0-671-46543-0, February 1984, with Timescape logo. 2.95   (4)   8
(B) #0-671-46543-0, numbered cover. 2.95   4   5
(C) #0-671-70095. 4.50   4   5

Triangle: Star Trek #9, 188 pages, novel by Sondra Marshak and Myrna Culbreath.
(A) #0-8398-2934, Gregg Press, 1986, hardcover. 11.95   12   15
Pocket Books, paperback:
(B) #0-671-83399-5, March 1983, Timescape logo. 2.95   4   5
(C) #0-671-49298-5, numbered cover. 2.95   (4)   5
(D) #0-671-60548-8, with Gertrude logo. 3.50   4   5
(E) #0-671-66251. 3.95   4   5

85

Star Wars, Star Trek and the 21st Century Christians (see section titled Books (Trek-Related)); *Startoons*; and *Star Wreck The Generation Gap.*

	Issue	Fair	Mint

Trillions of Trilligs: #0-394-83558-1, Random House, 1977, hardcover, by Christopher Cerf and Sharon Lerner and illustrated by Kay Wood. Fiction pop-up for kids with story told in 3-D cut-outs. This book had net sales of 12,537 copies.

	2.50	25	50

Trouble With Tribbles: Ballantine Books, paperback, 272 pages, by David Gerrold. Biographical information on behind-the-scenes TV Trek.

(A) #0-345-23402-2, May 1973, with black cover.

	1.50	10	(15)

(B) #0-345-23402-2, January 1974.

	1.50	5	10

(C) #0-345-23402-2, September 1974.

	1.50	5	8

(D) #0-345-23402-2, fourth printing.

	1.50	4	6

(E) #0-345-24942-9, September 1975, second edition with red cover.

	1.95	4	6

(F) #0-345-24942-9, sixth printing.

	1.95	4	6

(G) #0-345-24942-9, December 1977.

	1.95	3	5

(H) #0-345-27671-X, January 1978, red cover with Del Rey logo.

	2.25	3	5

The Truth Machine: Random House, hardcover, children's fiction by Christopher Cerf and Sharon Lerner and illustrated by Jane Clark. Net sale for this book were 18,345 for the retail edition and 6,788 for the Gibraltar binding edition.

	Issue	Fair	Mint

(A) #0-394-93576-6, original hardcover, 1977.

	3.99	15	25

(B) #0-394-83575-1, Gibraltar Library binding.

	3.99	10	(15)

(C) #0-394-83575-1, tradepaper, 1977.

	2.95	5	10

Uhura's Song: Star Trek #21, 373 pages, novel by Janet Hagan.

(A) #0-8398-2888-8, Gregg Press, 1985, hardcover.

	11.95	12	15

Pocket Books, paperback:

(B) #0-671-54730-5, January 1985.

	3.50	(4)	5

(C) #0-671-54730-5, with Gertrude logo.

	3.50	4	5

(D) #0-671-65227.

	3.95	4	5

Unseen Enemy: Star Trek #51, Pocket Books, paperback, novel by V. E. Mitchell.

	4.50	4	(5)

Vendetta: The Giant Novel #2, #0-671-74145-4, Pocket Books, May 1991, paperback, 400 pages, novel by Peter David.

	4.95	5	6

Vulcan: Bantam, paperback, 175 pages, novel by Kathleen Sky.

(A) #0-553-12137-5, September 1978.

	1.95	10	(15)

(B) Second printing, August 1979.

	1.95	5	10

(C) #0-553-24633-X, April 1984.

	2.95	5	8

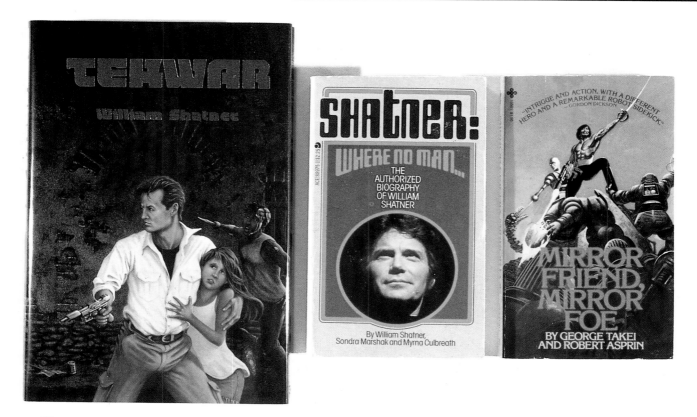

Shatner's limited edition (signed and numbered) *TekWar, Shatner: Where No Man...;* **and** *Mirror Friend, Mirror Foe* **by Takei.**

	Issue	Fair	Mint
(D) #0-553-24633-X, fourth printing.	2.95	4	6
(E) #0-553-24633-X, June 1985, with Spectra logo.	2.95	3	4

Vulcan Academy Murders: Star Trek #20, Pocket Books, 278 pages, novel by Jean Lorrah.

(A) #01529, Literary Guild Book Club, 1984, hardcover.	9.50	9	10

Science Fiction Book Club editions, 1984, hardcover:

(B) #064121, 1987.	4.98	5	6
(C) #064121, 1990.	5.98	5	6

Pocket Books, paperbacks:

(D) #0-671-50054-6, November 1984.	3.50	(4)	5
(E) #0-671-50054-6, second printing.	3.50	4	5
(F) #0-671-50054-6, third printing.	3.50	4	5
(G) #0-671-50054-6, with Gertrude logo.	3.50	4	5
(H) #0-671-64744-6.	3.95	4	5
(I) #0-671-72367.	4.50	4	5

Vulcan's Glory: Star Trek #44, #0-671-65667-8, Pocket Books, February 1989, paperback, 252 pages, novel by D. C. Fontana.

	3.95	(4)	5

The Truth Machine by Random House had a 25,000 copy run.

A selection of books by Leonard Nimoy: *Come Be with Me, We Are All Children Searching for Love*; *Will I Think Of You?*; and *You & I* (first edition).

	Issue	Fair	Mint

Warmed By Love: #0-88396-200-4, Blue Mountain Press, September 1983, hardcover, 157 pages, by Leonard Nimoy. A compilation of previously published poetry. **14.95 15 20**

We Are All Children Searching for Love: Blue Mountain Press, tradepaper, 63 pages, original poetry by Leonard Nimoy.
(A) #0-88396-024-9, 1977. **4.95 15 25**
(B) #0-88396-024-9, December 1977. **4.95 15 20**
(C) #0-88396-024-9, January 1979. **4.95 10 15**

The Web of the Romulans: Star Trek #10, Pocket Books, paperback, 220 pages, novel by M. S. Murdock.
(A) #0-8398-2833-0, Gregg Press, (G. K. Hall), 1983, hardcover. **10.95 10 15**
(B) #0-671-46479-5, June 1983, with Timescape logo. **2.95 (5) 8**
(C) #0-671-46479-5, second printing. **2.95 4 5**
(D) #0-671-60549-6, numbered cover. **3.50 4 5**
(E) #0-671-66501-6. **3.95 4 5**
(F) #0-671-70093. **4.50 4 5**

Will I Think Of You?: By Leonard Nimoy. Original poetry with photos.
(A) #0-912310-70-7, Celestial Arts, August 1974, tradepaper, 94 pages. **4.95 20 25**
(B) #0-440-5756-125, Dell, October 1975, paperback, 50 pages. **1.25 15 20**

World of Star Trek: By David Gerrold. Biographical writing on behind-the-scenes making of *Star Trek* for television.
Bluejay Press printings, tradepaper, 209 pages:
(A) #0-312-94463-2, May 1984. **8.95 10 (15)**
(B) #0-312-94463-2, second through fourth printings. **8.95 10 12**
Ballantine paperbacks, 276 pages:
(C) #0-345-23403-0, May 1973. **1.50 5 (10)**
(D) Second printing. **1.50 4 8**
(E) Third through fifth printings. **1.50 3 6**
(F) Sixth and seventh printings. **1.50 3 5**
(G) #0-345-24938-0, ninth printing, January 1975. **1.95 3 4**
(H) #0-345-28571-9, December 1979, second edition with silver artwork cover and Del Rey logo. **2.50 3 4**

World Without End: Bantam Books, paperback, 150 pages, novel by Joe Haldeman. The cover art for this book was done by Eddie Jones, who also drew the covers for *Best of Trek* #1-5 and #7.
(A) #0-553-12583-4, February 1979. **1.95 5 (10)**
(B) #0-553-24174-5, February 1985, with second edition artwork cover. **2.95 3 (5)**

Wounded Sky: Star Trek #13, Pocket Books, 255 pages, novel by Diane Duane. This was the last novel by Pocket to display a Timescape logo.

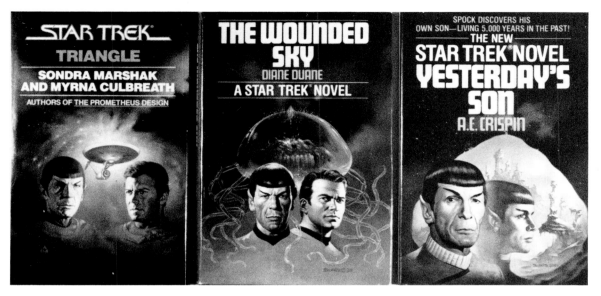

Three Star Trek novels by Pocket Books: *Triangle, The Wounded Sky,* **and** *Yesterday's Son.*

	Issue	Fair	Mint
A) Literary Guild Book Club, hardcover, 1983.	9.50	9	10

Science Fiction Book Club, 1983, hardcover:

	Issue	Fair	Mint
B) #025841, 1987.	4.98	5	6
C) #025841, 1990.	5.98	5	6

Pocket Books paperback editions:

	Issue	Fair	Mint
D) #0-671-47389-1, December 1983, with Timescape imprint.	2.95	4	5
E) #0-671-47389-1.	2.95	4	5
F) #0-671-60061-3.	3.50	4	(5)
G) #0-671-66735.	3.95	4	5

Yesterday's Son: Star Trek #11, 191 pages, novel by A. C. Crispin. This was the first of Pocket's novels to display a foil-stamped title on the cover.

	Issue	Fair	Mint
A) #0-8398-2830-6, Gregg Press (G. K. Hall), 1983, hardcover.	10.95	10	15
B) Literary Guild Book Club, hardcover, 1983.	9.50	9	10

Science Fiction Book Club, 1983, hardcover:

	Issue	Fair	Mint
C) #022558, 1987.	4.98	5	6
D) #022558, 1990.	5.98	5	6

Pocket Books paperback editions:

	Issue	Fair	Mint
E) 0-671-47315-8, August 1983, with Timescape logo.	2.95	(5)	8
F) 0-671-47315-8, numbered cover.	2.95	4	5
G) 0-671-60550-X.	3.50	4	5
H) 0-671-66110.	3.95	4	5
I) 0-671-72449.	4.50	4	5

You & I: 110 pages, by Leonard Nimoy. Original poetry and photos.

	Issue	Fair	Mint
(A) #0-9123310-27-8, Celestial Arts, January 1973, hardcover.	5.95	20	30
(B) #0-9123310-27-8, Celestial Arts, second through fourth printings.	5.95	20	25
(C) #0-9123310-27-8, Celestial Arts, December 1975, fifth printing.	5.95	15	20
(D) #0-91233026-X, Celestial Arts, January 1973, tradepaper.	2.95	20	25
(E) #0-38017616-0, Avon Books, December 1973, paperback.	1.50	10	15

Book Sets

The book sets in this section are listed by publishing company.

Ballantine Books: *Star Trek Logs,* #0-345-25341-8, 1975, paperback, by Alan Dean Foster. Boxed gift sets of *Star Trek Logs #1-4* and *Star Trek Logs #5-8* with cartoon covers. Packaged in slipcover cases.

	5	30	40

Bantam Books, 1975-1977:

(A) *Star Trek,* #0-553-25341, 1977, paperbacks, by James Blish. Boxed gift set of *Star Trek 1-4.* Packaged in slipcover case.

	6	25	35

(B) *Star Trek,* #0-553-24088, 1977, paperbacks, by James Blish. Boxed gift set containing *Star Trek 5-8.* Packaged in slipcover case.

	6	25	35

Four book sets: Bantam's *Great Adventures* and *Star Trek Lives! No. 1*, plus Pocket's *Star Trek Alpha Assortment* and *Star Trek 1*.

	Issue	Fair	Mint

(C) *Star Trek Fotonovel Assortment*, 1979, paperbacks. Boxed set including the first four fotonovels: *The City On The Edge Of Forever*, *Where No Man Has Gone Before*, *The Trouble With Tribbles*, and *A Taste Of Armageddon*. Slipcase features photos from the last two titles. **7.80 40 60**

(D) *Star Trek Lives! No. 1*, 1975, paperbacks, by James Blish. Six-volume boxed gift set which contains *Star Trek 1-6*. Packaged in slipcover case. **4.50 20 30**

(E) *Star Trek Lives! No. 2*, 1975, paperbacks, by James Blish. Six-volume boxed gift set including *Star Trek 7-11*. Packaged in slipcover case. **4.50 20 30**

(F) *Star Trek The Great Adventures #1-5*, #0-553-18616-7, 1979, paperbacks, by James Blish. Five-volume boxed gift set containing *Star Trek 1-5*. Packaged in slipcover case. **7.50 20 30**

(G) *Star Trek The New Voyages*, 1979, paperbacks. Four-volume fiction assortment. Includes the novels *Planet Of Judgement* and *Vulcan*. Packaged in slipcover case. **7.50 30 40**

Pocket Books, 1983-1989.

(A) *More Star Trek Adventure*, 1985, paperback. Set of four novels: *Ishmael*, *The Vulcan Academy Murders*, *Shadowland*, and *Web of the Romulans*. Packaged in slipcover case. **14 14 20**

(B) *Star Trek*, #0-671-90086-2, 1984, paperbacks. Set of four novels: *Abode of Life*, *Mutiny On The Enterprise*, *The Trellisane Confrontation*, and *The Wounded Sky*. Packaged in slipcover case. **11.80 12 20**

	Issue	Fair	Mint

(C) *Star Trek 1*, #0-671-92147-9, 1983, paperbacks. Set of four novels: *Dwellers In The Crucible*, *Chain Of Attack*, *Strangers From The Sky*, and *The Wounded Sky*. Packaged in slipcover case. **15.80 16 25**

(D) *Star Trek 2*, #0-671-92163-0, 1983, paperbacks. Set of four novels containing *Crisis On Centaurus*, *Dreams of Raven*, *Mindshadow*, and *My Enemy, My Ally*. Packaged in slipcover case. **15.80 16 25**

(E) *Star Trek Adventure*, #0-671-91017-5, 1985, paperbacks. Set of four novels: *My Enemy, My Ally*, *Tears of the Singers*, *Uhura's Song*, and *The Wounded Sky*. Packaged in slipcover case. **14 14 20**

(F) *Star Trek Alpha Assortment*, #0-671-98548-5, 1983, paperbacks. Set of four novels: *Black Fire*, *Covenant of the Crown*, *Triangle*, and *The Prometheus Design*. Packaged in slipcover case with artwork from *Yesterday's Son*. **11.80 12 20**

(G) *Star Trek Beta Assortment*, #0-671-98550-7, 1983, paperbacks. Set of four novels: *The Entropy Effect*, *The Klingon Gambit*, *Web of the Romulans*, and *Yesterday's Son*. Slipcover case includes artwork from *Prometheus Design*. **11.80 12 20**

(H) *Star Trek Classic Voyages*, 1987, paperbacks. Set of four novels: *Enterprise*, *The Prometheus Design*, *Battlestations!*, and *Dreadnought!*. Packaged in slipcover case with *Star Trek Trivia* bookcover art. **14.45 15 20**

(I) *Star Trek Classic Voyages 1*, #0-671-96368-6, 1989, paperbacks. Set of four novels: *IDIC*, *Yesterday's*

Two book sets: *Star Trek Logs 5-8* and *Logs 1-4.*

	Issue	Fair	Mint

˙on, *Covenant Of The Crown,* and *Enterprise.* Blue
lipcover case. **18 18 20**

J) *Star Trek Classic Voyages 2,* #0-671-96369-4,
'989, paperbacks. Set of four novels containing *The
Klingon Gambit, Black Fire, Web Of The Romulans,*
ˑnd *Demons.* Slipcover case included.
13.45 14 20

K) *Star Trek 20th Anniversary, Volume I,* #0-671-
ˑ1253-4, 1986, paperbacks. Four-volume book set
ˑontaining *Covenant of the Crown, Dwellers In The*

	Issue	Fair	Mint

Crucible, The Final Reflection, and *The Killing Time.*
Slipcover case included. **13.45 18 20**

(L) *Star Trek 20th Anniversary, Volume II,* #0-671-
91254-2, 1986, paperback. Set of four novels: *Crisis
on Centaurus, Mindshadow, Pawns and Symbols,* and
The Trellisane Confrontation. Packaged in slipcover
case. **13.45 14 20**

Science Fiction Book Club, Pocket books,
hardcover.

(A) Set of four books containing *Covenant of the
Crown, My Enemy, My Ally, Vulcan Academy Murders,* and *Yesterday's Son.* **22.50 23 25**

(B) #034850, four-volume set containing *Star Trek
Readers I-IV.* **25.98 25 35**

(C) #038620, two-volume set containing *Vulcan
Academy Murders* and *Yesterday's Son.*
9.98 10 15

(D) #157834, four-volume set with *Enterprise, The
Final Frontier, The Lost Years,* and *Strangers From
The Sky.* **29.98 30 35**

(E) #171595, three-volume set containing *How Much
For Just The Planet?, My Enemy, My Ally,* and *The
Wounded Sky.* **14.98 15 20**

(F) #184440, four-volume set containing *The Final
Frontier, Strangers From The Sky, Spock's World,* and
The Lost Years. **24.98 25 30**

Wanderer: *Star Trek II: The Wrath of Khan,* #0-
671-93230-6, 1982, tradepaper, by William Rotsler.
Special children's three-volume set which includes
Star Trek II Biographies, Star Trek II Distress Call,
and *Star Trek II Short Stories.* Slipcase packaging.
This is the only children's Trek gift book set ever
produced. **9.95 10 20**

Books (Translations And Foreign Editions)

Foreign book prices vary widely based on many
ˑechnical details which are involved in their produc-
ˑion. The problem of assessing their value in this
ˑountry is further compounded by import and export
ˑees which usually increase book prices substantially.
ˑor this reason, only the issue price in pence (p),
ˑounds (£), or francs is given if known. Dealers vary
ˑidely in their prices on foreign materials.

Collectors will also notice that in some cases the
ˑame title appears in simultaneous releases by mul-
ˑiple publishing houses. These overlaps result from
ˑtock overflows or the simultaneous exercising of co-

existing publishing contracts. In other instances, a
particular series of books appears to cross over between several different publishing subsidiaries
without ever having a complete set published at any
house.

Chain of Attack: Star Trek #1, United Kingdom,
Titan Books, 1987, paperback, by Gene DeWeese. 4"
x 6¾". **£2.95**

Chekov's Enterprise: United Kingdom, #0-7088-
1800-5, Futura Publications, April 1980, paperback,
by Walter Koenig. 4" x 6¾". **95p**

	Issue	*Fair*	*Mint*

Complete Visual Guide of Star Trek I: Japan, Super Visual Magazine. Tradepaper picture book. —

Corona: Japan, Hayakawa Publishing, Inc., 1988, 303 pages, by Greg Bear. —

Deep Domain: Star Trek #2, United Kingdom, #0-907610-86-2, Titan Books, May 1987, paperback, 275 pages, by Howard Weinstein. 4" x 6¾".
£2.95

Dreams of the Raven: Star Trek #3, United Kingdom, Titan Books, 1987, paperback, by Carmen Carter. 4" x 6¾". **£2.95**

Enterprise, The First Adventure: United Kingdom, #0-586-07321-3, Grafton Books, 1987, paperback, 371 pages, by Vonda McIntyre. 4¼" x 7".
£2.95

Enterprise, The First Adventure: Japan, Hayakawa Publishing, Inc., 1988, by Vonda McIntyre. Comes as a two-volume set.
(A) *Enterprise: The First Adventure, Volume 1*, 363 pages. —
(B) *Enterprise: The First Adventure, Volume 2*, 363 pages. —

Giant In The Universe: Columbia, (*Viaje A Las Estrellas: Un Gigante En El Universo*); Editorial Norma (Bogota), hardcover children's book by Kay Wood. —

Great Star Trek Trivia Book: United Kingdom, #0-7088-1780-7, Futura Publications, February 1980, paperback, by Rafe Needleman. 32 illustrations. 4" x 6¾". **95p**

How Much For Just The Planet?: Star Trek #5, United Kingdom, Titan Books, 1987, paperback, by John Ford. 4" x 6¾". **£2.95**

Making of Star Trek: United Kingdom, Pan Books, 1968, paperback, 416 pages, by Stephen Whitfield and Gene Roddenberry. Illustrated. 4" x 6¾".
75p

Monsters of Star Trek: United Kingdom, #0-7088-1779-3, Futura Books, February 1980, paperback, 144 pages, by Daniel Cohen. Illustrated. 4" x 6¾".
75p

Mudd's Angels: United Kingdom, #0-552-10865-0, Corgi Books, 1978, paperback, 177 pages, by J. A. Lawrence. 4" x 6¾". **85p**

Mudd's Angels: Japan, Hayakawa Publishing, Inc., 1985, 295 pages, by J. A. Lawrence. —

Mutiny On The Enterprise: Japan, Hayakawa Publishing, Inc., 1989, 286 pages, by Robert E. Vardman. —

Official Star Trek Trivia Book: United Kingdom, Futura Books, 1980, paperback, by Rafe Needleman. 4" x 6¾". —

Planet of Judgement: United Kingdom, #0-552-10622-4, Corgi Books, 1977, paperback, 151 pages, by Joe Haldeman. 4" x 6¾". **60p**

Price of the Phoenix: United Kingdom, Corgi Books, 1977, paperback, 182 pages, by Sondra Marshak. 4" x 6¾". **60p**

Raumschiff Enterprise: Set Edizioni Panini Modena Italy, 1979, softcover. Children's sticker book. See **Sticker Albums**.

Romulan Way: Star Trek #4, United Kingdom, Titan Books, 1987, paperback, by Diane Duane and Peter Morwood. 4" x 6¾". **£2.95**

Spock Messiah: United Kingdom, #0-552-10281-4, Corgi Books, January 1977, paperback, 192 pages, by Theodore Cogswell and George Spano. 4" x 6¾".
60p

Spock Must Die!: United Kingdom, paperback, 128 pages, by James Blish. 4" x 6¾".

(A) #0-552-09498-6, Corgi Books, April 1974.
30p

(B) #0-553-12589-3, Bantam Books, October 1979.
75p

Starless World: Japan, Hayakawa Publishing, Inc., 1981, 258 pages, by Gordon Eklund.

—

Star Trek: United Kingdom, by James Blish.

(A) #0-552-03459-2, Bantam Books, July 1967, paperback, 144 pages, 4" x 7". **25p**

(B) #0-552-03459-2, Corgi Books, July 1967, paperback, 144 pages, 4" x 7". **25p**

(C) #0-85617-888-8, White Lion, November 1974, hardcover, 136 pages, 6¾" x 7½".
£1.80

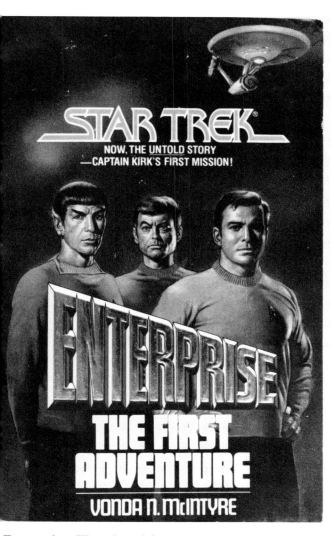

Enterprise, The First Adventure, United Kingdom, 1987.

	Issue	Fair	Mint

D) Severn House, hardcover, 5⅝" x 8¾".
—

Star Trek 1: Japan, Hayakawa Publishing, Inc. (Tokyo), 1977, 295 pages, by James Blish.
—

Star Trek 2: Japan, Hayakawa Publishing, Inc. (Tokyo), 1977, 298 pages, by James Blish.
—

Star Trek 2: United Kingdom, by James Blish.
(A) #0-552-63439-5, Bantam Books, August 1969, paperback, 128 pages, 4" x 7". **25p**
(B) #0-552-63439-5, Corgi Books, August 1969, paperback, 128 pages, 4" x 7". **25p**
(C) #0-85617-898-5, White Lion, May 1975, hardcover, 128 pages, 6¾" x 7½". **£2.50**
(D) Severn House, hardcover, 5⅝" x 8¾".
—

Issue   Fair   Mint

Star Trek 3: Japan, Hayakawa Publishing, Inc. (Tokyo), 1971, 279 pages, by James Blish.
—

Star Trek 3: United Kingdom, by James Blish.
(A) #0-552-64371-8, Bantam Books, August 1969, paperback, 128 pages, 4" x 7". **25p**
(B) #0-552-64371-8, Corgi Books, August 1969, paperback, 128 pages, 4" x 7". **25p**
(C) #0-85617-908-6, White Lion, August 1975, hardcover, 128 pages, 6¾" x 7½". **£2.50**
(D) Severn House, hardcover, 5⅝" x 8¾".
—

Star Trek 4: Japan, Hayakawa Publishing, Inc. (Tokyo), 1976, 281 pages, by James Blish.
—

Spock Must Die!, United Kingdom, 1979.

British version of *Star Trek 2* by James Blish.

	Issue	Fair	Mint

Star Trek 4: United Kingdom, by James Blish.

(A) #0-552-67009-X, Bantam Books, October 1971, paperback, 144 pages, 4" x 7". **25p**

(B) #0-552-09445-5, Corgi Books, October 1971, paperback, 144 pages, 4" x 7". **30p**

(C) #0-7278-0263-1, Severn House, March 1977, hardcover, 144 pages, 5⅝" x 8¾".
£3.15

(D) White Lion, hardcover, 6¾" x 7½".

—

Star Trek 5: Japan, Hayakawa Publishing, Inc. (Tokyo), 1978, 313 pages, by James Blish.

—

Star Trek 5: United Kingdom, by James Blish.

(A) #0-552-67300-5, Bantam Books, June 1972, paperback, 160 pages, 4" x 7". **30p**

	Issue	Fair	Mint

(B) #0-552-67300-5, Corgi Books, June 1972, paperback, 144 pages, 4" x 7". **30p**

(C) #0-7278-0271-2, Severn House, July 1977 hardcover, 144 pages, 5⅝" x 8¾".
£3.15

(D) White Lion, hardcover, 6¾" x 7½".

—

Star Trek 6: Japan, Hayakawa Publishing, Inc (Tokyo), 1978, 327 pages, by James Blish.

—

Star Trek 6: United Kingdom, paperback, 160 pages by James Blish. 4" x 7".

(A) #0-552-67364-1, Bantam Books, August 1972.
25p

(B) #0-552-09447-1, Corgi Books, August 1972.
30p

(C) Severn House, hardcover, 5⅝" x 8¾".

—

(D) White Lion, hardcover, 6¾" x 7½".

—

Star Trek 7: Japan, Hayakawa Publishing, Inc (Tokyo), 1979, 297 pages, by James Blish.

—

Star Trek 7: United Kingdom, paperback, 160 pages by James Blish. 4" x 7".

(A) #0-553-10815-8, Bantam Books, May 1973.
85p

(B) #0-552-09229-0, Corgi Books, May 1973.
30p

(C) Severn House, hardcover, 5⅝" x 8¾".

—

(D) White Lion, hardcover, 6¾" x 7½".

—

Star Trek 8: Japan, Hayakawa Publishing, Inc (Tokyo), 1978, 345 pages, by James Blish.

—

Star Trek 8: United Kingdom, by James Blish.

(A) #0-553-10816-6, Bantam Books, August 1973 paperback, 176 pages, 4" x 7". **85p**

(B) #0-552-09289-4, Corgi Books, August 1973, paperback, 176 pages, 4" x 7". **30p**

(C) #0-7278-0408-1, Severn House, October 1978 hardcover, 176 pages, 5⅝" x 8¾".
£3.75

(D) White Lion, hardcover, 6¾" x 7½".

—

Star Trek 9: Japan, Hayakawa Publishing, Inc (Tokyo), 1980, 371 pages, by James Blish.

—

Star Trek 9: United Kingdom, paperback, 192 pages by James Blish. 4" x 7".

Issue Fair Mint

A) #0-553-02238-5, Bantam Books, January 1974.
60p

B) #0-552-09476-5, Corgi Books, February 1974.
30p

C) Severn House, July 1977, hardcover, 5⅝" x 8¾".
—

D) White Lion, hardcover, 6¾" x 7½".
—

Star Trek 10: Japan, Hayakawa Publishing, Inc. (Tokyo), 1981, 339 pages, by James Blish.
—

Star Trek 10: United Kingdom, by James Blish.
A) #0-553-10796-0, Bantam Books, July 1974, paperback, 176 pages, 4" x 7".
75p
B) #0-552-09553-2, Corgi Books, July 1974, paperback, 176 pages, 4" x 7".
35p
C) #0-7278-0454-5, Severn House, May 1979, hardcover, 166 pages, 5⅝" x 8¾".
£3.95
D) White Lion, hardcover, 6¾" x 7½".
—

Star Trek 11: Japan, Hayakawa Publishing, Inc. (Tokyo), 1981, 355 pages, by James Blish.
—

Star Trek 11: United Kingdom, by James Blish.
A) #0-553-08717-7, Bantam Books, October 1975, paperback, 192 pages, 4" x 7".
75p
B) #0-552-09850-7, Corgi Books, October 1975, paperback, 192 pages, 4" x 7".
40p

Issue Fair Mint

(C) #0-7278-0504-5, Severn House, August 1979, hardcover, 192 pages, 5⅝" x 8¾".
£4.25
(D) White Lion, hardcover, 6¾" x 7½".
—

Star Trek 12: Japan, Hayakawa Publishing, Inc. (Tokyo), 1981, 356 pages, by James Blish.
—

Star Trek 12: United Kingdom, by James Blish.
(A) #0-552-10759-X, Corgi Books, June 1978, paperback, 192 pages, 4" x 7". **90p**
(B) #0-72778-0547-9, Severn House, December 1979, hardcover, 192 pages, 5⅝" x 8¾".
£4.25
(C) White Lion, hardcover, 6¾" x 7½".
—

Star Trek Annuals: United Kingdom. See **Comic Specials**.

Star Trek Blueprints: United Kingdom, #0-345-24471-0, Ballantine, June 1976, by Franz Joseph. 9" x 30" diagrams with twelve illustrations.
£2.50

Star Trek Catalog: United Kingdom, #0-448-14053-5, Grosset & Dunlap, September 1979, illustrated tradepaper, 160 pages, written by Turnbull. 7½" x 11¼".
£2.95

Star Trek Compendium: United Kingdom, #0-352-31355-2, Star Books, June 1983, illustrated tradepaper, 192 pages, by Allan Asherman. This British edition covers Star Trek through *ST II* and

Foreign Star Trek Foto Novels: Japan, Belgium, and South America.

Issue Fair Mint

contains twelve chapters. The first U.S. printings of this book ended with Chapter 10. 7½" x 11¼".
£4.95

Star Trek Concordance: United Kingdom, #0-345-25137-7, Ballantine, June 1977, illustrated tradepaper, 256 pages, by Bjo Trimble. 7½" x 11¼".
£3.50

Star Trek Fotonovels: Belgium, Mandala Productions, Antwerp/Orbis Books, 1978.
➤ #1, *The City On the Edge of Forever.*
➤ #2, *Where No Man Has Gone Before.*
➤ #3, *The Trouble With Tribbles.*
➤ #4, *A Taste of Armageddon.*
—

Star Trek Fotonovels: Japan, Mandala Productions, Tatsumi Mook, 1977.
➤ #1, *The City On the Edge of Forever.*
➤ #2, *Where No Man Has Gone Before.*
—

Star Trek Fotonovels: South America, GeoMundo, 1979.
(A) #3, #011779, *The Trouble With Tribbles.*
—

(B) #4, #011879, *A Taste Of Armageddon.*
—

Star Trek Fotonovels: United Kingdom, Mandala Productions, Corgi, illustrated paperback, 160 pages each. 4" x 6¾".
(A) #0-552-10673-9, *The City On the Edge of Forever,* January 1978. **85p**
(B) #0-552-61346-0, *Where No Man Has Gone Before,* March 1978. **85p**
(C) #0-552-61347-9, *The Trouble With Tribbles,* March 1978. **85p**
(D) #0-552-61348-7, *A Taste Of Armageddon,* April 1978. **85p**
(E) #0-553-11349-6, *Metamorphosis,* August 1978. **95p**
(F) #0-553-11350-X, *All Our Yesterdays,* September 1978. **95p**
(G) #0-553-12041-7, *The Galileo Seven,* October 1978. **95p**
(H) #0-553-12022-0, *A Piece Of The Action,* November 1978. **95p**
(I) #0-553-12021-2, *The Devil In The Dark,* December 1978. **95p**
(J) #0-553-12017-4, *Day Of The Dove,* January 1979. **95p**
(K) #0-553-12028-X, *The Deadly Years,* February 1979. **95p**
(L) #0-553-12012-3, *Amok Time,* March 1979. **95p**

Issue Fair Min

Star Trek Intragalactic Puzzles: United Kingdom #0-552-61083-6, Bantam, March 1978, tradepaper, 12 pages, by James Razzi. 7½" x 11¼".
£1.95

Star Trek Lives!: United Kingdom, #0-552-09914-, Corgi Books, October 1975, illustrated paperback, 28 pages, by Jacqueline Lichtenberg. 4" x 6¾".
60p

Star Trek Logs: United Kingdom, by Alan Dea Foster.
(A) Log One.
➤ #0-552-09747-0, Corgi Books, April 1975, pape back, 192 pages, 4" x 6¾". **40p**
➤ Severn House, hardcover, 5⅝" x 8¾".
£6.95
(B) Log Two.
➤ #0-552-09830-2, Corgi Books, July 1975, pape back, 192 pages, 4" x 6¾". **40p**
➤ #0-7278-0820-6, Log Two, Severn House, Jul 1982, hardcover, 192 pages, 5⅝" x 8¾".
£6.95
(C) Log Three.
➤ #0-552-10045-5, Corgi Books, December 197 paperback, 224 pages, 4" x 6¾".
45p
➤ Severn House, hardcover, 5⅝" x 8¾".
£6.95
(D) Log Four.
➤ #0-552-10107-9, Corgi Books, March 1976, pape back, 224 pages, 4" x 6¾". **50p**
➤ Severn House, hardcover, 5⅝" x 8¾".
£6.95
(E) Log Five.
➤ #0-552-10315-7, Corgi Books, November 197 paperback, 208 pages, 4" x 6¾".
60p
➤ Severn House, hardcover, 5⅝" x 8¾".
£6.95
(F) Log Six.
➤ Corgi Books, paperback, 4" x 6¾".
60p
➤ Severn House, hardcover, 5⅝" x 8¾".
£6.95
(G) Log Seven.
➤ Corgi Books, paperback, 4" x 6¾".
60p
➤ Severn House, hardcover, 5⅝" x 8¾".
£6.95
(H) Log Eight.
➤ Corgi Books, paperback, 4" x 6¾".
60p

 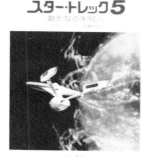

Japanese movie novelizations of *STTMP* through *ST V*.

	Issue	Fair	Mint

Severn House, hardcover, 5⅝" x 8¾".
£6.95

I) Log Nine.
Corgi Books, paperback, 4" x 6¾".
60p
Severn House, hardcover, 5⅝" x 8¾".
£6.95

J) Log Ten.
Corgi Books, paperback, 4" x 6¾".
60p
Severn House, hardcover, 5⅝" x 8¾".
£6.95

Star Trek Official Cooking Manual: United Kingdom, #0-553-11819-6, Bantam Books, November 1978, paperback, 224 pages, by Picard. 4" x 6¾".
95p

Star Trek Punchout Book: United Kingdom, #0-394-83277-9, Random House, June 1980, illustrated children's hardcover, 32 pages, by James Razzi. 8½" x 13½".
£1.75

Star Trek Puzzle Manual: United Kingdom, by James Razzi.

A) #0-553-12131-6, Bantam Books, January 1979, abridged edition, illustrated paperback, 128 pages, 4" x 6¾".
85p

(B) #0-552-99001-9, Corgi Books, December 1976, tradepaper, 128 pages, 7½" x 11¼".
£1.50

Star Trek Quiz Book: United Kingdom, #0-7221-1137-1, Sphere Books, October 1978, paperback, 160 pages, by Bart Andrews and Brad Dunning. 4" x 6¾".
85p

Star Trek Spaceflight Chronology 1980-2188: United Kingdom, #0-7088-1740-8, Phoebus (London), April 1980, tradepaper, by Stan Goldstein and Fred Goldstein. 7½" x 11¼".
£5.50

Star Trek Speaks: United Kingdom, #0-7088-1737-8, Futura Publications, February 1980, tradepaper, 160 pages, by Susan Sackett and Fred Goldstein. 5" x 7½".
£1.75

Star Trek Technical Manual: United Kingdom, #0-345-24730-2, Ballantine, June 1976, hardcover, 200 pages, by Franz Joseph. Illustrated, with diagrams. 7½" x 11¼".
£2.95

Star Trek The Motion Picture: France, Editions J'ai Lu, 1979, paperback, by Gene Roddenberry. 4" x 6¾".
7.01 francs

Issue   Fair   Mint

Star Trek: The Motion Picture: Japan, Hayakawa Publishing, Inc., 1982, 283 pages, by Gene Roddenberry. —

Star Trek The Motion Picture: Mexico, #968-458-022-3, Lasser Press (Mexico City), 1979, tradepaper, 228 pages, by Gene Roddenberry. 5" x 7½". A Spanish-language first edition limited to 12,000 copies. —

Star Trek The Motion Picture: United Kingdom, by Gene Roddenberry.
(A) #0-7088-1725-4, Futura Publications, December 1979, illustrated paperback, 208 pages, by Gene Roddenberry. 4" x 6¾". Includes special color photo section from the movie not in the U.S. edition.
£1.00
(B) #0-728-0611-9, Severn, May 1980, hardcover, 224 pages, 5⅝" x 8¾". **£4.95**

Star Trek The Motion Picture: West Germany, Playboy/Noewig (Munich), 1979, paperback, by Gene Roddenberry. 4" x 6¾". —

Star Trek The Motion Picture 14 Official Blueprints: United Kingdom, #0-7088-1765-3, Futura Publications, February 1980. Technical blueprints, 5⅝" x 8¾". **£3.50**

Star Trek The Motion Picture Peel Off Graphics: United Kingdom, #0-7088-1738-6, Future Books, April 1980, illustrated tradepaper, by Lee Cole. 7½" x 11¼". **£4.95**

Star Trek: The Motion Picture Pop-Up: Columbia, (Viaje A Las Estrellas), Editorial Norma (Bogota), 1979, hardcover children's book by Tor Lokvig and Chuck Murphey. —

Star Trek: The Motion Picture Pop-Up Book: United Kingdom, #0-361-04898-X, Purnell Books, March 1980, illustrated children's hardcover.
£2.50

Star Trek: The New Voyages: Japan, Hayakawa Publishing, Inc., 1983, 449 pages, by Sondra Marshak and Myrna Culbreath. —

Star Trek: The New Voyages: United Kingdom, #0-552-10233-4, Corgi Books, September 1976, paperback, 256 pages, by Sondra Marshak and Myrna Culbreath. 4" x 6¾". **65p**

Star Trek: The New Voyages 2: Japan, Hayakawa Publishing, Inc., by Sondra Marshak and Myrna Culbreath. Two-volume set.
(A) *Star Trek: The New Voyages 2, Part 1*, 1983, 274 pages. —

Who's Who In Star Trek by John Townsley, United Kingdom, 1988.

(B) *Star Trek: The New Voyages 2, Part 2*, 1983, 25[?] pages. —

Star Trek The New Voyages 2: United Kingdom, Corgi Books, 1978, paperback, 256 pages, by Sondra Marshak and Myrna Culbreath. 4" x 6¾". **65p**

Star Trek: The Next Generation: Encounter A[t] Farpoint: Japan, Hayakawa Publishing, Inc., 1987 282 pages, by David Gerrold. —

Star Trek II Short Stories: United Kingdom, #0 09-932230-7, Sparrow books, September 1983 children's tradepaper, 160 pages, by William Rotsler 5" x 7½". **£2.25**

Star Trek II: The Wrath of Khan: France, Edi tions J'ai Lu, 1982, hardcover, by Vonda McIntyre 5⅝" x 8¾". —

| | Issue | Fair | Mint |

Star Trek II: The Wrath of Khan: Japan, Hayakawa Publishing, Inc., 1982, 380 pages, by Vonda McIntyre. —

Star Trek II: The Wrath of Khan: West Germany, Heyne Bucher (Munich), 1982, paperback, by Vonda McIntyre. 4" x 6¾". —

Star Trek II: The Wrath of Khan: United Kingdom, 1982, by Vonda McIntyre.

A) Futura, paperback, 4" x 6¾". **£1.95**

B) MacDonald & Company, hardcover, 5⅝" x 8¾". —

Star Trek II: The Wrath of Khan Photo Story: United Kingdom, #0-416-43080-5, Methuen (A Magnet Special), 1982, paperback, 154 pages, by Richard Anobile. Anamorphic frame blow-ups in black and white with captions that narrate the movie story. 4" x 6¾". **£1.25**

Star Trek III: The Search for Spock: Japan, Hayakawa Publishing, Inc., 1984, 432 pages, by Vonda McIntyre. —

Star Trek III: The Search for Spock Short Stories: United Kingdom, #0-906-71059-0, Ravette, 1984, children's tradepaper, 126 pages, by William Rotsler. 5" x 7½". **£2.25**

Star Trek III: The Search for Spock Story Book: United Kingdom, Ravette (London), 1984, paperback, by Lawrence Weinstein. 5" x 7½". —

Star Trek III Vulcan Treasure: United Kingdom, #0-906-50138-0, Ravette, 1984, tradepaper, 117 pages, by William Rotsler. 5" x 7½". **£2.25**

Star Trek IV: The Voyage Home: Japan, Hayakawa Publishing, Inc., 1987, 432 pages, by Vonda McIntyre. —

Star Trek V: The Final Frontier: Japan, Hayakawa Publishing, Inc., 1990, 392 pages, by J. M. Dillard. —

Trillions of Trilligs: Columbia (Viaje A Las Estrellas: La Invasion De Los Robots), Editorial Norma (Bogota), 1977, children's hardcover, by Christopher Cerf and Sharon Lerner. —

Vulcan: Japan, Hayakawa Publishing, Inc., 1986, 280 pages, by Kathleen Sky. —

Web of the Romulans: Japan, Hayakawa Publishing, Inc., 1986, 321 pages, by M. S. Murdock. —

Who's Who In Star Trek: United Kingdom, #0-352-32186-5, W. H. Allen & Company (Star Books) (London), 1988, paperback, 109 pages, by John Townsley. Updated reprint of the small press book of the same title. Trek reference with alphabetical character listings for *Star Trek* and *Star Trek: The Next Generation*. **£2.50**

World Without End: Japan, Hayakawa Publishing, Inc., 1986, 239 pages, by Joe Haldeman. —

Yesterday's Son: Japan, Hayakawa Publishing, Inc., 1985, 308 pages, by Ann C. Crispin. —

Books (Trek-Related)

This section contains books that, while not devoted to Trek topics, contain some portion of Trek-related material.

Age of Wonders: Exploring the World of Science Fiction: By David Hartwell. A nonfiction examination of science fiction literature and its media phenomenon. Pages 33-35, 133, and 199 review Star Trek and the Trekkie movement, the design of the Enterprise, and the naming of the U.S. shuttle.

A) #0-8027-0808-0, Walkers & Company, 1984, hardcover, 205 pages. **15.95 16 17**

B) #0-97-02693-7, McGraw Hill, 1985, paperback, 224 pages. **3.95 4 5**

American Monomyth: Hardcover, by Robert Jewett and John Shelton Lawrence. A study of the American myth syndrome, pop culture, and the media artists. Chapter 1 is titled "Star Trek and the Bubblegum Fallacy" and Chapter 2 is titled "Trekkie Religion and the Werther Effect." Pages 1-39 are Trek-related with two black and white photos.

(A) #0-385-12203-9, Anchor Press (Doubleday), 1977, 263 pages. **8.95 9 15**

(B) 1988, University Press of America, 331 pages, with introduction dedicated to Gene Roddenberry. **17.95 18 20**

American Vein: E. P. Dutton, 1979, 261 pages, by Christopher Wicking and Tise Vahimagl. Biographies

	Issue	Fair	Mint

of famous TV directors. Includes bios on Gene Roddenberry, Gene L. Coon, Joseph Pevney, James Daniels, James Goldstone, and Ralph Senensky.

(A) #0-525-05420-0, hardcover. **9.95** **10** **15**

(B) #0-525-47603-2, tradepaper.
6.95 **7** **10**

Best of Science Fiction TV: #0-517-56650-8, Harmony Books, 1987, tradepaper, 144 pages, by John Javna. Reviews of TV science fiction. Reviews *Star Trek* on pages 11-15 and contains pictures and trivia about the show throughout. Color tint photo of Spock on cover. **8.95** **9** **10**

Celebrity Cookbook: #2301, Playmore Inc. (Moby Books), 1981, tradepaper, by Johna Blinn. Illustrated recipe book with personal favorites of the stars. Includes William Shatner's "Steak Picado" on pages 200-201. There is also an interview about futuristic diets.
7.95 **7** **10**

Close Encounters: Film, Feminism & Science Fiction: University of Minnesota Press, 1990, 250 pages, by Constance Penley. Women in Star Trek.

(A) #0-8166-1911-5, hardcover.
39.95 **40** **42**

(B) #0-8166-1913-3, tradepaper.
12.95 **13** **14**

Complete Directory to Prime Time Network Television Shows, 1946-Present: Ballantine, 1,006 pages, by Tim Brooks and Earle Marsh. An alphabetical listing of TV programs, their histories, and followers. *Star Trek* is discussed on pages 708-709.

(A) $0-345-29587-0, hardcover, 1979.
19.95 **20** **24**

(B) #0-345-29588-9, tradepaper, 1981.
12.95 **13** **15**

Cosmic Dancers, Exploring the Science in Science Fiction: #0-97-023867-7, McGraw Hill, 1986, tradepaper, by Amit Goswani. An investigation of science fiction technology as it relates to fact. Star Trek philosophies examined include time travel, matter transporters, matter/anti-matter drive, and drive logic on pages 8, 113-114, 157, 213, and 247.
7.95 **7** **10**

Cult TV: St. Martins Press, 1985, tradepaper, 256 pages, by John Javna. Contains "A viewer's guide to the shows America can't live without." Trivia snips on Star Trek with black and white photos. Show lists on pages 54-57. Black and white photo insert of Spock on cover. **12.95** **13** **15**

Draw 50 Famous Stars: Doubleday & Company, 1983, 30 pages, by Lee J. Ames. Learn to draw famous characters via outlined panel sketches as

	Issue	Fair	Mint

selected by Rona Barrett's *Hollywood Magazine*. Included are nine panel frames of Mr. Spock.

➢ #0-385-15688-X, tradepaper.

➢ #0-385-15689-B, prebound with jacket.

Price for each. **8.95** **8** **10**

Encyclopedia of Science Fiction Movies: Woodbury Press, 1984, hardcover, 408 pages, by Phil Hardy. A year-by-year chronology of science fiction films up until 1985, with reviews and photos. Contains information on *STTMP*, *ST II*, and *ST III*.
12.98 **12** **15**

Encyclopedia of TV Science Fiction: United Kingdom, 1990, tradepaper, 600 pages, by Roger Fulton. Import containing both U.S. and British listings of sci-fi/fantasy shows. Includes over 400 series, mini-series, specials, and animated shows with air dates, production credits, and information. Cover shows Ruk and Kirk (LG). **39.95** **40** **45**

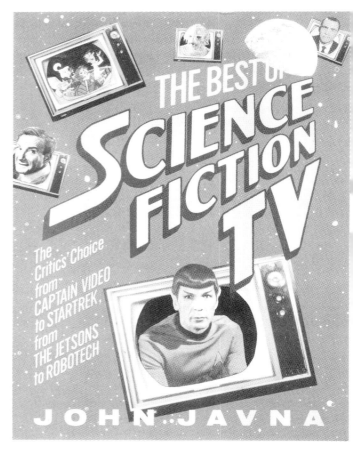

The Best of Science Fiction TV, **Harmony Books, 1987.**

Issue Fair Mint

Famous Spaceships of Fact and Fantasy: #0-89024-539-8, (#12038 tradepaper), Kalmbach Publishing Company, 1984, tradepaper, 88 pages, by Editors. Shows how to build famous spaceships; pages 64-73 detail various modificatinos for the Enterprise. Color picture of the Enterprise on cover.
8.50   9   10

Fandom is for the Young: Or One Convention Too Many: #0-553-04416-2, Vantage, 1981, hardcover, by Karen Flanery and Nina Gramick. Autobiographical nonfiction about attending science fiction conventions.   **8.95   8   12**

Fantastic Television: Harmony Books, 1977, 192 pages, by Gary Gerani and Paul Schulman. A pictorial history of science fiction and fantasy films on the screen. Star Trek movies included on pages 100-114 with nine pages of commentary and a five-page episode guide. There are also 27 black and white Trek photos. Book jacket has photo of Spock.

A) #0-517-52646-8, hardcover.
12.95   12   18

B) #0-517-52645-X, tradepaper.
8.95   8   12

Films of the Seventies: #0-8065-0927-9, Citadel Press, tradepaper, 1982, 328 pages, by Robert Bookinder. Covers *STTMP* on pages 283-288, plus photos.   **9.95   9   12**

Film Magic, The Art And Science of Special Effects: #0-13-314774-6, Prentice Hall Press, 1987, tradepaper, 140 pages, by David Hutchison. *ST IV* review on pages 126-128.   **12.95   13   15**

From Jules Verne To Star Trek: #0-8473-1458-8, Drake Publishers, 1977, tradepaper, 147 pages, by Jeff Rovin. A guide to the 100 best TV and movie science fiction. Includes a synopsis on Trek on pages 139-143 with three black and white photos of Trek's exotic women. Also a full-color portrait of Spock.
6.95   6   10

Great Science Fiction From The Movies: #0-671-82974-9, Archway (Pocket Books), 1976, paperback, 149 pages, by Edward Edelson. Star Trek information.   **1.95   3   5**

Hake's Guide To TV Collectibles: #0-87069-571-1, Wallace-Homestead Book Company, 1990, tradepaper, 185 pages, by Ted Hake. Price listings for television memorabilia. Includes Star Trek merchandise.
14.95   15   17

Heroes of the Spaceways: #3960-3, Quick Fox, 1981, tradepaper, 127 pages, by Bill Harry.
6.95   7   10

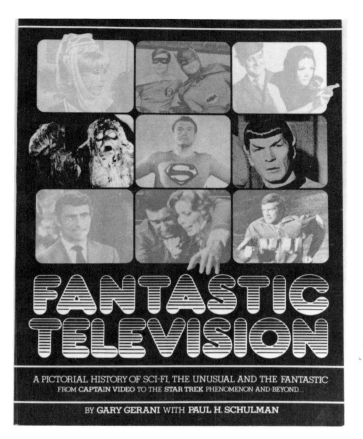

Fantastic Television, **Harmony Books, 1977.**

Issue   Fair   Mint

How You Can Explore Higher Dimensions of Space And Time, An Introduction to the New Science of Hyperspace for Trekkies of All Ages: #0-13-444035-8, Prentice Hall, Inc., 1984, tradepaper, 188 pages, by T. B. Pawlicki. Trek philosophies as applied to alternate realities and paranormal phenomenon.   **6.95   6   8**

Mad Look At The 60's: #35499, Warner, September 1968, 414 pages, by Nick Meglin. —   **20   30**

Mirror Matter: Pioneering Antimatter Physics: #0-471-62812-3, John Wiley Publishers, 1988, hardcover, 262 pages, by Robert L. Forward. Nonfiction discussion on technology and sci-fi themes, Star Trek included.   **18.95   19   22**

Model Building Handbook: Chilton Craft & Hobby Books, 1981, tradepaper, 176 pages, by Brick Price. Explores the making of hand-crafted models and props. Includes photos of *STTMP* helmet made of fiberglass and auto putty, a phaser's wooden master for vacuum forming, and professional machinery used to create prop-quality starship models.

How You Can Explore Higher Dimensions of Space and Time, Prentice Hall, 1984.

	Issue	Fair	Mint
(A) 0-8019-6862-3.	12.95	12	15
(B) 0-8019-6862-1.	9.95	9	12

Omni's Screen Flights, Screen Fantasies: #0-385-19202-9, Dolphin Books (Doubleday), 1984, tradepaper, 310 pages, edited by Danny Peary. A review of famous science fiction movies with information on *STTMP*, *ST II*, and *ST III*.
17.95   17   20

Official TV Trivia Quiz Book #2: Signet, 1976, paperback, 152 pages, by Bart Andrews.
2.95   3   5

Pictorial History of Science Fiction Films: #0-8065-0537-0, Citadel Press, 1975, tradepaper, by Jeff Rovin. Brief history and photos of TV Trek on pages 205-208.
9.95   9   12

Science Fiction: #0-688-00842-9, William Morrow & Company, 1984, hardcover, 400 pages, edited by Phil Hardy. A pictorial review of science fiction films. Includes *STTMP* on page 354, *ST II* on page 377, plus black and white photos and a full-page color centerfold from *STTMP*. Front color jacket shows photo from *ST II*.
25   25   30

Science Fiction Collector's Catalog: #0-498-02562-4, A. S. Barnes & Company, Inc., 1984, tradepaper, 181 pages, by Jeff Rovin. Collector information on science fiction memorabilia which include Trek comics and magazines. Pages 146-157 (Chapter 14) covers Trek collectibles in detail.
12.95   12   20

Science Fiction Fantasy: #0-451-13930-5, 1985, paperback, 128 pages, by Editor of *Video Times*. Video reviews. Pages 92-103 cover Trek disks, tapes and CDs.
1.95   2

Science Fictionary: Wideview Books (Putnam), 1980, 200 pages, by Ed Naha. A comprehensive dictionary for TV films and writers. Biographies included for Gene Roddenberry, Fontana, and former fanzine writer Juanita Coulsen. Also recaps Star Trek as series, animated cartoon, and movies.
(A) #0-872-23-6196, hardcover. 16.95   16   20
(B) #0-872-23-6293, tradepaper.
10.95   10   15

Screening Space: The American Science Fiction Film: #0-8044-6886-9, Ungar Publishing Company, 1987, tradepaper, 345 pages, by Vivian Solcak. Originally published as *Limits of Infinity* circa 1980. A review and analysis of *STTMP*, *ST II*, and *ST III*.
14.95   14   15

S-F 2: A Pictorial History of Science Fiction Films, 1975-Present: #0-8065-0875-2, Citadel Press, 1984, hardcover, 256 pages, by Richard Meyers. A dictionary of films plus a "Where No Man Has Gone Before" review on pages 153-161. Contains twelve black and white photos and a two-page photo spread.
12.95   12   15

Second Whole Kids Catalog: Bantam Books, 1980, 250 pages, by Peter Cardozo. Children's game and craft book. Pages 236-239 are devoted to Trek items.
(A) #0-872-23-6196, hardcover.
16.95   16   20
(B) #0-872-23-6293, tradepaper.
10.95   10   15

Six Science Fiction Plays: #0-671-48766-3, Washington Square Press, 1976, 388 pages, by Roger Elwood. Features the uncut script of Harlan Ellison's "City On The Edge Of Forever" on pages 3-138. Introduction by Ellison. This is the first time the uncut version was printed anywhere.

	Issue	Fair	Mint
(A) Hardback, library edition.	6.95	10	15
(B) Paperback.	1.95	5	10

Space Adventure Collectibles: #0-87069-565-7, Wallace-Homestead Book Company, 1990, tradepaper, 224 pages, by T. N. Tumbusch. Science fiction collectible guide which includes a chapter on Trek memorabilia. Also contains numerous black and white and some color photos. **19.95 20 21**

Space and Science Fiction Plays for Young People: #0-8238-0252-3, Editor Plays, Inc., 1981, hardcover, 220 pages, by Sylvia E. Kamerman. A collection of one-act, royalty-free plays for the classroom. An unabridged screenplay for Gerrold's "The Trouble With Tribbles" designed for junior and senior high school age students appears on pages 40-72. **12.95 12 15**

Space Trek: The Endless Migration: 223 pages, by Jerome Clayton Glenn and George S. Robinson. Historical background is examined through technology and used to project what the future of human migration into space will be like. The efforts of Trek fans of Enterprise Frontiers to name the U.S. space shuttle after the famous TV starship are chronicled on pages 62-63 and 79-84.

(A) #0-8117-158-7, Stackpole Books, 1978, hardcover. **9.95 9 12**

(B) #0-446-91122-4, Warner Books, paperback. **2.50 2 8**

Special Effects In The Movies: #0-345-28605-5, Hilltown Press (Ballantine), 1981, tradepaper, 184 pages, by John Culhane. Information and photos about STTMP on pages 164-165. **11.95 11 15**

Starlog Science Fiction Trivia: #0-451-14397-3, Signet (New American Library), September 1986, paperback, 208 pages, by the editors of Starlog Magazine. Adult trivia book. Star Trek questions on pages 40-44, plus two black and white photos and a cartoon drawing. The cover has a photo insert of Spock. **2.95 2 5**

Star Wars, Star Trek and the 21st Century Christians: #693400, Bible Voice, Inc., 1978, paperback, 91 pages, by Winkie Pratney. Reviews Christian ethics as portrayed in Star Trek and Star Wars with black and white photos throughout. **1.75 5 10**

	Issue	Fair	Mint

State of the Art: #0-525-48186-9, Dutton, 1985, tradepaper, by Pauline Kael. A movie review of ST II and ST III on pages 196-198. **12.95 12 14**

Super T.V. Trivia: #0-451-13507-5, Signet, 1985, paperback, 154 pages, by Bart Andrews. A compilation of three books in one. Contains Super Trivia #1-3. Star Trek questions and photo quizzes. Cover has drawing of Spock. **3.95 3 5**

T.V. Addict's Nostalgia Trivia and Quiz Book: #0-517-44836-X, Greenwich House, 1984, hardcover, by Bart Andrews. Contains "Trekkie Fever" on pages 134-137. **6.98 6 10**

T.V. In The 60's: #0-345-31866-8, Ballantine, 1985, paperback, 271 pages, by Tim Brooks. Pages 222-225 discuss TV Trek. **3.50 3 5**

T.V. Nostalgia Quiz and Puzzle Book: #0-8092-5425-5, Contemporary Books, 1984, paperback, 299 pages, by Bruce Nash. Star Trek "Tube Teasers" on pages 151-153. **6.95 6 10**

T.V. Theme Song Sing-Along Song Book: #0-312-78215-2, St. Martin's Press, 1984, tradepaper, 64 pages, by John Javna. Lyrics, music, and trivia from famous TV shows. Pages 102-103 spotlight Star Trek. **5.95 5 8**

T.V. Trivia, Thirty Years of Television: #0-517-46367-9, Beekman House, 1984, hardcover, 64 pages, by editors of Consumer Guide. Original book edition of the magazine version by Entertainment Today. Pages 52-53 contain questions about Trek, plus color photos. **4.98 4 6**

Television: #0-394-56401-4, Educational Broadcasting Corporation, 1988, hardcover, 372 pages, by Michael Winship. A companion book to the PBS series. Includes special Gerry Finnerman coverage and has a large black and white photo of Star Trek. Cover has color insert. **19.95 20 22**

Watching T.V.: 4 Decades of American Television: #0-07-010268-6, McGraw Hill, 1982, hardcover, 314 pages, by Harry Castleman and Walter Podrazik. A synopsis of TV Trek on pages 195-197. **22.95 22 25**

When We Were Young: An Album of Stars: Prentice Hall, 1979, tradepaper, 64 pages, by Pat Fortunato. **2.95 3 5**

Yesterday's Tomorrow: #0-671-54133-1, Summit Books, 1984, tradepaper, 158 pages, by Joseph C. Corn and Brian Horrigan. A nonfiction review of culture and technology of the future as projected from fact, fiction, and the Big Screen. Page 31 briefly summarizes TV Trek. **17.95 15 20**

Star Trek Bop Bag, AHI, 1975.

Bop Bag

	Issue	*Fair*	*Min*

Star Trek Bop Bag: #1073, Azrak-Hamway International (AHI), 1975. Mr. Spock cartoon figure imprinted on an inflatable, plastic punching bag. Stands 50" high. The box features "Star Trek" logo from the Gold Key Comics series with cartoon Enterprise and bag photos.

	3	50	7!

Brush And Comb

Star Trek Brush and Comb Set: Gabil, 1977. Includes oval children's brush with comb. Transfer on brush reverse side shows affiliation with Trek. Se comes inside plastic case. Blue, 3" x 6".

	2.95	20	2!

Bumper Stickers

Beam Me Up Scottie: Printline Corporation, 1987. Oddly-spelled variety of sticker, which may be adapted to college logos and school colors. 3" x 11½".

Issue   Fair   Mint

➤ "Beam me up Scottie," black paint-slash lettering on chartreuse.

➤ "Beam me up Scottie," #FL0557, orange paint-slash lettering on blue, University of Florida gator logo on right side.

Price for each.   **1.50   2   3**

Beam Me Up Scotty: H & L Enterprises, 1987. "Beam me up Scotty. There's no intelligent life down here." Two styles, 3" x 11".

➤ Black letters on red and white background.
➤ Black letters on blue and white background.

Price for each.   **1   1   2**

Convention Bumper Sticker: Star Trek Convention, New York City, 1972. Fluorescent orange lettering on black stock. Lettered "Star Trek Lives!" The popularity of this slogan has its origins at the Star Trek Con held at the Statler-Hilton Hotel in New York City in January 1972. Although repeatedly printed over the years, this slogan has never again appeared in this color combination.   **.50   5   8**

Spock It To Me: Star Trek Enterprises, 1968. Black lettering on fluorescent Day-Glo stock. 4" x 13".
                                              .75   3   5

Star Fleet Academy Parking Permit: Hollywood On Location, 1985. Bumper sticker designed to resemble a parking sticker.   **1   2   3**

SST: Star Trek Enterprises, 1968. Official bumper sticker of the Save Star Trek campaign when Paramount threatened to cancel the TV series after its second year. Lettered "Save Star Trek — Write NBC" in fluorescent green letters on black stock. 4" x 13".   **.35   5   10**

Star Trek Bumper Stickers: April Publications, 1984. Humorous sayings on self-sticking and removable stickers. Saturn blue lettering on Day-Glo yellow stock. 3¾" x 14".

➤ "Caution... I brake for tribbles"
➤ "Honk, if you like Star Trek"
➤ "I've visited Vulcan — Home of Spock"
➤ "Live long and prosper"
➤ "Star Trek lives!"
➤ "This vehicle equipped with warp drive"
➤ "Vulcan power"

Price for each.   **1.50   1   2**

Star Trek Bumper Stickers: Aviva Enterprises, 1979. Bumper stickers in assorted color stocks and lettering. 2½" x 11".

➤ "Beam me up Mr. Spock" (blue and white on orange).
➤ "Dr. McCoy doesn't make housecalls" (profile of McCoy on left side, blue and white on orange stock).

➤ "I am a Trekkie" (profile of Spock on left side).
➤ "Live long and prosper" (with Vulcan hand salute, black on white).
➤ "Star Trek" (with Enterprise and Spock giving Vulcan salute on left side).

Price for each.   **1   2   3**

Star Trek Bumper Stickers: Fan-produced, 1984. 2½" x 11".

➤ "Don't honk! I only do warp 2"
➤ "We're one happy fleet"

Price for each.   **1   1   2**

Star Trek Bumper Stickers: Fantasy Traders, 1984. Standard-sized stickers.

➤ "Beam me up Scotty. This place has no intelligent life."
➤ "Beam me up Scotty. This planet sucks."
➤ "Klingon Property: Violators will be dismembered"
➤ "This car boldly goes where no car has gone before"
➤ "Warp 5: A speed we can live with"

Price for each.   **1   2   3**

Star Trek Bumper Stickers: Lincoln Enterprises, 1984. All brilliant Day-Glo fluorescent stock with black lettering. 4" x 15".

➤ #0151, "Star Trek lives"
➤ #0152, "Live long and prosper"
➤ #0153, "I Grok Spock / Star Trek"
➤ #0154, "I reserve the right to arm Klingons"
➤ #0155, "Government vehicle / Vulcan Embassy"
➤ #0156, "Take a human to lunch" with Vulcan IDIC
➤ #0157, "Smile... if you like Star Trek"
➤ #0158, "Vote YES on Star Trek"
➤ #0159, "Caution — Endangered species" with Earth symbol.
➤ #0160, "Jaws is a Klingon minnow" with shark head.
➤ #0161, "Mr. Spock for President," black on orange.
➤ #0162, "Don't tailgate, This is a Klingon War Cruiser"
➤ #0165, "Trekker on board"
➤ #0166, "Mr. Spock phone home"

Price for each.   **1.25   2   3**

Star Trek Bumper Stickers: Starbase Central, 1984. Bumper stickers in assorted colors and styles. Various sizes.

➤ "Don't Honk, I only have impulse power"
➤ "Earthers beware .... Klingon Battle Cruiser" with Klingon ship above.
➤ "Follow me where no man has gone before" on starfield.

Issue   Fair   Mint

➤ "Graduate of Star Fleet Academy" with three rank insignias on left side.

➤ "I have a one Trek mind" with Enterprise on left side.

➤ "I operate on impulse power"

➤ "I study Horta culture" with artwork by Fasson of Spock studying Horta on his hands and knees.

➤ "It is the will of Landru"

➤ "Keep on Trekkin'"

➤ "Klingon staff car"

➤ "Phasers on stun" with Enterprise firing twin beams.

➤ "Powered by tribbles" with tribbles dropping out of Volkswagen Beetle on left side.

➤ "Space Place"

➤ "Space... The Final Frontier" with crescent shapes on right.

➤ "Spock for President" with row of stars below lettering.

➤ "Starfleet Recruiting Office"

➤ "Star Trek fans make better lovers!"

➤ "Star Trek Lives! / U.S.S. Enterprise NCC 1701" with Enterprise on left side.

➤ "Star Trek Lives!" with Enterprise in upper left and Klingon ship in lower right.

➤ "This vehicle powered by matter/anti-matter," legend in dark lettering with ragged edging.

➤ "Watch it! Photon torpedos armed" with front view of Enterprise on right side.

Price for each.   **1   2   3**

Star Trek Bumper Stickers: T-K Graphics, 1984. Black lettering on white stock. 2¾" x 11".

➤ "Beam me up Scotty! This planet has no intelligent life!"

➤ "Live long and prosper" with Vulcan salute.

➤ "Star Fleet Headquarters / Official vehicle"

➤ "Spock lives on!"

➤ "U.S.S. Enterprise Veteran"

➤ "Vulcan Embassy / Official vehicle"

➤ "Vulcan Embassy / Staff vehicle"

Price for each.   **.75   1   2**

Star Trek Fanta-Sticks: Mere Dragons, 1988. Colorful vinyl bumper stickers in assorted colors. 3" x 12".

➤ "At warp speed 9 — They all look green to me" with traffic light design.

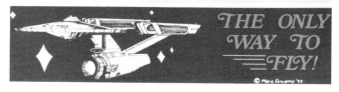

Bumper stickers: H & L Enterprises, Printline Corporation, and Mere Dragons.

➤ "Beam me up Scotty — It ate my phaser!"

➤ "Brought to you by the Klingon Anti-Earth league"

➤ "Caution: This vehicle equipped with photon torpedoes & trigger happy helmsman"

➤ "Engine by Scotty. 0 to warp 7 in fifteen seconds"

➤ "Federation Mobile Security Unit"

➤ "He's dead Jim — You grab his tricorder, I'll get his wallet," red and blue on white.

➤ "I'd rather be: squishing tribbles; fleecing the Federation; annoying Earthers; guzzling Romulan ale" with checkbox design.

➤ "I'd rather be exploring: The Final Frontier, Solving the Labyrinth, Time Traveling," with checkbox design.

➤ "If you can read this, You are in phaser range" with Enterprise on left, yellow on black.

➤ "It's a bird, it's a plane, it's super Spock"

➤ "Join the Colonial Marines; Keeping the peace by high-tech intimidation. See your local recruiter" with United States Marine Corps emblem.

➤ "My other car is a starship," with stars, white on blue.

➤ "Nobody knows the tribbles I've seen"

➤ "Official Starfleet personnel transport"

➤ "Official Vulcan Embassy limousine"

➤ "Property of Klingon rollerball team," black on red.

	Issue	*Fair*	*Mint*

➢ "The only way to fly" with Enterprise on left, red on blue.

➢ "There are few problems in the Galaxy that can't be solved by a suitable application of concentrated phaser fire"

➢ "Vulcan purveyor of logical enlightenment"
Price for each.   1   1   2

Star Trek Mini-Bumper Stickers: T-K Graphics, 1984. Black lettering on fluorescent red, green, orange, or chartreuse stock. 3¼" x 5½".
➢ "Honk if you're a Trekker"
➢ "Join the Enterprise — See the future"
➢ "Space — The Final Frontier"
➢ UFP Janus head emblem design
➢ "U.S.S. Enterprise" with schematic drawing
Price for each.   .50   .50   1

Star Trek Multi-Color Bumper Stickers: T-K Graphics, 1984. Red and black lettering on white stock unless specified. 2¾" x 11".
➢ "I brake for tribbles," with Enterprise silhouette, red and black on blue.
➢ "Star Fleet HQ staff vehicle" with Janus head emblem, red and black on green.
➢ "Star Trek lives!" with Enterprise silhouette, red and black on green.
➢ "The saga continues" with Enterprise silhouette, red and black on yellow.
➢ "U.S.S. Enterprise shuttlecraft" with Enterprise silhouette.
Price for each.   1   1   2

***Star Trek The Motion Picture* Bumper Stickers:** Lincoln Enterprises, 1984. Day-Glo fluorescent stock with black lettering. 4" x 15".
➢ #0163, "I am a carbon unit"
➢ #0164, "The human adventure is just beginning"
Price for each.   1.25   2   3

***Star Trek III* Bumper Stickers:** Fan-produced, 1984. 2½" x 11".
➢ "Spock is dead? Long live Star Trek"

	Issue	*Fair*	*Mint*

➢ "Spock is dying to be in Star Trek III"
Price for each.   1   1   2

***Star Trek III* Bumper Stickers:** Lincoln Enterprises, 1984. Black on Day-Glo color stock. 4" x 15"
➢ "Bring back the Enterprise," black on yellow.
➢ "We want Star Trek III"
Price for each.   1.25   2   3

***Star Trek IV* Bumper Sticker:** Paramount Home Video, 1988. Special video promotional sticker. Lettered "I love whales."   N/A   3   5

***Star Trek: The Next Generation* Bumper Sticker:** Mere Dragons, 1990. Lettered "I was expendable, I was stupid, I went — T. Yar."
    1.50   1   2

***Star Trek: The Next Generation* Bumper Stickers:** Lincoln Enterprises, 1988. Day-Glo fluorescent stock with black lettering. 4" x 15".
➢ #0168, "Don't tailgate — This is a Ferengi Cruiser"
➢ #0169, "Star Trek The Next Generation welcome to the 24th Century"
➢ #0170, "*Star Trek The Next Generation* — The 24th Century is just beginning"
➢ #0171, "I am fully functional — Data"
➢ #0172, "Support your local android — Data"
Price for each.   1.25   2   3

Trekfest Bumper Stickers: Riverside Area Community Club, 1984. Bumper stickers commemorating the annual Trekfest on Riverside, Iowa.
➢ "Trek — Riverside, Iowa, The future birthplace of James T. Kirk," with solar system schematic.
➢ "Trek — Riverside, Iowa, Where it all begins," with solar system schematic.
Price for each.   1.50   2   3

William Shatner Fan Club Bumper Stickers: William Shatner Fan Club, 1984. Blue lettering on white vinyl. 3¼ x 11".
➢ "Bring back our Enterprise"
➢ "Trekkers do it under the stars"
Price for each.   2   2   4

Business Cards

Beam Me Up Scotty Business Cards: Once Upon A Planet, 1987. Humorous cards with balloon dialogue. Card shows Earth on blue starfield. Blurb reads, "Beam me up Scotty. There's no intelligent life down here." Packaged in cellophane wrap with six cards per pack. 2" x 3".
Price per pack.   .50   1   2

Star Trek Business Cards: April Publications, 1984. Collector's four-set series with colorful raised lettering on Lusterkote cardstock. 2½" x 3½".
(A) No. 1, ten-card set.
➢ Captain Kirk
➢ Mr. Spock
➢ Dr. McCoy
➢ Scotty
➢ Lieutenant Uhura

	Issue	*Fair*	*Mint*

➤ Scotty
➤ Lieutenant Uhura
➤ Cyrano Jones!
➤ Harry Mudd
➤ Bela Oxmyx
➤ Kang
➤ Gary Seven
(B) No. 2, ten-card set.
➤ Lieutenant Sulu
➤ Ensign Chekov
➤ Nurse Chapel
➤ Yeoman Janice Rand
➤ Landru
➤ T'Pring
➤ Edith Keeler
➤ Sarek of Vulcan
➤ Korob & Sylvia
➤ Koloth
(C) No. 3, ten-card set.
➤ Captain Pike
➤ Lt. Kevin Riley

	Issue	*Fair*	*Mint*

➤ T'Pau
➤ Apollo
➤ Trelane
➤ Nomad
➤ Vaal
➤ Hengist
➤ Miramanee
➤ Garth of Izar
(D) No. 4, ten-card set.
➤ Admiral Kirk
➤ Spock of Vulcan
➤ Dr. McCoy, Retired
➤ Commander Decker
➤ Lieutenant Ilia
➤ Dr. Chapel
➤ Chief Janice Rand
➤ Sonak
➤ Admiral Nogura
➤ Commander Branch

	Issue	Fair	Mint
Price per set.	1.25	1	3

Buttons (Photo)

Bridge Crew Button: Paramount Pictures Corp., 1966. Unusual rectangular button with a black and white photo cut-out of TV crew on the bridge. Includes Chekov, McCoy, Scotty, and Spock seated around Kirk. Blue background and PPC licensing information along the rim. This is the same as the rectangular mirror also produced by Paramount at the same time. 2⅛" x 3⅛". — 5 8

Enterprise Cut-Out: Circa 1970s. Unusual button trimmed into the shape of the TV Enterprise (port side). Artwork Enterprise is silver and blue on white plastic background. Pin clip backing. 1¼" x 3½". — 3 5

Kirk and Spock Promo Button: Paramount Pictures Corp., 1966. Black and white cut-outs of Spock and Kirk on blue background. White and black letters above profiles read "Star Trek." Clip pin backing on polished steel, laminated, 2¼" diameter. — 5 8

Spock Buttons: Virgil Finlay, 1973. These convention buttons appeared at the 1973 Star Trek Con and featured a portrait of early Spock by fan artist Virgil Finlay. Metal with stick pin-style clasp. Green with black and white line drawing. 1¼" diameter. These pins were advertised extensively in the *Monster Times* magazine during 1973-74. Set of three buttons. 1 3 6

Star Trek Buttons: Button-Up Company, 1984. Assorted color photo buttons from TV Trek. On each button is the legend "Star Trek" in white letters along the rims or near the edges. Clip pin backs. 1½" diameter.
➤ Enterprise with second Federation ship
➤ Kirk with communicator
➤ Kirk and McCoy
➤ Kirk and Spock in civilian clothes
➤ Kirk, McCoy, and Uhura
➤ Kirk, Spock, and McCoy
➤ McCoy (TSP)
➤ Sulu, close-up

	Issue	Fair	Mint
Price for each.	1	2	3

Star Trek Buttons: California Dreamers, 1987. Set of twelve photo buttons from TV Trek, which sported partial legends the same as those appearing on the California Dreamers greeting cards (see **Greeting Cards**). The pins were distributed nationally at Waldenbooks and came mounted on blue 2" x 3" cardstock suitable for counter displays. 1½" diameter.
➤ #253266, "Energize," Spock, Kirk, Yeoman, and two crewman in transporter room.
➤ #253273, "Seek Out Strange New Worlds," Spock, Uhura, and Kirk on bridge.
➤ #253280, "Live Long and Prosper," Spock giving Vulcan salute.

Issue   Fair   Mint

➤ #253297, "Fire All Phaser Weapons," Spock and Kirk in Engineering with phasers drawn.

➤ #253303, "The Captain," close-up of Kirk.

➤ #253310, "Beam Me Up Scotty," Kirk with communicator in hand.

➤ #253327, "Spock For President," close-up of Spock with smile.

➤ #253334, "Superior Being," Spock in his quarters.

➤ #253341, "Keep Your Shields Up," Spock, Kirk, and Chekov on bridge.

➤ #253358, "I Hate Mondays," Chekov with hands over ears.

➤ #253365, "Hang In There," Spock manacled against stone wall, scene from Cp.

➤ #253372, "Space, The Final Frontier," Enterprise over Earth-type planet.

Price for each.   1   1   2

Star Trek Buttons: Starpost, 1987. Set of color picture buttons from TV Trek. These may be either photos or color art pictures. Sizes vary.

(A) 2¼" photo buttons.

➤ #555, Spock

➤ #557, Vian

➤ #558, Talosian

➤ #559, Mugato

Price for each.   .75   1   2

(B) 2¼" art buttons.

➤ #687, U.S.S. Enterprise   .79   1   2

➤ #688, Kirk, Spock, McCoy, and Enterprise
                                         .99   1   2

(C) 3" photo button, #720, Spock
                                         .99   1   2

Star Trek Character Buttons: Lincoln Enterprises, 1976. Colorful photo buttons featuring portraits from classic Trek. The words "Star Trek" are lettered on the tops, along with the name of the

Assorted photo and slogan buttons.

	Issue	Fair	Mint

character beside the photo. Clip pin backs. 2¼" in diameter.

➤ #2470A, Kirk
➤ #2470B, Spock
➤ #2470C, Dr. McCoy
➤ #2470D, Scotty
➤ #2470E, Uhura
➤ #2470F, Sulu
➤ #2470G, Chekov
➤ #2470H, Chapel
➤ #2470I, Enterprise

Price for each. **1 2 4**

Star Trek Episode Buttons: Langley Associates, 1976. Set of 60 assorted laminated photo buttons showing photos from the TV series. Only one button shows any lettering. This set was officially licensed by Paramount Pictures Corporation. 2¼" in diameter.

➤ #1, Enterprise with "Star Trek" title credit
➤ #2, Enterprise firing twin phasers
➤ #3, Enterprise counter-clockwise over blue planet
➤ #4, Enterprise counter-clockwise over green planet
➤ #5, Enterprise clockwise over magenta planet and its moon
➤ #6, Enterprise approaching amoeba (IS)
➤ #7, Romulan Bird of Prey (BT)
➤ #8, Klingon Cruiser
➤ #9, Spock, close-up in dress uniform
➤ #10, Spock, close-up in regular uniform
➤ #11, Spock laughing (blooper)
➤ #12, Bearded Spock (MM)
➤ #13, Kirk, close-up in dress uniform
➤ #14, Kirk, close-up
➤ #15, Kirk, buried in tribbles
➤ #16, McCoy, close-up
➤ #17, Scotty, close-up
➤ #18, Chekov at science station
➤ #19, Sulu at helm with remote viewer extension
➤ #20, Uhura at station
➤ #21, Spock, close-up
➤ #22, Natira, close-up (FW)
➤ #23, Spock, close-up
➤ #24, Sarek, close-up (JB)
➤ #25, Sulu, close-up
➤ #26, male Romulan Commander, close-up (BT)
➤ #27, female Romulan Commander, close-up (EI)
➤ #28, shuttle docking
➤ #29, Marta, close-up (WGD)
➤ #30, Spock at station
➤ #31, Chekov and security guards
➤ #32, Vina, close-up (Me)
➤ #33, Kirk on transporter pad

	Issue	Fair	Mint

➤ #34, Zarabeth, close-up (AY)
➤ #35, Odona, close-up (MG)
➤ #36, Spock, close-up
➤ #37, Balok's dummy (CMn)
➤ #38, Sulu, close-up
➤ #39, Janice Rand, close-up (CX)
➤ #40, Balok's dummy, close-up (CMn)
➤ #41, Keeper, close-up (Me)
➤ #42, Deela, close-up (WE)
➤ #43, Sylvia, close-up (Cp)
➤ #44, Spock, close-up
➤ #45, Chekov, close-up
➤ #46, McCoy, close-up in medical tunic
➤ #47, Kor, close-up (EM)
➤ #48, Nurse Chapel, close-up
➤ #49, Losira, close-up (Dv)
➤ #50, Chekov, close-up
➤ #51, McCoy, close-up
➤ #52, Kang, close-up (Dv)
➤ #53, Ruk and Kir, close-up (LG)
➤ #54, Khan, close-up (SS)
➤ #55, Marlena Moreau in alternate universe (MM)
➤ #56, Zephram Cochrane, close-up (Mt)
➤ #57, Spock, close-up of his smile (TSP)
➤ #58, Uhura at her station (MM)
➤ #59, Shras, close-up (JB)
➤ #60, Kirk with communicator, close-up

Price for each. **.50 3 5**

Star Trek The Motion Picture Buttons: Aviva, 1979. A set of eleven full-color and enameled buttons with clip pin-style backs. Each button has either the new movie lettering or just the *STTMP* logo above the photo. 2¼" in diameter.

➤ Admiral Kirk, close-up with *STTMP* legend.
➤ Admiral Kirk, right profile with *Star Trek* legend.
➤ Admiral Kirk in corridor with *STTMP* legend.
➤ Admiral Kirk in corridor with *Star Trek* legend.
➤ Eleven-member bridge crew with *STTMP* legend.
➤ Spock and McCoy next to seated Kirk with *STTMP* legend.
➤ Spock, McCoy, and Kirk on bridge with *Star Trek* legend.
➤ Spock in Vulcan robes, head-to-waist view with *STTMP* legend.
➤ Spock in Vulcan robes, with *Star Trek* legend.
➤ Spock at station with *STTMP* legend.
➤ Spock at station with *Star Trek* legend.

Price for each. **1 2 3**

Star Trek The Motion Picture Buttons: Starpost, 1980. Set of six full-color photo buttons from *STTMP*. Laminated with pin clip back. 2¼" in diameter.

➤ #140, Kirk

	Issue	*Fair*	*Mint*

➢ #141, Spock
➢ #142, Kirk and Spock
➢ #143, Chapel
➢ #144, Ilia
➢ #145, Rand

Price for each.	.69	1	2

***Star Trek II: The Wrath of Khan* Buttons:** Image Products, Inc., 1982. Set of five full-color and enameled photo buttons with characters from *ST II*. Each button has the letter logo from the movie in white near the bottom. Clip pin backs. 3" in diameter.

➢ Admiral Kirk, close-up
➢ Spock in Vulcan robes, extra lettering reads "Spock Lives!"
➢ Khan, close-up
➢ Full nine-member bridge crew

➢ Enterprise, front view	1.50	3	5

***Star Trek III: The Search for Spock* Buttons:** Button-Up Company, 1984. Assorted color photo buttons featuring the crew and aliens from the movie cast. Each button has the "Star Trek III" letter logo on its circumference in either white or black. Clip pin backs. 1½" in diameter.

➢ Chekov, facing right, close-up
➢ Kirk, looking left, close-up
➢ Kirk in uniform
➢ Kruge, close-up with red tint
➢ Kruge, in Command chair
➢ Marcus, close-up with black lettering
➢ McCoy, close-up with blue tint
➢ Saavik, close-up
➢ Spock, close-up in white robe
➢ Spock, looking left and in white robe
➢ Uhura, pointing phaser, black lettering
➢ *Star Trek III* logo, white letters on black

Price for each.	1	2	3

***Star Trek III: The Search for Spock*:** Starpost, 1984. These buttons come in two different sets of different sizes. Clip pin backs.

(A) Set of 2¼" buttons.

➢ #200, Enterprise
➢ #201, Saavik
➢ #202, David Marcus
➢ #203, Kruge
➢ #211, Kirk
➢ #212, Uhura
➢ #213, Chekov
➢ #214, Sarek
➢ #215, McCoy
➢ #216, Sulu
➢ #217, Kirk and McCoy
➢ #218, David and Saavik
➢ #220, Kirk and Kruge
➢ #221, Spock

Price for each button.	.79	2	3

(B) 3" buttons.

➢ #700, Klingon Bird of Prey
➢ #701, Kruge
➢ #702, Kirk
➢ #703, Uhura
➢ #704, Chekov
➢ #705, David Marcus
➢ #706, U.S.S. Grissom
➢ #707, McCoy
➢ #708, U.S.S. Excelsior
➢ #709, Kirk, Chekov, and Scotty
➢ #710, Kirk and group on Genesis
➢ #711, Kirk and Kruge
➢ #712, Saavik
➢ #713, Sulu
➢ #714, Sarek
➢ #715, group on Vulcan

Price for each button.	.99	2	3

Buttons (Slogan)

April Publication Buttons: 1984, 1988. Plastic laminated with metal, safety pin-style backs. 2¼" in diameter.

A) 1984.

➢ "He Touched Me," with profile of Spock giving Vulcan salute.
➢ "Spock It To Me"
➢ "I Studied With The Vulcan Masters"
➢ "My Tribble Loves Me"
➢ "I Have Been Where No Man Has Gone Before"
➢ "Vulcan Power"

(B) 1988.

➢ "Beam Me Up Scotty"

Price for each.	1	1	2

Button-Up Button: 1986. Laminated slogan pin with safety pin latch. "Beam Me Up, Scotty!" lettered in black on square yellow background with blue perimeters, comes clipped to a yellow cardstock back suitable for counter displays.

	1	1	2

Fan Issue Buttons: Intergalactic Traders (IT), Star Tech (ST), 1983-present. Hundreds of unlicensed slogan buttons have been produced by fan retailers

An assortment of Langley Associates photo buttons from 1976.

and distributors, some of which have been identified. Others have no identifying imprints or issue dates. A few prominently distributed buttons are included here. All are 2¼" in diameter.

(A) *Star Trek* buttons, all produced by Star Tech.

➢ "Beam Me Up!"

➢ "Closet Trekkie"

➢ "He's Dead Jim"

➢ "I'd Rather Be Watching Star Trek"

➢ "I'm a Trekker Not A Trekkie"

➢ "May Your Tribbles Always Purr"

➢ "My Favorite Doctor Is The Real McCoy"

➢ Star Trek Twentieth Anniversary Logo

➢ "They Make Such A Nice Sound When You Squish Them," with artwork of Klingon stepping on tribble.

	Issue	Fair	Mint

➤ United Federation of Planets shield
➤ "Vulcan Power"

Price for each. **1 1 2**

(B) *Star Trek III: The Search for Spock* buttons, all produced by Star Tech.
➤ "Don't Call Me Tiny!"
➤ "How Can You Have A Yellow Alert In Space Dock?"
➤ "I Don't Believe In No-Win Scenarios"
➤ "I Know Engineers — They Love To Change Things"
➤ "Let Them Eat Static"
➤ "Nobody's Perfect"
➤ "Sir, Someone Is Stealing The Enterprise!"
➤ "The Word is No. I am Therefore Going Anyway"
➤ "The More They Overthink The Plumbing, The Easier It Is To Stop Up The Drain"
➤ "This is Revenge For All Those Arguments He Lost"
➤ "Up Your Shaft"
➤ "Who's Been Holding Up the Damn Elevator?"

Price for each. **1 1 2**

(C) *Star Trek IV: The Voyage Home* buttons.
➤ "A Double Dumb-Ass On You!" (IT)
➤ "Angels and Ministers of Grace Defend Us" (IT)
➤ "Are You Sure It Isn't Time for a Colorful Metaphor?" (IT)
➤ "By The Book!" (ST)
➤ "Damage Control Is Easy. Reading Klingon, That's Hard" (ST)
➤ "Everybody Remember Where We Parked" (IT)
➤ "Guessing Is Not In My Nature" (ST)
➤ "He Did A Little Too Much LDS" (ST)
➤ "Hello Alice, Welcome To Wonderland" (IT)
➤ "He's A Wee Bit In A Snit Isn't He?" (ST)
➤ "He's Not Exactly Working On All Thrusters" (IT)
➤ "How Do You Feel?" (IT)
➤ "I Do Not Understand The Question" (ST)
➤ "I Don't Think These Kids Can Steer" (ST)
➤ "I Just Hope We Can Cloak The Stench" (ST)
➤ "I Prefer Common Sense" (ST)
➤ "Is That a Lot?" (ST)
➤ "Is That The Logical Thing To Do?" (ST)
➤ "It's A Miracle These People Ever Got Out of the 20th Century" (IT)
➤ "It Must be The Radiation" (ST)
➤ "Klingon Justice Is A Unique Point of View" (ST)
➤ "May Fortune Favor The Foolish" (IT)
➤ "No Ma'am. No Dipshit." (IT)
➤ "Oh Joy!" (IT)
➤ "Pavel Chekov: Rank Admiral" (ST)
➤ "Scotty, Now Would Be A Good Time" (IT)

➤ "Somebody's Got To Keep An Eye On Him" (ST)
➤ "So Much For The Little Training Cruise" (ST).
➤ "The Hell They Did!" (ST)
➤ "The Question Is Irrelevant" (ST)
➤ "Too Much LDS" (IT)
➤ "What Is This The Dark Ages?" (ST)
➤ "What Is What?" (ST)
➤ "Where The Hell Are We?" (ST)
➤ "Whoever Said the Human Race Was Logical" (ST)
➤ "You Could Exaggerate" (ST)
➤ "You Really Have Gone Where No Man Has Gone Before" (IT)
➤ "You're Not Exactly Catching Us At Our Best" (IT)
➤ "You've Got To Do Better" (ST)
➤ "You Wouldn't Want To Show Me Around Your Spaceship Would You" (ST)

Price for each. **1 1 2**

(D) *Star Trek V: The Final Frontier* buttons, all produced by Star Tech.
➤ "Bourbon and Beans — An Explosive Combination"
➤ "Do You Not Know A Jailbreak When You See One?"
➤ "Don't Trust Anyone!"
➤ "Excuse Me — I'd Just Like To Ask A Question"
➤ "Hi Bones. Mind if We Drop In For Dinner?"
➤ "Hold Your Horse Captain!"
➤ "I Always Wanted To Play To A Captive Audience"
➤ "I Apologize!"
➤ "I Do Not Think You Realize The Gravity of the Situation"
➤ "I Expect That's Klingon For 'Hello'"
➤ "I Know This Ship Like The Back of My Hand!"
➤ "I Liked Him Better Before He Died"
➤ "I'm A Nervous Wreck!"
➤ "Please Captain — Not In Front of the Klingons!"
➤ "Please Tell Me The Transporters Are Working"
➤ "What Are You Doing In This Neck Of The Woods?"
➤ "Why Don't You Go Out and Pester Dr. McCoy For A While?"
➤ "We're Lost But We're Making Good Time"
➤ "Were We Having A Good Time?"
➤ "You Call This A Shore Leave?"
➤ "You Were Never Alone"

Price for each. **1 1 2**

H & L Enterprises Button: 1988. Unusual giant-sized button. "Beam Me Up Scotty. There's No Intelligent Life Down Here" lettered in black on an orange and yellow background. Safety pin clasp. 5" in diameter. **2.99 3 4**

Leonard Nimoy National Association of Fans Buttons: 1969-71. Special slogan buttons available

	Issue	*Fair*	*Mint*

through club membership to LNNAF during its first three years. Stick pin backs. 1½" in diameter.
1969:

(A) "I Grok Mr. Spock," black lettering on bright green. **.25 4 6**

(B) "Turn On To Nimoy," green lettering on white, slogan runs in circles. **.15 3 5**

(C) "What's A Leonard Nimoy," black lettering on white. **.25 4 6**

1971:

(D) "Star Trek Lives!," the official button of the 1972 Star Trek Con, black letters on orange. **.35 5 6**

Lincoln Enterprises Buttons: 1984. Slogan buttons of assorted sizes. Safety clip latch.

➤ "It is Illogical," black lettering on blue, 2¼".
➤ "Keep On Trekkin'," black lettering on yellow, 2¼".
➤ "Live Long and Prosper," black lettering on green, 3".
➤ "Paramount Is A Klingon Conspiracy," black lettering on red, 2½".
➤ "Star Trek Lives," black lettering on yellow, 1½".
Price for each. **.25 2 3**

Pocket Books Promo Buttons: 1985-89. Special promo buttons given away at bookstores to promote the release of Star Trek novels and books by the publisher.

➤ "Read The Klingon Dictionary," 1985.
➤ "Star Trek, The Only Logical Books To Read," 1986, orange with black and white photo cut-out of Spock signing his name.
➤ "Star Trek, The Only Logical Books To Read," 1989, navy with Star Trek logo.
Price for each. **Free 2 3**

Star Trek Convention Buttons: Circa 1970s. Special buttons made up primarily for promotional purposes. These come in assorted sizes.

(A) "Star Trek Lives!," Star Trek Con 1973, green refractive lettering and TV Enterprise (port side view) on black background, safety pin clasp, 2" in diameter. **1 2 4**

(B) The Star Trek Convention 1975, Tellurian Enterprises, Inc., 1975, black silhouette artwork of TV Enterprise (starboard side) over city skyline, safety pin clasp, 2½" in diameter. **1 2 4**

(C) Trekfest, Riverside Area Community Club, Riverside, Iowa, 1986, set of two commemorative buttons, 2" in diameter.

➤ Riverside, Iowa, "Where The Trek Begins," Trekfest 1986, with star design.

	Issue	*Fair*	*Mint*

➤ Riverside, Iowa, "Future Birthplace of Captain James T. Kirk," Trekfest 1986, without star design.
Price per pin. **1.50 1 2**

Star Trek Glitter Buttons: Fan issue, 1984. Set of buttons constructed as TV character busts with a refractive paper design. Backgrounds are black with square silver foil insets within the Trek drawing.

➤ Kirk, 2½"
➤ Spock, 2½"
➤ McCoy, 2½"
➤ UFP Janus head, 2¼"
Price for each. **1 1 2**

Star Trek Love Buttons: Star Tech, 1987. Specialty buttons with black lettering on a white background with red heart centers. Safety pin clasps. 2¼" in diameter.

➤ "I Love Star Trek"
➤ "I Love James Kirk"
➤ "I Love William Shatner"
➤ "I Love Spock"
➤ "I Love Dr. McCoy"
➤ "I Love DeForest Kelley"
➤ "I Love Sulu"
➤ "I Love George Takei"
➤ "I Love Chekov"
➤ "I Love Walter Koenig"
➤ "I Love Uhura"
➤ "I Love Nichelle Nichols"
➤ "I Love Scotty"
➤ "I Love James Doohan"
➤ "I Love Gene Roddenberry"
➤ "I Love Saavik"
Price for each. **1 1 2**

Star Trek Stick Pin Buttons: Fan-produced, circa 1970s. Assorted buttons with colorful paper backgrounds. The backs, however, instead of being the usual safety pin style, are simply metal tongs without a bottom clasp, which allows the entire clip device to be rotated around the interior button rim to any position for pinning onto clothes. 1½" in diameter.

➤ "Star Trek," Specialties Inc., Gaithersburg, Maryland. White block lettering with white artwork outline of the TV Enterprise on royal blue background.
➤ "Star Trek Is!," black lettering on blue.
➤ "Star Trek Lives!," black lettering on orange.
➤ "Vulcan Power," blue lettering on white.
Price for each. **.50 2 3**

***Star Trek V: The Final Frontier* Promo Button:** Paramount Pictures Corporation, 1988. Special rectangular movie promo button for *ST V*. Navy rec-

	Issue	*Fair*	*Mint*

cangle with light blue movie letter logo across the center. 2¾" x 1¾". **2   2   4**

Star Trek: The Next Generation Buttons: Vision Aeries, 1988. Assorted slogans in many colors taken from *STTNG*, 2¼" in diameter.
- "If you prick me, do I not leak?"
- "It was an adult who did it!"
- "Children are not allowed on the bridge."
- "I am programmed in multiple techniques, a broad variety of pleasuring."
- "There was a young lady from Venus, whose body was shaped like a ..."
- "What's so damn troublesome about not having died?"
- "I'm fully functional."
- "Sharing an orbit with God is no small experience."
- "Edo make love at the drop of a hat. Any hat."
- "Capital punishment on our world is no longer considered a justifiable deterrent."
- "There can be no justice so long as the laws are absolute."
- "I must restrain myself too much."
- "I'm an Earth woman and I'm not that fragile."
- "I want Lt. Yar to become my first one."
- "Nice to meet you, Pinocchio."
- "I'm only going to tell you this just once. It never happened."
- "It's elementary, my dear Riker."
- "We no longer enslave animals for food purposes."
- "Even Klingons need love now and then."
- "I hope you have a lot of pretty boys on board because I'm willing and waiting."
- "Klingons are so unusual in their reactions, aren't they?"
- "Space and time and thought aren't the separate things they appear to be."
- "I'm with Starfleet. We don't lie."
- "I know my way around starships."

Price for each. **1   1   2**

Taco Bell Promo Buttons: 1984. Issued in conjunction with the promotion of *ST III* glassware by Taco Bell. Buttons have yellow lettering on royal blue background. Safety pin clasp. 3" in diameter.
- "Beam Home With The Crew of the Enterprise"
- "Beam Home With Kruge"
- "Beam Home With Spock"
- "Beam Home With T'Lar"

Price for each. **1   3   5**

T-K Graphics Buttons: 1983-present. A variety of slogan buttons with safety pin-style clasps. 2¼" in diameter.

(A) Star Trek buttons.
- "Beam Me Up Scotty, This Place Has No Intelligent Life."
- "Kiss Me I'm a Trekker"
- "Live Long and Prosper"
- "Remember Spock"
- "Space... The Final Frontier"
- "Spock Lives!," black lettering on gold
- "Star Trek," black lettering on green, with Enterprise schematic
- "Star Trek Fans Make Better Lovers"
- "Star Trek Lives!," with Command insignia
- "U.S.S. Enterprise Veteran," black lettering on gold
- "Vulcans Never Bluff"

Price for each. **1   1   2**

(B) *Star Trek The Motion Picture* buttons.
- "Carbon-Based Unit"
- "The Human Adventure Is Just Beginning"

Price for each. **1   1   2**

(C) *Star Trek II: The Wrath of Khan* buttons.
- "I Don't Like To Lose"
- "I Exaggerated"
- "I Have Been And Always Will Be Your Friend"
- "Nobody's Perfect"
- "Revenge Is A Dish Best Served Cold"
- "Survivor Kobayashi Maru Test"
- "The Needs of the Many Outweigh the Needs of the Few Or the One"
- "There Are Always Possibilities"

Price for each. **1   1   2**

Vision Aeries Buttons: 1988. Assorted humorous slogan buttons in a variety of colors. Safety pin clasps. 2¼" in diameter.
- "Here's Mudd In Your Eye"
- "Nobody Knows the Tribbles I've Seen," with artwork of tribble in martini glass.
- "Pon Farr Research Department Test Subject"
- "Spock Me!"
- "Spock You!"
- "To Hell with the Prime Directive. Let's Kill Something."
- "Tribble In Paradise," with artwork of tribble wearing sunglasses and lounging on the beach.
- "Tribble Motto — If At First You Don't Suck Seed, Try, Try A Grain"
- "Vulcanized Rubber," with artwork of birth control device with Vulcan ears.

Price for each. **1   2   3**

Cachets

Enterprise Space Shuttle Cachet: Palmdale, California, September 17, 1976. Commemorative first-day cover souvenir of the "roll-out of Space Shuttle Enterprise OV-101." Features canceled 13¢ postage stamp on illustrated envelope. The pictures show the shuttle, the first four-man crew, and Leonard Nimoy. Attending at the ceremonies were Leonard Nimoy, George Takei, DeForest Kelley, and Gene Roddenberry. President Gerald Ford and Senator Barry Goldwater spoke. **.18   10   15**

Star Trek Cachets: Star Trek Association of Towson, Incorporated, Hunt Valley, Maryland. Special, First Day of Issue stamped envelopes sold at Shore Leave conventions IX and X in Maryland. Each cachet features a canceled postal stamp, embossed lettering explaining Star Trek's contribution to the space program, and rubber-stamped pictures of a Enterprise ship.

(A) Set #1, includes three cachets from Shore Leave IX (July 10, 11, and 12, 1987). Each features one of the U.S. Postal Service space stamps released in 1975 and carries an April 4, 1975 / Pasadena, California cancellation date. Also features inked picture of movie Enterprise.

	Issue	Fair	Min.
Price for each.		2	2
Price for complete set.		6	15	20

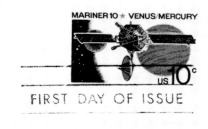

Star Trek Association of Towson cachet from Shore Leave IX.

	Issue	*Fair*	*Mint*

(B) Set #2, includes four cachets from Shore Leave X, (July 7, 8, 9, and 10, 1988). Each carries a U.S. Postal Service 22¢ stamp with a secondary Domestic E issue stamp to cover a sudden jump in the mailing rate from 22¢ to 25¢. Cancellation date is March 28, 1988 from Hollywood, California. Also features inked picture of

the *STTNG* Enterprise. Of special interest to collectors is the July 9, 1988 cachet which was hand-carried to the bridge of the *STTNG* TV set by Senior Illustrator Andrew Probert on March 25, 1988.

	Issue	*Fair*	*Mint*
Price for each.	2	2	5
Price for complete set.	8	20	25

Calculators

Star Trek Checkbook Calculator: #J2472, Lincoln Enterprises, 1987. Maroon, plush vinyl checkbook holder with calculator included. Calculator has automatic memory and when turned off, will remember your previous checking balance, displaying it once it is turned on again. Available with or without the Star Trek insignia. **19.95 20 25**

Star Trekulator: Mego Corporation, 1976. Functional nine-digit display calculator with six functions (addition, subtraction, division, multiplication, percentiles, and square root). Features LED display with Enterprise scenes. Requires four AA batteries. Box front shows cartoon Spock at science station and Enterprise. Rear of box illustrates the calculator. 6" x 10" boxed. **10 100 150**

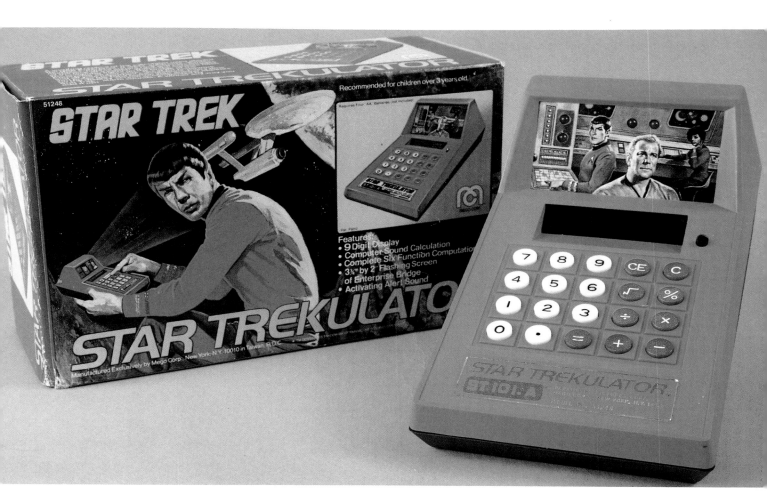

Star Trekulator, Mego Corporation, 1976.

Calendars

Leonard Nimoy Calendars: Blue Mountain Arts. Set of two wall calendars promoting the poetry of Leonard Nimoy.

	Issue	Fair	Mint

(A) Leonard Nimoy Calendar 1980, #0-88396-052-4, cover is yellow and gold-toned with sepia photo of Nimoy reclining. Stapled. **4.95 15 25**

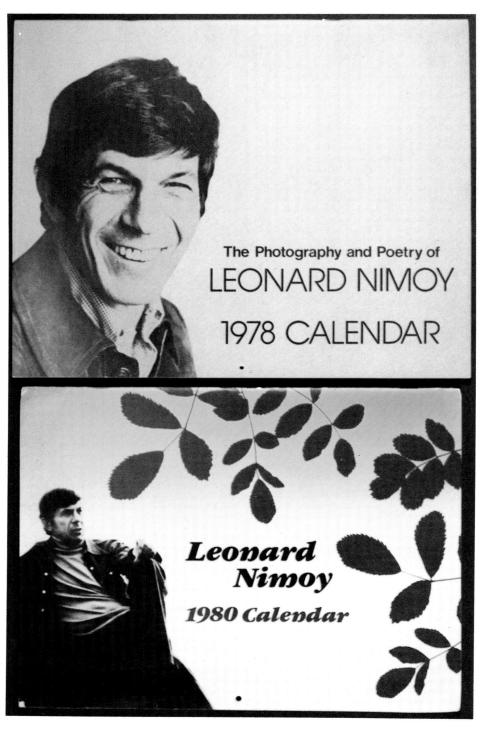

Two rare Leonard Nimoy calendars from 1978 and 1980, Blue Mountain Arts.

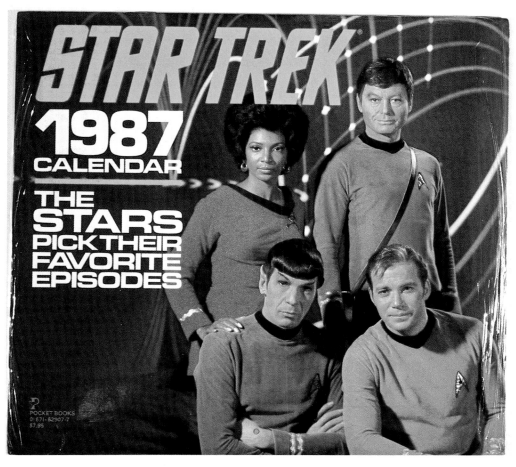

1987 *Star Trek* calendar, Pocket Books.

	Issue	Fair	Mint

(B) Leonard Nimoy Calendar 1981, #0-88396-086-9, cover is yellow and gold-toned with leaf design. Lacks any photos. Spiral-bound. **4.95 15 25**

Photography and Poetry of Leonard Nimoy Calendar 1978: Celestial Arts, 1978. Photos taken by Nimoy are featured with his written verse. Cover is yellow with black and white photo cut-out of Nimoy. Stapled. 10¼" x 12½". **3.95 20 30**

Star Trek Animated Calendar 1975: #0104, Lincoln Enterprises. Full-color calendar showing the equipment used by members of the Enterprise crew from the cartoon series. **4.95 15 20**

Star Trek Calendar 1973: Lincoln Enterprises. Odd calendar that runs from April 1973 to March 1974. Features six full-color Trek photos from the series. 8½" x 11". **2.50 15 20**

Star Trek Calendars: Pocket Books. Full-color wall calendars with centerfolds. Each contains twelve photo scenes from either TV Trek or the movies. Packaged in cellophane wrap. 12" x 13".

	Issue	Fair	Mint

(A) *Star Trek The Motion Picture* Calendar 1980, #0-671-790986, centerfold of movie cast. **5.95 20 30**

(B) Star Trek Stardate Calendar 1981, #0-671-79142-7, twelve scenes from *STTMP*, centerfold of Spock and Kirk. **5.95 15 20**

(C) Star Trek Stardate Calendar 1982, twelve scenes from *STTMP*. **5.95 20 30**

(D) *Star Trek II: The Wrath of Khan* Stardate Calendar 1983, #0-671-45611-3, twelve scenes from *ST II*, centerfold of Enterprise firing on Reliant. **6.95 15 20**

(E) Star Trek Stardate Calendar 1984, #0-671-47939-3, Timescape logo with twelve scenes from the TV series, centerfold features Enterprise crew. **6.95 (15) 20**

(F) *Star Trek III: The Search for Spock* Stardate Calendar 1985, #0-671-52789-4, twelve scenes from *ST III*, centerfold of Enterprise at Spacedock. **6.95 15 20**

(G) Star Trek Stardate Calendar 1986, #0-671-60435-X, twelve photo profiles of the crew from the first

1989 *Star Trek: The Next Generation* calendar, Pocket Books.

	Issue	Fair	Mint

three movies, centerfold of Kirk and Spock from *STTMP* promo poster. **7.95 10 15**

(H) Star Trek Calendar 1987, The Stars Pick Their Favorite Episodes, #0-671-62907-7, special 20th Anniversary calendar on glossy stock, Trek photos of the cast's favorite shows, centerfold chart lists 70 episodes by title, air date, and production number. **7.95 (15) 20**

(I) Star Trek Celebration Calendar 1988, #0-671-64476-9, fourteen color photos from the TV series, centerfold of Enterprise crew. **7.95 10 15**

(J) Star Trek Celebration Calendar 1989, #0-671-66661-4, twelve color photos from classic TV Trek episodes, centerfold has the ships of Star Trek. **7.95 (10) 15**

(K) *Star Trek V: The Final Frontier* Calendar 1990, #0-671-68512-0, twelve photos from *ST V*. **8.95 9 10**

(L) Star Trek Calendar 1991, #0-671-70914-3, twelve photos from all the movies. **8.95 9 10**

	Issue	Fair	Mint

(M) Star Trek 25th Anniversary Calendar, 1992, #0-671-74263-9, twelve months of classic Trek photographs. **9.95 10 11**

Star Trek Cloth Calendar: Franco Manufacturing, Incorporated, Rumania, 1977. Beige linen wall hanging with dated months arranged in 3" x 4" squares along the bottom half. Top portion is decorated with colorful art rendition of Kirk and Spock portraits in shades of orange, gold, black, blue, and white. Picture includes a mountain landscape, large blue moon, starfield, and TV Enterprise. Comes in envelope. **3 40 50**

Star Trek Historical Calendars: Datazine Publications. Fan-produced calendars consisting of a collection of black and white cartoon drawings by artist Don Harden and data compiled by Tim Farley. Important data is posted on the day of its anniversary as the events pertain to Star Trek. Black ink on white stock. 24 pages.

➤ Star Trek Historical Calendar 1985, cover features cartoon drawing of the *ST III* cast around T'Lar.

	Issue	*Fair*	*Mint*

Centerfold is also an artwork drawing.

➤ Star Trek Historical Calendar 1986, cover features cartoon of cigar-smoking Kirk leading heavily-armed Trek crew behind him. Legend reads "The E Team."

Price for each.	4.95	5	10

Star Trek Hysterical Calendars: Datazine Publications. Calendars portraying black and white cartoon illustrations and humorous balloon dialogue by Michael C. Goodwin (author of *My Stars!* and *Starry Night*). 24 pages.

(A) Star Trek Hysterical Calendar 1987. Cover is cartoon of *ST IV* crew standing at vending machine.

	4.95	5	8

(B) Star Trek Hysterical Calendar 1989. Cover art shows McCoy with Spock ears.

	4.95	5	6

(C) Star Trek Hysterical Calendar 1990. Cover shows picture of McCoy, Spock, Sybok, and Kirk from *ST V*.

	4.95	5	6

Star Trek Hysterical S.F. Calendar: Datazine Publications. Cartoon illustrations by Mike Fisher which cover all types of science fiction media topics. Cover shows Klingon (*ST V*) poking fingers into Spock's eyes as he tries to give Vulcan nerve pinch. Balloon caption reads "Foiled Again!" 24 pages.

	4.95	5	6

Star Trek Pocket Calendars 1984: T-K Graphics. Wallet-sized, mini-calendars printed on colored cardstock. 2¾" x 4¼". Two styles.

➤ #X037, UFP Janus head
➤ #X038, U.S.S. Enterprise silhouette

Price for each.	.25	1	2

Star Trek Poster Calendars: See **Posters.**

Star Trek Stardate Calendars: Ballantine Books. Full-color wall calendars with twelve photo scenes from TV Trek, plus centerfold. 12" x 13" in mailing box. Set of four.

(A) #0-345-24729-9, 1976, with color collage centerfold.

	4.95	35	50

(B) #0-345-25136-9, 1977, with Spock portraits as centerfold.

	4.95	25	35

(C) #0-345-27249-8, 1978, with monthly dates set in ovals and black and white photo insets, plus centerfold with Spock profiles.

	4.95	25	35

(D) #0-345-278121-6, 1979, with centerfold of Enterprise orbiting red planet.

	4.95	25	35

***Star Trek The Motion Picture* Calendar 1980:** T-K Graphics, 1979. Wall calendar with a full-color photo of the eleven-member movie bridge crew from *STTMP*. Bottom lists the entire year's dates with holidays marked. 11" x 17".

	2	4	6

Star Trek: The Next Generation Calendars: Pocket Books. Full-color 12" x 13" wall calendars with centerfolds. Contain twelve monthly photographs from *STTNG*. Shrink-wrapped.

(A) *Star Trek: The Next Generation* 1991 Calendar, #0-671-70914-3, contains photographs from the early seasons.

	9.95	10	12

(B) *Star Trek: The Next Generation* 1992 Calendar, #0-671-74262-0, includes photographs from the later seasons.

	9.95	10	11

Star Trek The Next Hysterical Calendars: Datazine Publications. Wall calendars with black and white cartoon illustrations by Michael Goodwin. 24 pages. Focuses on *STTNG* themes.

➤ Star Trek The Next Hysterical Calendar 1988. Cover shows Worf with rubber dart on head.

➤ Star Trek The Next Hysterical Calendar 1989. Cover art features picture of *STTNG* Enterprise heading into nebula with nacelles under the saucer disc.

➤ Star Trek The Next Hysterical Calendar 1990. Artwork cover shows Data as Sherlock Holmes.

Price for each.	4.95	5	6

Star Trektennial Calendar 1976-1978: #1004, Lincoln Enterprises. Interesting three-year revolving calendar which covers January 1976 to December 1978 and features twelve photo scenes from TV Trek. Cover has photo scene of castle from "The Menagerie." 9" x 12".

	4	5	10

Star Trek Three Year Calendar 1982-1984: #1004, Lincoln Enterprises. Re-release of the three-year revolving calendar from 1976 because the dates coincide again. Features twelve scenes from the series.

	4.95	5	10

U.S.S. Enterprise Officer's Official Date Book — 1980 Desk Calendar: Wallaby (Pocket Books), 1979. White, spiral-bound engagement book featuring *STTMP* photos. Right-hand pages show dates one week at a time. Left-hand side is illustrated with black and white or color photos. Approximately 41 pictures in black and white, twelve in color. 5½" x 8".

	6.95	15	20

William Shatner Calendars: William Shatner Fan Club. Fan-issue calendar with twelve never-seen-before shots of Shatner. Glossy lithography format with special date reminders. Stapled, 8" x 10".

➤ William Shatner Calendar 1984.
➤ William Shatner Calendar 1985, includes twelve cartoons by fan artist LaVena K. Kidd.

Price for each.	15	20	25

Card games: Fizzbin Game from episode PA (second version, 1990), *STTMP* playing cards (1979), *Star Trek II* fir
and second edition boxes (1982), and the *ST IV* promotional premium cards from TWA (1986).

	Issue	Fair	Mint

Your Star Trek Pictorial Calendar: Star Trek Enterprises, 1968. Rare six-page calendar showing scenes from the TV series in assorted color tints. Two entire months are featured per page with a single overhead photo. Stapled, 7¾" x 9¾". Photos include:

Black and white — chess scene with Kirk and Spock (WNM)

Green — Spock and Kirk (AE)

Brown — Kirk, Uhura, and McCoy on bridge.
Purple — Kirk and McCoy aboard Sleeper Ship (SS)
Blue — Spock with Nomad (Cg)
Red — Kirk and Uhura

Note: This calendar was offered in late 1967 as part of a Star Trek souvenir kit previewed through Star Trek Enterprises. (See **Souvenir Kits**.)

—	50	75

Card Games

Fizzbin Game:

(A) Zolke and Davis, 1976. Card deck and playing rules for the game "Fizzbin" introduced by Kirk in the TV episode PA. Photo cardbacks show a collage of four scenes from the classic television show.

	6	25	35

(B) John Brock, 1990. New release of the classic TV episode game. Deck is boxed and blister-packed to cardstock. Contains playing instructions.

	10	10	15

***STTMP* Enterprise Deck:** Aviva, 1979. Plastic-coated cards with movie-vintage starship on the cardbacks. Blue starfield box with gray movie title logo is blister-packed to 7¾" x 4¼" cardstock showing

movie rainbow promo poster.

	4	12	15

***ST II* Official Playing Cards:** Movie Players, Ltd., 1982. Complete card deck featuring 52 different photo portraits and action scenes from the second movie. Two releases.

(A) First edition. Lettered "Star Trek Wrath of Khan" inside blue glow on black box.

	2.50	25	35

(B) Second edition. Lettered "Star Trek II Wrath of Khan" printed on black box.

	3	15	25

***ST IV* Playing Card Premium:** TWA Give-Away premium in conjunction with the fourth movie.

Free	10	15

Starpool Inc.'s *ST II* kinetic passengers, Kirk and Spock, 1982.

Car Hangers And Kinetic Passengers _____

	Issue	Fair	Mint

Beam Me Up, Scotty Car Hanger: #50, H & L Enterprises, 1986. Sign designed for vehicular rear windows and patterned after the faddish "Baby On Board" yellow and black caution signs. Plastic square with black lettering. Clear, rubber suction cup included. 5" x 5".   **1.27**   **2**   **4**

Beam Me Up, Scotty Miniature Car Hanger: #22, H & L Enterprises, 1987. Same style as above, but reduced in size to 2½" x 2½". "Beam Me Up" in red letters, "Scotty" in black. Suction cup included.   **.99**   **1**   **3**

Beam Me Up Scotty Car Hanger: Stravina, Inc., 1985. Yellow caution sign with red letters. Suction cup included.   **2**   **3**   **5**

Beam Me Up Scotty! Car Hanger: #908, Weaver Works, 1986. Standard yellow plastic square with black lettering. Suction cup included. 5" x 5".   **2.95**   **3**   **4**

Star Trek Car Hangers: Vision Aeries, 1988. Yellow caution signs with black lettering. Comes with suction cup.
➤ #01HNG031, "Tribble On Board"
➤ #01HNG032, "Spock You!"
➤ #01HNG033, "Shuttle Craft"
Price for each.   **2**   **2**   **4**

***Star Trek II* Kinetic Passengers:** Starpool, Inc., 1982. Set of two *ST II* movie charactures designed for attachment to the rear windows of cars. Spring-

	Issue	Fair	Mint

loaded devices cause the hands to wave when the car is in motion.
- Kirk with communicator
- Spock giving Vulcan salute

Price for each. **8.95 20 35**

Certificates

Flight Deck Certificates: Lincoln Enterprises, 1968-80. Certificate making you an honorary member of the U.S.S. Enterprise crew and signed by James T. Kirk and Gene Roddenberry. Certificates have superimposed image of the TV Enterprise in the center.
(A) #1401, plain certificate, blue starfield with white Enterprise. **.50 5 8**
(B) #1402, deluxe certificate, parchment-like paper with insignia sticker and two-color ribbon. **1 5 10**

Honorary Flight Deck Award: Produced by Bjo Trimble, Frederick Pohl/*Galaxy* and *Analog* magazines, 1969. Special award sent to fans who responded to the SST (Save *Star Trek*) mail-in campaign. Certificate is the same as the regular Flight Deck Certificate #1401 sold by Star Trek Enterprises, but with the addition of a gold insignia sticker in the corner. Participating fans had their names enrolled on the Starship crew rosters. **Free 10 20**

Kolinahr Discipline Certificate: April Publications, 1988. New gold-lithographed certificate. 8½" x 11". **1 1 2**

Star Fleet Awards: Altair Scientific Foundation, 1990. Set of seven 8½" x 11" standard, specific, or personalized awards given by the United Federation of Planets High Council. Come in clear plastic protectors.
- #A1, Federation Medal of Valor
- #A2, Vulcan Award of Technical Achievement
- #A3, Organian Peace Award
- #A4, Altair Arts & Science Award
- #A5, Star Fleet Meritorious Award
- #A6, Vulcan Science Award
- #A7, Aldebaran Medal of Valor

Price for each standard award (details to be added). **2 2 3**
Price for each specific award (details already printed). **3 3 4**
Price for each personalized award (name printed). **4 4 5**

Star Fleet Licenses: Altair Scientific Foundation, 1990. Set of three 8½" x 11" licenses or permits issued from the ASF. Come in clear plastic protectors.

Trekkie On Board Car Hanger: H & R Records, 1987. Yellow plastic sign with black letters. Suction cup included. 5" x 5". **2.95 3 4**

- #L1, Tradesman-at-Large License
- #L2, Merchant's Permit
- #L3, Planetary Advisor's License

Price for each standard license. **3 3 4**
Price for each custom certificate. **4 4 5**

Star Fleet Professional Certificates: Altair Scientific Foundation, 1990. Standard or custom designed 8½" x 11" certificates for those with commissioned skills, as issued by Altair Scientific Foundation. Graphics included. Come in clear plastic protector.
- #P1, Ship's Master's Papers
- #P2, Pilot's Papers
- #P3, Navigator's Papers
- #P4, Engineer's Papers
- #P5, First Officer's Papers

Price for each standard certificate. **3 3 4**
Price for each custom certificate. **4 4 5**

Star Fleet Ship Commissioning's Certificates: Altair Scientific Foundation, 1990. Standard or custom made 8½" x 11" certificates for commissioned class starships. Include a variety of graphics and come in clear plastic protector.
- #C1, Enterprise Class, Heavy Cruiser
- #C2, Nimitz Class, through Deck Carrier
- #C3, Reliant Class, Science Vessel
- #C4, Knox Class, Frigate
- #C5, Rickover Class, Fast Frigate
- #C6, Monoceros Class, Scout

Price for each standard certificate. **3 3 4**
Price for each custom certificate. **4 4 5**

Star Fleet Skill Certificates: Altair Scientific Foundation, 1990. Standard or custom designed 8½" x 11" certificates representing the professional fields as issued by the Altair Scientific Foundation, Institute for Advanced Learning. Many graphic varieties included. Come in clear plastic protectors.
- #S1, Phaser Fire Control Specialist
- #S2, Offensive Weapons Specialist
- #S3, Defensive Weapons Specialist
- #S4, Navigational Systems Specialist
- #S6, Life Support Systems Specialist

Issue	Fair	Mint

➤ #S7, Propulsion Systems Specialist
➤ #S8, Warp Drive Systems Specialist
➤ #S9, Medical Technician
➤ #S10, Bio-Medical Associate
➤ #S11, Medical Technician Specialist
➤ #S12, Hand Weapons Specialist (Star Fleet Marine)
➤ #S13, Hand To Hand Combat Specialist (Star Fleet Marine)
➤ #S14, Space Assault Specialist (Star Fleet Marine)
➤ #S15, Armored Assault Specialist (Star Fleet Marine)
➤ #S16, Counter-Terrorist Specialist (Star Fleet Marine)

Price for each standard certificate.

	3	3	4

Price for each custom certificate.

	4	4	5

Star Trek Animated Fan Club Certificate: Lincoln Enterprises, 1975. Certificate came with membership in the fan organization and granted the bearer full citizenship in the Federation and free passage on any starship. Same as the UFP certificate. Annual membership $3.50.

	N/A	5	8

Star Trek Certificates: April Publications, 1984. Assorted certificates lithographed in gold and suitable for framing. 8½" x 11".

	Issue	Fair	Mint
(A) Delta Oath of Celibacy	1	1	2
(B) Enterprise Crew Member	1	1	2
(C) Federation Birth	1	1	2
(D) Klingon Captain	1	1	2
(E) Phaser Marksmanship	1	1	2
(F) Spock's Death	1	1	2
(G) Starfleet Admiral	1	1	2
(H) Starfleet Oath	1	2	4

Star Trek bean bag chair, Paramount Pictures Corporation, 1976.

	Issue	Fair	Mint
(I) Starfleet Officer's Club	1	1	2
(J) Starfleet Operations	1	1	2
(K) Starship Captain	1	1	2
(L) Tribble Pedigree	1	1	2
(M) Vulcan Birth	1	1	2
(N) Vulcan Land Lease	1	2	4
(O) Vulcan Officer's Club	1	1	2

Star Trek The Official Fan Club Certificate of Membership: STTOFC, 1986. Certificate acknowledges participation in the fan club and the news of exclusive information direct from Paramount, as well as entitles them to purchase fan club merchandise. Annual fee $10. 5" x 7".

	N/A	1	2

	Issue	Fair	Mint

Starfleet Certificate of Membership: Starfleet Fan Club, 1984. Special recognition for joining the Starfleet Fan Club. Annual Fee $10.

	N/A	2	3

United Federation of Planets Certificate: Star Trek Enterprises, 1968. Grants the bearer full citizenship in the UFP and free passage on any starship. Black lettering in italics and printed on parchment-like paper. Free with the annual $3 membership to Star Trek Interstellar Fan Club. 8" x 11".

	N/A	5	10

Vulcan Marriage License Certificate: April Publications, 1984. Gold-lithographed certificate. 8½" x 11".

	1	1	2

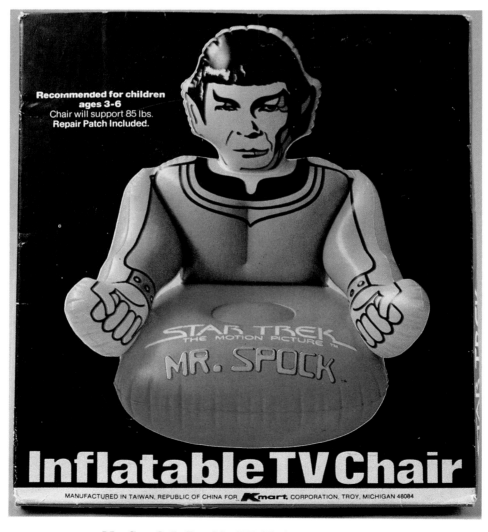

Mr. Spock Inflatable TV Chair, K-Mart, 1979.

Chairs

| | *Issue* | *Fair* | *Mint* |

Bean Bag Chairs:

(A) Paramount Pictures Corporation, 1976. "Star Trek" with Enterprise design. Styrofoam pellet-filled traditional bean bag chair with blue and white stitched vinyl sections. Design stencil "Star Trek" lettering and TV starship in blue. — **75 175**

(B) Decorion Fun Furnishings, 1979. "Star Trek The Motion Picture" with crew design. Adult-sized yellow vinyl-covered bean bag filled with white styrofoam pellets. Seat front is imprinted with blue color swatch background and art illustration of *STTMP* bridge crew in light blue movie uniforms: Spock, Scotty, McCoy, Sulu, Ilia, Uhura (wearing yellow tunic) around seated

Kirk in chair. Lettering is in white below. Boxed. — **75 150**

Director's Chair — *ST IV*: STTOFC, 1987. White metal-framed director's chair in traditional style. Royal blue canvas seat and back with official *ST IV* movie title logo in white outline stencil and "Star Date: 1986, How On Earth Can They Save the Future?" printed in small white letters above. Boxed for shipping and requires assembly. **49 45 50**

Inflatable Chair — "Mr. Spock": K-Mart, 1979. *STTMP*-vintage child's chair featuring a cartoon imprint of Spock in movie blue uniform with lettering on the seat. Chair has armrests. 8" x 9" box is black and has photo of chair. **3.96 20 30**

Charms

Charm jewelry has always been popular for bracelets. Collectors should note that so-called small or miniature pendants may actually be charms (or sometimes even earrings) provided with a chain and should try to avoid duplication in their collections. More confusion arises when descriptions are vague and multiple titles for the same piece proliferate. A good example of this is the hand offering the split-finger Vulcan sign, referred to as the Vulcan Salute, the Vulcan Hand of Peace, or the Vulcan Greeting. Charms, probably due to their small size, were one of the first pieces of jewelry to make the quantum leap in quality from costume to fine and very expensive works.

Classic Charms

Enterprise Design: Star Trek / Lincoln Enterprises, 1970. Introduced in *Star Trek Catalog No. 2* as one of the earliest forms of Trek jewelry. 1¾" TV Enterprise in starboard profile relief has back side flat. Metal ship has hole punched in top for clasp. 22K gold-plated. **5 10 20**

Enterprise Design: Star Trek / Lincoln Enterprises, 1976, ST-10. Star Trektennial 3-D ship similar to miniature one introduced in the TV episode Cp. 1¾" full-view ship:
(A) #J2401, charm **4 8 10**
(B) #J2402, charm and bracelet **9 17 20**

IDIC Design: #2304, Lincoln, 1976. Rendition of the Vulcan symbol in gold- and silver-toned metals with a central synthetic gemstone. Originally released with bracelet. **5.50 12 15**

Insignia Design: Lincoln Enterprises. Plain Command Star, ½".
(A) #2352, 1976, 22K gold-plated with 18" chain. **4 6 7**
(B) #2362, 1976, sterling silver with 18" chain. **8 15 17**
(C) #J2371G, 1987, 14K gold with diamond center. **89.95 85 95**
(D) #J2375GD, 1987, 14K gold with pavé diamonds. **300 290 310**
(E) #J2478G, 1987, insignia executed as an outline charm in 14K gold wire. **99.95 95 105**

Vulcan Hand: #2414, Lincoln Enterprises, 1980. 3-D right-handed palm and wrist in gold plate showing salute. Includes an 18" chain. **3.95 5 8**

Movie Charms

STTMP **Enterprise Design:** Lincoln Enterprises, 1987. ¾" movie starship in 3-D miniature. Fine detailing of ship registered NCC-1701A.
(A) #J2404A, gold-plated, includes 24" chain. **7.95 10 12**
(B) #J2404GH, 14K gold. **125 120 130**
(C) #J2404KD, 14K gold with diamonds. **300 280 320**

STTMP **Movie Title Premium Charm Bracelet:** DuBarry Fifth Avenue, Inc., 1989. Child's I.D. bracelet in link chain. Engraved and personalized up to eight letters, lettered with movie title logo. Cereal box-back coupon from General Mills (expired 11/30/80) offered charm for payment plus proof from Lucky Charms cereal. **1.25 8 12**

	Issue	Fair	Mint

ST IV Whale Charms: Lincoln Enterprises, 1987. Assorted whales alone or together and posed in a variety of renditions.

(A) #J2476, George (swimming down). Gold-plated.
| | 7.95 | 8 | 10 |

(B) #J2476G, George as above in 14K gold.
| | 175 | 170 | 180 |

(C) #J2477, Gracie (flipped). Gold-plated.
| | 7.95 | 8 | 10 |

(D) #J2479, both whales over insignia cut-out.
| | 12.95 | 13 | 14 |

(E) #J2479G, above in 14K gold.
| | 150 | 145 | 155 |

(F) #J2480, two small whales together. Plated.
| | 8.95 | 9 | 10 |

(G) #J2480G, above in 14K gold solid.
| | 89.95 | 85 | 95 |

(H) #J2481, two small whales "kissing." Plated.
| | 8.95 | 9 | 10 |

(I) #J2481G, above in 14K gold solid.
| | 89.95 | 85 | 95 |

(J) #J2482, small George. Plated.
| | 5.95 | 6 | 8 |

	Issue	Fair	Mint

(K) #J2482G, above in 14K gold solid.
| | 50 | 45 | 55 |

(L) #J2483, small Gracie. Plated.
| | 5.95 | 6 | 8 |

(M) #J2483G, above in 14K gold solid.
| | 50 | 45 | 55 |

(N) #J2464, 7" bracelet. Costume quality.
| | 3.95 | 5 | 6 |

(O) #J2464G, 18" necklace in 14K gold.
| | 39.95 | 35 | 45 |

Star Trek: The Next Generation Charms

STTNG Enterprise Design:
(A) Lincoln Enterprises, 1987. 3-D miniature STTNG starship NCC-1701-D in ¾" size.
➤ #J2405A, gold-plated with 18" chain.
| | 7.95 | 8 | 10 |

➤ #J2405GH, 14K gold solid.
| | 125 | 120 | 130 |

➤ #J2405KD, 14K gold with diamonds.
| | 300 | 280 | 320 |

(B) Intergalactic, distributor, 1990. Miniature replica of STTNG ship in silver plate.
| | 7.95 | 8 | 10 |

Checkbook Covers

Star Trek Address Book / Checkbooks: Reed Productions, 1988. Photo-style checkbooks with black and white TV Trek photocards or *ST V* photocards inserted into a clear plastic vinyl pocket front. Set of eight.
➤ Kirk (TV)
➤ Kirk and Spock (TV)
➤ Kirk, Spock, and McCoy (TV)
➤ Kirk and Spock in transporter (TV)
➤ Enterprise (*ST V*)
➤ Enterprise crew (*ST V*)
➤ Kirk and Spock over El Capitan (*ST V*)
➤ Kirk, Spock, McCoy, and Sybok (*ST V*)
Price for each.
| | 6 | 6 | 7 |

Star Trek Checkbook Calculator: See **Calculators.**

Star Trek Checkbook Covers: T-K Graphics, 1984. Vinyl, polyester-lined covers in brown and tan with silk-screened designs. Folder-style. 3¼" x 6½".
➤ Star Fleet Academy
➤ Star Fleet Command Intelligence Division
➤ Star Fleet HQ Tactical Operations
➤ UFP Diplomatic Service, with Janus head emblem
➤ U.S.S. Enterprise, with starship schematic design
➤ U.S.S. Enterprise NCC-1701
➤ Vulcan Science Academy
Price for each.
| | 2.50 | 5 | 8 |

Chess Sets

3-D Chess Game: #PR9050, New Eye Studios, 1990. Three-level chess game complete with instructions and chess pieces. Each prop replica is handmade with custom hardwood armatures.
| | 99 | 75 | 100 |

3-D Chess Game: Field Manufacturing Company, 1967. All-plastic chess set featuring three successive levels of chess playing and strategy for all ages. Each gridded platform is supported by a branching arma-

ture and closely resembles the famous 3-D chess set seen on the *Star Trek* TV series. Comes with instructions and standard chess pieces. This item was one of the first prop replicas ever produced.
| | — | 200 | 250 |

3-D Chess Set: Dimensional Games, Inc., 1990. Remake of the 1967 game by Lynn R. Johnson. Includes three square base levels supported by a curved

3-D chess set from Dimensional Games, Inc., 1990. Remake of the 1967 game.

	Issue	*Fair*	*Mint*

tree stand. Playing levels are etched, transparent plastic with a chessboard design. Rule book included. Boxed in white cardstock with orange and white sticker front. 9" x 15".

	39.95	**40**	**45**

Star Trek Chess Set: The Franklin Mint, 1990. This chess set is officially sanctioned by Paramount and authenticated by Gene Roddenberry. Includes complete 32-piece set of playing pieces plus a custom-designed playing board. Kirk, Spock, McCoy, and other members of the Federation face the evil forces of the Klingons, Romulans, and Khan himself. Federation characters are crafted of 24K gold electroplate over pewter. The nasties are crafted of sterling silver electroplate over pewter. Pieces are approximately 2½" high and are set into crystal bases.

An advertisement for the Franklin Mint's Star Trek chess set, 1990.

Issue Fair Mint

The playing board is made from aluminum and glass, and depicts a dimensional star system. Playing board measures 16" x 16" x 3". Offered on time payments of two new playing pieces every other month (billed as one piece per month) for $29.50 each. Chess board provided at no extra charge.   **944   950   1025**

Issue Fair Mint

Strato Chess: Starbase Central, 1984. 3-D chess set made from plastic gaming grids and brushed aluminum armatures. The armatures oppose one another between levels one and two, and levels two and three. Plastic playing pieces included.   **25   50   75**

Clocks

Classic Clocks

Crew Portrait Clocks: Untitled. 1979.

Note: This same faceplate appears on a Star Trek theme watch and pocket watch (see **Watches**). However, only on the electric wall clock does the box packaging read "Westclox, Tally Industries, 1979."

(A) "Star Trek" Alarm Clock. Traditional round table clock with large face numbers and photo of Kirk, McCoy, and Spock on face. Time set and alarm features, second hand.   **15   35   40**

(B) #26379, "Star Trek" Wall Clock. Traditional-style kitchen clock in same faceplate design as alarm clock above. Electric cord and works by Accent Electric. Packaged in open-window heavy cardboard shipping box.   **19   45   60**

Enterprise Clock: ASA, Inc., 1974. Traditional kitchen clock with 8" diameter face. Plastic case had deep outer rim shroud. Starfield faceplate has "Star Trek" lettering over starboard starship firing twin phasers. Electrical cord.   **—   50   65**

Issue Fair Mint

Insignia Clock: Sweda, Lincoln Enterprises, distributor, 1983. Travel clock that folds out and compacts to fit in wallet. Gold-toned finish, digital display, and alarm. Includes a leatherette carrying case and jeweler's battery. Decorated with classic Command Star insignia in gold-tone mounted in the upper left-hand corner. **24.95   20   30**

Commemorative Clocks

ST-10 "1966-1986 Star Trek — 20 Years": STTOFC, 1987. Traditional round kitchen clock with white case, large numbered face, and red center design of the 20th Anniversary official circle letter logo. Analog-quartz movement. **28   25   30**

Issue Fair Mint

Movie Clocks

***STTMP* — Crew Portrait Clock:** Zeon, England, 1980. Twin-bell alarm clock lettered "Star Trek" in movie letter logo style below poster photo of front view of movie Enterprise and busts of Kirk and Spock below. Double chrome bell alarms on top. **8   75   100**

***ST V* — Enterprise:** Paramount Special Effects, 1989. Wall clock with laser print photo of rearward movie ship against black and shimmering blue nebula-world on face. Rectangular beveled glass face with two hands in gold-toned metal and no numerals. Quartz movement. Lifetime warranty. Flush front face measures 9" x 11". **48   45   50**

STTMP Crew Portrait alarm clock (Zeon, 1980) and two styles of the Classic Crew Portrait clock, circa 1979.

Coaster

| Issue | Fair | Mint |

***Star Trek IV* Movie Video Release Coaster:**
Metro Video, Los Angeles, 1988. Leather 4" diameter
coaster with movie title logo. Regional promotional
item in conjunction with Paramount Home Video's
release of the *ST IV* video tape.

Free   2   5

Coins

This listing includes mint-struck precious metal
coins fashioned in commemoration of the Star Trek
television show, its characters, or the subsequent
movies. Coins listed in this section may be mint-
boxed or be designed for use as jewelry in the form
of coin medallions mounted in permanent or detachable rim holders. Some include jewelry chains. Since
all of the coin commemoratives tend to follow similar
designs featuring Kirk and Spock, or other character
busts with obverses showing the starship Enterprise,
they are difficult to distinguish from each other using
a design criteria. For this reason the coins are listed
below by their dates and the mint that produced them.
For non-coin jewelry with chains, see the listing titled
Pendants.

Classic Design Coin Commemoratives

1974 Hanover Mint Coins: Obverse Kirk and Spock
busts, reverse Enterprise, lettered "Five year mission
. . . Where No Man Has Gone Before." Series includes
three styles in mint-strike coins, differing in metal
content. Approximately half-dollar size.

(A) Series 1. Silver .999 pure with serial edge numbers in a clean strike, with detachable rim mount.

75   250   500

(B) Series 2. Bronze. Same minting as above
without serial numbers and detachable rim mount.
Includes chain.

30   100   130

(C) Series 3. Bronze. Struck as above with rim
struck as solid part of the coin. Permanent non-
detachable coin mount medallion jewelry.

20   30   40

(D) Replica (circa 1980s). Non-precious metal casting
for an inexpensive rendition of the above.

14.95   15   18

1975 New York Star Trek Convention Coin:
Bronze. Obverse reads "Star Trek 1975" over starfield, reverse lettered "U.S.S. Enterprise" with front
profile of TV ship. 1 9/16" diameter.

5   25   35

Star Trek IV: The Voyage Home **promotional coaster,
1988.**

| Issue | Fair | Mint |

1976 ST-10 Anniversary Commemorative Coins:
Lincoln Enterprises, 1976. Bronze, antiques with bas
relief. "10th Anniversary Commemoration — Star
Trek 1966-1976," obverse with busts of Kirk, Spock,
McCoy, and Scotty; reverse shows "Space the Final
Frontier . . . Where No Man Has Gone Before" legend
with profile starboard Enterprise ship over planet.

(A) #2460, coin   **4.50   12   14**

(B) #2460A, with 24" chain and mount

5   13   15

1989 Rarities Mint: Series of seven crew character
profiles minted in three different metals. Coins are
struck in high relief. Obverse shows one of seven
character busts in brushed finish over mirrored background. Common reverse of TV Enterprise in starboard profile with legend "Where No Man Has Gone
Before."

(A) Gold — 24K Limited Edition. Minting of 250 coin
sets struck in 1/4 troy ounce .999 gold. Packaged in
airtight black-backed Lucite capsule for display.
Coins are boxed individually in blue velvet case with
letter of authenticity, serial numbers. Coins depict
Kirk, Spock, McCoy, Scotty, Uhura, Sulu, or Chekov.
Price for each.   **349   450   550**

(B) Gold — 24K. Same set as above limited to twenty
sets in 1 troy ounce gold. All seven character coins
in proof set as listed in (A). Price for each.

1349   2000   3000

	Issue	*Fair*	*Mint*

(C) Sterling silver. Limited 10,000 issue set of seven crew coins struck as above in 1 troy ounce silver. Includes Lucite display capsule, velvet box, serialized letter of authenticity. All seven character coins in proof set as listed individually in (A). Price for each.

44.95   50   55

(D) Silver medallion mounted coins. Struck as above in option of non-precious content: ⅒ ounce silver with rhodium plate. Spock, Kirk, or McCoy.

15.95   16   18

Movie Design Coin Commemoratives

1984 *ST III* Coin Medallion: Lincoln Enterprises. Zinc-cast with clear enamel coating. "Star Trek III: Search For Spock" on obverse with busts of Kirk (turned slightly sideways) and Spock (facing full front). Reverse reads "Kirk — Of All the Souls I have Encountered, His Was the Most Human" with lettering inside an outer ring circling the rim. Center is starboard movie Enterprise viewed from bottom of saucer below Genesis planet. 1½"-diameter coin is mounted in gold-plated rim holder.

(A) #2461, originally included a 24" chain.

12.95   13   15

(B) Sold currently without the chain.

—   12   14

1986 ST-20 Anniversary Coin: #J2462, Lincoln Enterprises. Zinc cast with clear enamel coating. "1966-1986 / 20th Anniversary Commemorative." Obverse is bas-relief *STTMP* vintage busts of Kirk and Spock (both facing front). Reverse is starboard movie Enterprise viewed from over the saucer above planets.

A sample of coins and pendants (see Pendants section). **Top row:** *STTNG* Starfleet Academy Pendant in pewter; *ST IV* Challenger Commemorative Coin Pendant in bronze; and ST-25 Anniversary Commemorative Coin in silver (box below). **Bottom Row:** Classic *Star Trek* Crew Coin Pendant in silver; classic *Star Trek* Crew Coin Pendant in Bronze; and two classic *Star Trek* Crew Coins in silver.

	Issue	*Fair*	*Mint*

Available in pewter or bronze.

(A) Originally sold with 24" chain.

	14.95	25	30

(B) Sold currently without the chain.

	—	14	16

1986 *ST IV* Challenger Commemorative: Lincoln Enterprises. Remember the Seven. "Star Trek IV The Voyage Home" on obverse in circle above/below bas relief detailed Golden Gate Bridge, two whales, and Enterprise scene. Reverse is full crew 36-word movie dedication to the men and women of the Space Shuttle Challenger inscribed over the shuttle's image. Olympic-size medallion attached to ribbon of gold, sil-

	Issue	*Fair*	*Mint*

ver, and white colors (the IDIC symbol colors). Multiple strikes.

(A) #J2463A, bronze	19.95	17	24
(B) #J2464, gold 24K plate	59.95	55	65
(C) #J2465, gold and silver plate	79.95	80	85
(D) #J2466, pewter plate	29.95	30	35

1991 ST-25 Silver Anniversary Coin: Franklin Mint, 1990. Official commemorative 25th anniversary coin is mint-strike, detailed in brushed and polished finish. Front shows a central insignia with clockwise portraits of TV Enterprise, McCoy, Kirk, and Spock. Reverse is lettered "Star Trek" with Enterprise and

Mounted coins, from left to right: *ST III* Coin (1984); Star Trek Commemorative Series 3 (1974); Star Trek Commemorative Series 2 (1974); ST-20 Anniversary Commemorative Coin in bronze (1986); ST-10 Anniversary Commemorative Coin (1976); and ST-20 Anniversary Commemorative Coin in pewter (1986).

	Issue	Fair	Mint
(A) Silver (2500 grains)	175	175	190
(B) Pewter	49.50	50	60

shows a calendar of the year 1991. Rim reads "Star Trek 25th Anniversary 1966-1991." Available in two strike metals. 76mm diameter.

Colorforms

Star Trek Adventure Set: Colorforms, 1975. Sticker board set showing cartoon transporter chamber, bridge stations, and Captain's chair. Red, blue, white, and yellow colorform parts recreate action game with crew and aliens. Boxed with cover illustration of Enterprise, Spock, Kirk, and McCoy.

3.50	25	35

Coloring Kits

How Do You Doodle Set: #2081, Open Door Enterprises, 1976. Poster coloring set which includes two black and white line drawings designed for coloring with felt markers. Set includes five fine-tip markers. Drawings are 12" x 18". Packaged in plastic pocket.

➤ Journeys of the Enterprise, action scene.

➤ Tour of the Enterprise, crew, and Enterprise.

Price for complete set, uncolored.

3.95	20	30

How Do You Doodle Set: #2081, Open Door Enterprises, 1976. Includes two black and white line drawings and five colored markers. Drawings are 12" x 18".

➤ Enemies of the Federation

Star Trek Adventure Set by Colorforms, 1975.

#192, Star Trek Space Design Center, Avalon, 1979.

	Issue	Fair	Mint

➢ Star Trek Lives

Price for complete set, uncolored.

	3.95	20	30

Pen-A-Poster Kits: Open Door Enterprises, 1976. Set of four individually-packaged pen and poster sets. Each black and white line drawing poster came flat in a cardboard pocket with shrink wrapping. Included a coloring guide and six markers per set. Poster size 14½" x 22".

➢ #2411, Star Trek Lives, crew shot.

➢ #2412, Enemies of the Federation, battle scenes.

➢ #2413, Tour of the Enterprise, crew.

➢ #2414, Journeys of the Enterprise, crew, and Enterprise.

Price for each.

	3.50	5	10

Pen-A-Poster Kits: Open Door Enterprises, 1976. Paired sets of the above posters. Each of these shrink-wrapped, black and white line drawing poster sets included two posters and five markers for coloring. Size 14½" x 22".

	Issue	Fair	Mint

➢ #ST2411, Enemies of the Federation and Journeys of the Enterprise

➢ #ST4211, Enemies of the Federation and Star Trek Lives

➢ #ST2411, Star Trek Lives and Tour of the Enterprise

Price per set.

	3	10	15

Pen-A-Poster Kit Deluxe: Open Door Enterprises, 1976. Contains four black and white Trek Pen-A-Poster sheets, which were also sold separately, plus ten non-toxic felt pens. Boxed and shrink-wrapped. Poster size 12" x 18".

➢ Enemies of the Federation

➢ Journeys of the Enterprise

➢ Star Trek Lives

➢ Tour of the Enterprise

Price for complete set, uncolored and boxed.

	5	20	30

Star Trek Chalk & Play Activity Board: Hasbro, circa 1960s. Children's blackboard featuring sticker decals of time clock, the alphabet, and a number line,

Star Trek: The Motion Picture 3-D Poster Bulletin Board, Whiting / Milton Bradley, 1979.

	Issue	Fair	Mint

plus Kirk and Spock running and Enterprise over planet. Lettering in upper right-hand corner. 16" x 24".

	Issue	Fair	Mint
	—	200	500

Star Trek Magic Slates: Whitman, circa 1970s. Magic drawing slates with TV Trek artwork headers. Set of four.

(A) #4481A, yellow Spock and Kirk with "Guardian of Forever" time portal.

	Issue	Fair	Mint
of Forever" time portal.	.69	5	8

(B) #4481B, yellow TV Enterprise over planets, starboard view.

	.69	5	8

(C) #24443-1, blue Kirk and planets.

	.59	5	8

(D) #24443-2, blue TV Enterprise firing at planet, top view.

	.59	5	8

Star Trek Magic Slates by Whitman, circa 1970s: #4481B and #24443-1.

	Issue	Fair	Mint

Star Trek Numbered Pencil & Paint Set: Hasbro, 1967. Coloring kit containing eight water color paint tablets and twelve pre-sketched pictures, plus eight colored pencils. Box front shows starboard profile of Enterprise and cut-outs of Kirk and Spock. Very similar to the cover of the Hasbro Paint-By-Number kits. Box sized 11" x 15". — **50 100**

Star Trek Space Design Center: #192, Avalon, 1979. Artist's design kit associated with *STTMP*. Includes plastic work tray to hold play cards, markers, and color pallets. Also has a project book of ideas for designing clothes, plus Kirk, Spock, Ilia, and Acturian stand-up figures to outfit. Box shows entire kit with child at work. Box sized 3½" x 14½" x 18½". — **25 35**

	Issue	Fair	Mint

***Star Trek The Motion Picture* Color 'N Recolor Game Cloth:** Avalon, 1979. Boxed game printed on reusable plastic mat. Includes seven different games with eight crayons. Mat size 36" x 40". **2.95 15 25**

***Star Trek The Motion Picture* 3-D Poster Bulletin Board:** Crafts by Whiting/Milton Bradley, 1979. Preprinted and die-cut cardboard canvas with action scene from *STTMP*. Included four non-toxic marker pens. Canvas size 11" x 17". **10 20 30**

***Star Trek The Motion Picture* Pen and Poster Set:** #4006, Aviva, 1979. Set of three black and white drawings from *STTMP* with seven markers. **4.95 10 15**

Comic Books

Star Trek Television Series

Star Trek: Gold Key, 1967-79, Western Publishing Company. The complete set consists of 61 issues and spans a total of twelve years. Despite the lengthy lifetime of these comics, they were relatively unpopular. The series was plagued by numerous format inconsistencies when compared to the previously established Trek universe of the TV series. Problems began with the very first issues drawn by Alberto Gioletti, who resided in Italy and had never seen a *Star Trek* episode. His only information about the show came from a limited quantity of episode photographs. The result was an accumulative series of negative factors that destroyed the credibility of the comic. One of Gioletti's biggest blunders was the proposed ability of the Enterprise to come in for ground landings. Even later, Gold Key artists labored under rigid format specifications, including an edict

Star Trek Gold Key Comic #1.

	Issue	Fair	Mint

which proposed a limit of only 25 words per cartoon panel and the fact that no character from the TV series could be resurrected unless it was a central cast character. Collectors should note that there was an occasional interchange between Gold Key and Whitman as comic covers exist in both types for certain issues. Generally speaking, the Whitman covers are reprint issues that exhibit different coloration than their Gold Key counterparts. In rarer cases, Whitman cover printings are actually reversed, but there is no appreciable value difference between either logo editions with the same issue number.

No. 1, 1967, Parts I and II, "The City of No Return." This issue was reprinted as Star Trek Comic #29. Photo cover of Spock holding beaker with Kirk, Sulu, and Enterprise. **.10   40   100**

No. 2, #10210-806, 1968, Part I, "The Devil's Isle of Space"; Part II, "The Secret of Execution Asteroid." Photo cover. **.12   20   60**

No. 3, #10210-112, 1968, Part I, "Invasion of the City Builders"; Part II, "The Bridge to Catastrophe." Photo cover. **.15   20   60**

No. 4, #10210-906, June 1969, "The Peril of Planet Quick Change"; Part I, "The Creatures of Light"; Part II, "The Sinister Guest." Photo cover. This issue was later reprinted as Star Trek comic #35. **.15   20   60**

No. 5, #10210-909, September 1969, "The Ghost Planet," Parts I and II. Photo cover. This issue was later reprinted as Star Trek comic #37. **.15   20   60**

No. 6, #10210-912, December 1969, "When Planets Collide." Photo cover. **.15   20   40**

No. 7, #10210-003, March 1970, "The Voodoo Planet," Chapters I and II. Photo cover. This issue was reprinted as Star Trek comic #45. **.15   15   40**

No. 8, #10210-004, September 1970, "The Youth Trap," Parts I and II. Photo cover. **.15   15   40**

No. 9, #10210-102, February 1971, "The Legacy of Lazeus," Parts I and II. Photo cover. **.15   15   40**

No. 10, #10210-105, May 1971, "Sceptre of the Sun," Parts I and II. This comic began the first of the artwork covers and contained photo inserts of Kirk and Spock. It also underwent extensive transmutations as the Khan Noonian Singh antagonist envisioned by comic writer Len Wein was forbidden by strict Paramount guidelines. Singh was transformed into the evil Chang. **.15   10   25**

	Issue	Fair	Mint

No. 11, #10210-108, August 1971, "The Brain Shockers," Parts I and II. Artwork cover.
.15   10   25

No. 12, #10210-111, November 1971, "The Flight of the Buccaneer," Parts I and II. Artwork cover. Len Wein originally conceived the lovable space rogue Harcourt Fenton Mudd as a protagonist for this issue, but publishing mandates forced the idea to be scrapped.
.15   10   25

No. 13, #10210-202, February 1972, "Dark Traveler," Parts I and II. Artwork cover. .15   10   25

No. 14, #90210-205, May 1972, "The Enterprise Mutiny," Parts I and II. Artwork cover.
.15   10   25

No. 15, #90210-208, August 1972, "Museum at the End of Time," Parts I and II. Artwork cover.
.15   10   25

No. 16, #90210-211, November 1972, "Day of the Inquisitors," Parts I and II. Artwork cover.
.15   10   25

No. 17, #90210-302, December 1972, "The Cosmic Caveman," Parts I and II. Artwork cover.
.15   10   25

No. 18, #90210-305, January 1973, "The Hijacked Planet," Parts I and II. Artwork cover.
.15   10   25

No. 19, #90210-307, July 1973, "The Haunted Asteroid," Parts I and II. Artwork cover.
.20   10   25

No. 20, #90210-309, September 1973, "A World Gone Mad," Parts I and II. Artwork cover.
.20   10   25

No. 21, #90210-311, November 1973, "The Mummies of Heitus VII," Parts I and II. Artwork cover.
.20   8   20

No. 22, #90210-401, January 1974, "Siege in Superspace," Parts I and II. Artwork cover.
.20   8   20

No. 23, #90210-403, March 1974, "Child's Play," Parts I and II. Artwork cover. .20   8   20

No. 24, #90210-405, May 1974, "The Trial of Captain Kirk," Parts I and II. Artwork cover.
.20   8   20

No. 25, #90210-407, July 1974, "Dwarf Planet," Parts I and II. Artwork cover. .25   8   20

No. 26, #90210-409, September 1974, "The Perfect Dream," Parts I and II. Artwork cover.
.25   8   20

No. 27, #90210-411, November 1974, "Ice Journey," Parts I and II. Artwork cover. .25   8   20

No. 28, #90210-501, January 1975, "The Mimicking Menace," Parts I and II. Artwork cover.
.25   8   20

No. 29, #90210-503, March 1975, "The Planet of No Return," Parts I and II. This issue is a reprint of Star Trek comic #1, but carries an artwork cover.
.25   8   20

No. 30, #90210-505, May 1975, "Death of a Star," Parts I and II. Artwork cover. .25   8   20

No. 31, #90210-507, July 1975, "The Final Truth," Parts I and II. Artwork cover. .25   5   15

No. 32, #90210-508, August 1975, "The Animal People," Parts I and II. Artwork cover.
.25   5   15

No. 33, #90210-509, September 1975, "The Choice," Parts I and II. This issue was reprinted in 1978 as a Whitman Dynabrite comic along with issue #41. Artwork cover. .25   5   15

No. 34, #90210-510, October 1975, "The Psychocrystals." This issue was reprinted in 1978 as a Whitman Dynabrite comic along with Star Trek comic #36. Artwork cover. .25   5   15

No. 35, #90210-511, November 1975, "The Peril of Planet Quick Change," Parts I and II. A reprint of Star Trek #4. Artwork cover. .25   5   15

No. 36, #90210-603, March 1976, "A Bomb in Time." This comic was reprinted in 1978 as a Whitman Dynabrite comic along with Star Trek comic #34. Artwork cover. .25   5   15

No. 37, #90210-605, May 1976, "The Ghost Planet," Parts I and II. This issue is a reprint of Star Trek comic #5. Artwork cover. .25   5   15

No. 38, #90210-607, July 1976, "One of Our Captains is Missing." Artwork cover. .25   5   15

No. 39, #90210-608, August 1976, "Prophet of Peace." Artwork cover. .25   5   15

No. 40, #90210-609, September 1976, "Furlough to Fury." Artwork cover. Alden McWilliams began his artwork panels for the series with this issue and they are considered some of the best in the Gold Key collection. .30   5   15

No. 41, #90210-611, November 1976, "The Evictors." This issue was reprinted in 1978 as a Whitman Dynabrite comic along with Star Trek comic #33. Artwork cover. .30   3   10

No. 42, #90210-701, January 1977, "World Against Time." Artwork cover. .30   3   10

No. 43, #90210-702, February 1977, "The World Beneath the Waves." Artwork cover.
.30   3   10

No. 44, #90210-705, May 1977, "Prince Traitor." Artwork cover. .30   3   10

| | *Issue* | *Fair* | *Mint* |

No. 45, #90210-707, July 1977, "The Voodoo Planet," Chapters I and II. This issue is a reprint of Star Trek comic #7. Artwork cover. .30 3 10

No. 46, #90210-708, August 1977, "Mr. Oracle." Artwork cover. .30 3 10

No. 47, #90210-709, September 1977, "This Tree Bears Bitter Fruit" by George Kashdan, A. McWilliams, and Doug Drexler. Artwork cover. .30 3 10

No. 48, #90210-710, October 1977, "Murder on the Enterprise" by Arnold Drake, A. McWilliams, and Doug Drexler. Artwork cover. .30 3 10

No. 49, #90210-711, November 1977, "A Warp in Space" by George Kashdan and A. McWilliams. Artwork cover. .30 3 10

No. 50, #90210-801, January 1978, "Planet of No Life" by Arnold Drake and A. McWilliams. Artwork cover. .30 3 10

No. 51, #90210-803, March 1978, "Destination Annihilation" by George Kashdan and A. McWilliams. Artwork cover. .35 3 10

No. 52, #90210-805, May 1978, "And A Child Shall Lead Them" by George Kashdan and A. McWilliams. Artwork cover. .35 3 10

No. 53, #90210-807, July 1978, "What Fools These Mortals Be" by George Kashdan and A. McWilliams. Artwork cover. .35 3 10

No. 54, #90210-808, August 1978, "Sport of Knaves" by George Kashdan and A. McWilliams. Artwork cover. .35 3 10

No. 55, #90210-809, September 1978, "A World Against Itself," by Arnold Drake and A. McWilliams. Artwork cover. .35 3 10

No. 56, #90210-810, October 1978, "No Time Like the Past" by George Kashdan and A. McWilliams. Artwork cover. .35 3 10

No. 57, #90210-811, November 1978, "Spore of the Devil" by Arnold Drake and A. McWilliams. Artwork cover. .35 3 10

No. 58, #90210-812, December 1978, "The Brain Damaged Planet" by George Kashdan and A. McWilliams. Artwork cover. .35 3 10

No. 59, #90210-901, January 1979, "To Err is Vulcan" by Arnold Drake and A. McWilliams. Artwork cover. .35 3 10

No. 60, #90210-902, February 1979, "The Empire Man" by John Warner and A. McWilliams. This issue featured the first of two cartoon-style Star Trek comics. Artwork cover. .35 3 10

No. 61, #90210-903, March 1979, "Operation Con Game" by George Kashdan and A. McWilliams. Second of two cartoon-style artwork covers. .35 3 10

Star Trek Annual: No. 1, 1985, D.C. Comics Incorporated. "All Those Years Ago" by Mike Barr, David Ross, Bob Smith, Carl Gafford, and Marv Wolfman. A special flashback adventure occurring before *STTMP*. 1.25 2 5

Star Trek Annual: No. 2, 1986, D.C. Comics Incorporated. "The Final Voyage" by Mike Barr, Dan Jurgens, Bob Smith, Agustin Mas, and Michele Wolfman. This special edition chronicles the last mission of the Enterprise before *STTMP*. 1.25 2 5

Star Trek Annual: No. 3, 1988, D.C. Comics Incorporated. "Retrospect" by Peter David, Curt Swan, Ricardo Villagran, Janice Chang, and Michele Wolfman. Special TV series edition. 1.25 2 5

Who's Who In Star Trek: #1, March 1987, D.C. Comics Incorporated, 48 pages. Special issues consisting of complete character bios of the Star Trek universe. Includes both TV Trek and the movies. 1.50 2 5

Who's Who In Star Trek: #2, April 1987, D.C. Comics Incorporated, 48 pages. By Allan Asherman, Steve Bove, Carl Gafford, and Michele Wolfman. 1.50 2 5

Star Trek Movie Series

Star Trek: Marvel Comics Group, 1980-82. A complete set of eighteen issues. Poor sales and stringent publishing limitations, which dictated that only material from the first two Star Trek motion pictures could be used, rather than characters, aliens, etc. from the TV series, helped to terminate this comic in less than two years. Collectors should note that Marvel covers may have issue numbers enclosed either in diamond boxes with a Spiderman logo or issue numbers enclosed within square boxes with vertical bar codes. Spiderman issues were sold directly from the publisher to a comic book dealership. Bar-coded comics were purchased by retail outlets from licensed, independent distributors. There is no distinction in collector prices between the two cover types.

No. 1, April 1980, Stan Lee Presents "Star Trek: The Motion Picture," Part I by Mary Wolfman, Dave Cockrum, Klaus Janson, and Marie Severin. The first of three comics devoted to *STTMP*. .40 3 6

No. 2, May 1980, "V'ger" by Mary Wolfman, Dave Cockrum, Klaus Janson, John Constanza, and Marie Severin. *STTMP* adaptation Part II. .40 2 5

	Issue	Fair	Mint

No. 3, June 1980, "Evolutions" by Mary Wolfman, Dave Cockrum, Klaus Janson, John Constanza, and Marie Severin. *STTMP* adaptation Part III.
.40 2 5

No. 4, July 1980, "The Haunting of Thallus" by Mary Wolfman, Dave Cockrum, Klaus Janson, Carl Gafford, and Jim Novak. .40 2 4

No. 5, August 1980, "The Haunting of the Enterprise" by Mike Barr, Dave Cockrum, Klaus Janson, John Constanza, and Carl Gafford. .40 2 4

No. 6, September 1980, "The Enterprise Murder Case," Mike Barr, Dave Cockrum, Klaus Janson, Rick Parker, and Carl Gafford. .50 2 5

No. 7, October 1980, "Tomorrow or Yesterday" by Tom DeFalco, Mike Nasser, Klaus Janson, and Ray Burzon. .50 2 5

No. 8, November 1980, "The Expansionist Syndrome" by Martin Pasko, Dave Cockrum, Ricardo Villamonte, Ray Burzon, and Carl Gafford. .50 2 5

No. 9, December 1980, "Experiment in Vengeance" by Martin Pasko, Dave Cockrum, Frank Springer, John Constanza, and Carl Gafford. .50 2 5

No. 10, January 1981, "Domain of the Dragon God" by Michael Fleiner, Leo Duranona, Klaus Janson, Rick Parker, and Carl Gafford. .50 2 5

No. 11, February 1981, "Like A Woman Scorned" by Martin Pasko, Joe Brozowski, Tom Parker, Carl Gafford, and Joe Rosen .50 2 5

No. 12, March 1981, "Eclipse of Reason" by Alan Bremmert, Martin Pasko, Luke McDonnell, Tom Palmer, Joe Rosen, and Carl Gafford.
.50 2 5

No. 13, April 1981, "All the Infinite Ways" by Martin Pasko, Joe Brozowski, Tom Palmer, Joe Rosen, and Carl Gafford. .50 2 5

No. 14, June 1981, "We Are Dying, Egypt, Dying" by Martin Pasko, Luke McDonnell, Gene Gray, John Morelli, and Carl Gafford. .50 2 5

No. 15, August 1981, "The Quality of Mercy" by Martin Pasko, Gil Kane, John Morelli, and Carl Gafford.
.50 2 5

No. 16, October 1981, "There's No Space Like Gnomes" by Martin Pasko, Luke McDonnell, Sal Trapani, Janice Chang, and Carl Gafford. .50 2 5

No. 17, December 1981, "The Long Night's Dawn" by Mike Barr, Ed Hannigan, Tom Palmer, and Carl Gafford. .50 2 5

No. 18, February 1982, "A Thousand Deaths" by D. M. Matteis, Joe Brozowski, Sal Trapani, and Shelly Leperman. .60 2 5

Star Trek: #0-939766-00-0, Marvel Comics Group, 1982. Special paperback edition by Stan Lee. Three Marvel Star Trek comic reprints. Includes Marvel #12, "Eclipse of Reason"; #11, "Like A Woman Scorned"; and #7, "Tomorrow or Yesterday."
2.50 5 10

Star Trek: D.C. Comics, 1984-88, D.C. Comics Incorporated. The complete set consists of 56 comics.

No. 1, February 1984, Chapter I, "The Wormhole Connection" by Mike Barr, Tom Sutton, Ricardo Villagran, John Constanza, and Michele Wolfman. This comic series continues Trek adventures after the events of *ST II*. .75 3 7

No. 2, March 1984, Chapter II, "The Only Good Klingon" by Mike Barr, Tom Sutton, Ricardo Villagran, John Constanza, and Michele Wolfman.
.75 2 5

No. 3, April 1984, Chapter II, "Errand of War" by Mike Barr, Tom Sutton, Ricardo Villagran, John Constanza, and Michele Wolfman. .75 2 5

No. 4, May 1984, "Deadly Allies" by Mike Barr, Tom Sutton, Ricardo Villagran, John Constanza, and Michele Wolfman. .75 2 5

No. 5, June 1984, "Mortal Gods" by Mike Barr, Tom Sutton, Sal Amendola, John Constanza, and Michele Wolfman. .75 2 5

No. 6, July 1984, "Who Is Enigma?" by Mike Barr, Tom Sutton, Ricardo Villagran, John Constanza, and Michele Wolfman. .75 2 5

No. 7, August 1984, "Pon Far" by Mike Barr, Ed Barreto, Ricardo Villagran, John Constanza, and Michele Wolfman. .75 2 4

No. 8, November 1984, "Blood Fever" by Mike Barr, Tom Sutton, Ricardo Villagran, John Constanza, and Michele Wolfman. .75 2 4

No. 9, December 1984, Chapter I, "...Promises To Keep" and "New Frontiers" by Mike Barr, Tom Sutton, Ricardo Villagran, John Constanza, and Michele Wolfman. .75 2 4

No. 10, January 1985, Chapter II, "Double Image" by Mike Barr, Tom Sutton, John Constanza, and Michele Wolfman. .75 2 4

No. 11, February 1985, Chapter III, "Deadly Reflection" by Mike Barr, Tom Sutton, Ricardo Villagran, John Constanza, and Michele Wolfman.
.75 2 4

No. 12, March 1985, Chapter IV, "The Tantalus Trap" by Mike Barr, Tom Sutton, Ricardo Villagran, Carrie Spiegel, and Michele Wolfman. .75 2 4

No. 13, April 1985, Chapter V, "Masquerade" by Mike Barr, Tom Sutton, Ricardo Villagran, Carrie Spiegel, and Michele Wolfman. .75 2 4

No. 14, May 1985, Chapter VI, "Behind Enemy Lines" by Mike Barr, Tom Sutton, Ricardo Villagran, John Constanza, and Michele Wolfman.
.75 2 4

Original cover artwork by Tom Sutton (on left) for Star Trek DC Comic #15, June 1985 (on right).

	Issue	Fair	Mint

No. 15, June 1985, Chapter VII, "The Beginning of the End" by Mike Barr, Tom Sutton, Ricardo Villagran, John Constanza, and Michele Wolfman.
.75 2 4

No. 16, July 1985, Chapter VIII, "Homecoming..." by Mike Barr, Tom Sutton, Ricardo Villagran, John Constanza, and Michele Wolfman. .75 2 4

No. 17, August 1985, "The D'Artagnan Three" by L. B. Kellogg, Tom Sutton, Ricardo Villagran, John Constanza, and Michele Wolfman. .75 2 4

No. 18, September 1985, "Rest & Recreation!" by Ricardo Villagran, Agustin Mas, and Michele Wolfman. .75 2 4

No. 19, October 1985, "Chekov's Choice," Walter Koenig, Dan Speigle, C. Speigle, Michele Wolfman, and Marv Wolfman. This issue was a special adventure set between the events of *STTMP* and *ST II*.
.75 2 4

No. 20, November 1985, "Giri" by Wenonah Woods, Tom Sutton, Ricardo Villagran, Agustin Mas, and Michele Wolfman. .75 2 4

No. 21, December 1985, "Dreamworld" by Bob Rozakis, Tom Sutton, Ricardo Villagran, A. Mas-Layi, and Michele Wolfman. .75 2 3

Issue	Fair	Mint

No. 22, January 1986, Part I, "Wolf on the Prowl" by Tony Isabella, Tom Sutton, Ricardo Villagran, A. Mas-Layi, and Michele Wolfman.   .75   2   3

No. 23, February 1986, Part II, "Wolf At the Door" by Tony Isabella, Tom Sutton, Ricardo Villagran, A. Mas-Layi, and Michele Wolfman.   .75   2   3

No. 24, March 1986, Part I, "Double Blind" by Diane Duane, Tom Sutton, Ricardo Villagran, Agustin Mas, and Michele Wolfman. Special issue written by Diane Duane (author of Star Trek novels).   .75   2   4

No. 25, April 1986, Part II, "Double Blind" by Diane Duane, Tom Sutton, Ricardo Villagran, A. Mas-Layi, and Michele Wolfman.   .75   2   4

No. 26, May 1986, "The Trouble with Transporters" by Bob Rozakis, Tom Sutton, Ricardo Villagran, Agustin Mas, and Michele Wolfman.   .75   2   3

No. 27, June 1986, "Around the Clock" by Robert Greenberger, Tom Sutton, Ricardo Villagran, Agustin Mas, and Michele Wolfman.   .75   2   3

No. 28, July 1986, "The Last Word" by Diane Duane, Gray Morrow, Agustin Mas, and Michele Wolfman. Special issue by Trek author Duane.   .75   2   4

No. 29, August 1986, "Last Stand" by Tony Isabella, Tom Sutton, Ricardo Villagran, Agustin Mas, and Michele Wolfman.   .75   2   3

No. 30, September 1986, "Uhura's Story" by Paul Kupperbers, Ricardo Villagran, Carmine Infantino, Agustin Mas, and Michele Wolfman.   .75   2   3

No. 31, October 1986, "Maggie's World" by Tony Isabella, Len Wein, Tom Sutton, and Ricardo Villagran.   .75   2   3

No. 32, November 1986, "Judgement Day" by Len Wein, Tom Sutton, Ricardo Villagran, Agustin Mas, and Michele Wolfman.   .75   2   3

No. 33, December 1986, "Vicious Circle" by Len Wein, Tom Sutton, and Ricardo Villagran. Special anniversary issue celebrating 29 years of Star Trek.   .75   2   5

No. 34, January 1987, "The Doomsday Bug," Chapter I, "Death Ship" by Len Wein, Tom Sutton, Ricardo Villagran, Agustin Mas, and Michele Wolfman.   .75   2   3

No. 35, February 1987, Chapter II, "Stand Off!" by Len Wein, Gray Morrow, Agustin Mas, and Michele Wolfman.   .75   2   3

No. 36, March 1987, Chapter III, "The Apocalypse Scenario" by Len Wein, Gray Morrow, Agustin Mas, and Michele Wolfman.   .75   2   3

No. 37, April 1987, "Choices" by Len Wein, Curt Swan, Pablo Marcos, and Shelly Eiber.   .75   2   3

No. 38, May 1987, "The Argon Affair" by Michael Fleisher, Adam Kubert, Ricardo Villagran, Agustin Mas, and Michele Wolfman.   .75   2   3

No. 39, June 1987, "When You Wish Upon A Star" by Len Wein, Tom Sutton, Ricardo Villagran, Agustin Mas, and Michele Wolfman.   .75   2   3

No. 40, July 1987, "Mudd's Magic" by Len Wein, Tom Sutton, Ricardo Villagran, Agustin Mas, and Michele Wolfman.   .75   2   3

No. 41, August 1987, "What Goes Around" by Tom Sutton, Ricardo Villagran, Agustin Mas, and Michele Wolfman.   .75   2   3

No. 42, September 1987, "The Corbomite Effect" by Mike Carlin, Tom Sutton, Ricardo Villagran, Agustin Mas, and Michele Wolfman.   .75   2   3

No. 43, October 1987, "Paradise Lost," Part I, "The Return of the Serpent" by Michael Carlin, Tom Sutton, Ricardo Villagran, Agustin Mas, and Michele Wolfman.   .75   2   3

No. 44, November 1987, Part II, "Past Perfect" by Michael Carlin, Tom Sutton, Ricardo Villagran, Helen Veslik, and Michele Wolfman.   .75   2   3

No. 45, December 1987, Part III, "Devil Down Below" by Michael Carlin, Tom Sutton, Ricardo Villagran, Helen Veslik, and Michele Wolfman.   .75   2   3

No. 46, January 1988, "Getaway" by Michael Carlin, Tom Sutton, Ricardo Villagran, Helen Veslik, and Michele Wolfman.   .75   2   3

No. 47, February 1988, "Idol Threats" by Michael Carlin, Tom Sutton, Ricardo Villagran, Helen Veslik, and Michele Wolfman.   .75   2   3

No. 48, March 1988, "The Stars In Secret Influence" by Peter David, Tom Sutton, Ricardo Villagran, Helen Veslik, and Michele Wolfman.   .75   2   3

No. 49, April 1988, "Aspiring To Be Angels" by Peter David, Tom Sutton, Ricardo Villagran, Helen Veslik, and Michele Wolfman.   1   2   3

No. 50, May 1988, "Marriage of Inconvenience" by Peter David, Tom Sutton, Ricardo Villagran, Helen Veslik, and Michele Wolfman. Special anniversary issue.   1.50   2   4

No. 51, June 1988, "Haunted Honeymoon" by Peter David, Tom Sutton, Ricardo Villagran, Tim Harkins, and Michele Wolfman.   1   2   3

No. 52, July 1988, "Hell In A Hand Basket" by Peter David, Tom Sutton, Ricardo Villagran, Tim Harkins, and Michele Wolfman.   1   2   3

No. 53, August 1988, "You're Dead Jim" by Peter David, Gordon Purcell, Ricardo Villagran, Tim Harkins, and Michele Wolfman.   1   2   3

	Issue	Fair	Mint

No. 54, September 1988, "Old Loyalties" by Peter David, Gordon Purcell, Ricardo Villagran, Tim Harkins, and Michele Wolfman.   **1   2   3**

No. 55, October 1988, "Finnegan's Wake" by Peter David, Tom Sutton, Ricardo Villagran, Tim Harkins, and Michele Wolfman.   **1   2   3**

No. 56, November 1988, "A Small Matter of Faith" by Martin Pasko, Gray Morrow, Tim Harkins, and Michele Wolfman. This issue was the first of a proposed Five Year Mission series, which never materialized.   **1   2   4**

Star Trek: D.C. Comics, 1989-present, D.C. Comics Incorporated. After the sudden disappearance of D.C.'s first line of Trek comics, this series made its debut a year later.

No. 1, October 1989, "The Return" by Peter David, James W. Fry, Arne Starr, Bob Pinaha, and Tom McCraw.   **1.50   1   2**

No. 2, November 1989, "The Sentence" by Peter David, James W. Fry, Arne Starr, Bob Pinaha, and Tom McCraw.   **1.50   1   2**

No. 3, December 1989, "Death Before Dishonor" by Peter David, James W. Fry, Arne Starr, Bob Pinaha, and Tom McCraw.   **1.50   1   2**

No. 4, January 1990, "Repercussions" by Peter David, James W. Fry, Arne Starr, Bob Pinaha, and Tom McCraw.   **1.50   1   2**

No. 5, February 1990, "Fast Friends" by Peter David, James W. Fry, Arne Starr, Bob Pinaha, and Tom McCraw.   **1.50   1   2**

No. 6, March 1990, "Cure All" by Peter David, James W. Fry, Arne Starr, Bob Pinaha, and Tom McCraw.   **1.50   1   2**

No. 7, April 1990, "Not Sweeney!" by Peter David, Marie Fry's Son, Arne Starr, Bob Pinaha, and Tom McCraw.   **1.50   1   2**

No. 8, May 1990, "Going, Going..." by Peter David, James W. Fry, Arne Starr, Bob Pinaha, and Tom McCraw.   **1.50   1   2**

No. 9, June 1990, "...Gone" by Peter David, James W. Fry, Arne Starr, Bob Pinaha, and Tom McCraw.   **1.50   1   2**

No. 10, July 1990, "The First Thing We Do..." by Peter David, James W. Fry, Arne Starr, Bob Pinaha, and Tom McCraw.   **1.50   1   2**

No. 11, August 1990, "Let's Kill All The Lawyers" by Peter David, James W. Fry, Arne Starr, Bob Pinaha, and Tom McCraw.   **1.50   1   2**

No. 12, September 1990, "Trial and Error" by Peter David, Gordon Purcell, Arne Starr, Bob Pinaha, and Tom McCraw.   **1.50   1   2**

No. 13, October 1990, "The Return of the Worthy," Part I; "Rude Awakening" by Bill Mumy, Peter David, Gordon Purcell, Arne Starr, Bob Pinaha, and Tom McCraw.   **1.50   1   2**

No. 14, December 1990, "The Return of the Worthy," Part II; "Great Expectations" by Peter David, Bill Mumy, Arne Starr, Bob Pinaha, and Tom McCraw.   **1.50   1   2**

No. 15, January 1991, "The Return of the Worthy," Part III; "Tomorrow Never Knows!" by Peter David, Bill Mumy, Gordon Purcell, Arne Starr, Bob Pinaha, and Tom McCraw.   **1.50   1   2**

No. 16, February 1991, "Worldsinger" by J. Strczynski, Gordon Purcell, Arne Starr, Bob Pinaha, and Tom McCraw.   **1.50   1   2**

No. 17, March 1991, "Partners?" by Howard Weinstein, Ken Hooper, Bob Dvorak, Bob Pinaha, and Tom McCraw.   **1.50   1   2**

No. 18, April 1991, "Partners?" Part II by Howard Weinstein, Ken Hooper, Bob Dvorak, Bob Pinaha, and Tom McCraw.   **1.50   1   2**

No. 19, May 1991, "Once A Hero" by Peter David, Gordon Purcell, Arne Starr, Bob Pinaha, and Tom McCraw.   **1.50   1   2**

Star Trek Annual: #1, D.C. Comics Incorporated, 1990. "So Near the Touch" by George Takei, Peter David, Gray Morrow, Bob Pinaha, and Tom McCraw. Special edition co-written by actor George Takei.   **2.95   2   4**

Star Trek III: The Search for Spock: D.C. Comics Incorporated, 1984. A D.C. movie special containing the comic adaptation of *ST III* by Mike W. Barr, Tom Sutton, Ricardo Villagran, John Constanza, and Michele Wolfman.   **1.50   2   5**

Star Trek IV: The Voyage Home: D.C. Comics Incorporated, 1987. A special comic adaptation of *ST IV* by Mike W. Barr, Tom Sutton, Ricardo Villagran, Agustin Mas, and Michele Wolfman.   **2   2   5**

Star Trek V: The Final Frontier: Movie Special No. 1, D.C. Comics Incorporated. Official comics adaptation of *ST V* by Peter David, James W. Fry, Arne Starr, Bob Pinaha, and Tom McCraw.   **2   2   5**

Star Trek: The Next Generation Series

Star Trek: The Next Generation: February 1988-July 1988, D.C. Comics Incorporated. Special six-issue mini-series release based on the TV show.

Original comic artwork, authographed by Denise Crosby (on left) and D.C Comics *Star Trek: The Next Generation* Comic #5.

	Issue	Fair	Mint

No. 1, February 1988, "...Where No Man Has Gone Before" by Michael Carlin, Pablo Marcos, Carlos Garzon, Arne Starr, Bob Pinaha, and Carl Gafford.
1.50   2   4

No. 2, March 1988, "Spirit In The Sky" by Michael Carlin, Pablo Marcos, Carlos Garzon, Arne Starr, Bob Pinaha, and Carl Gafford.
1   3   6

No. 3, April 1988, "Factor Q" by Michael Carlin, Pablo Marcos, Carlos Garzon, Arne Starr, Bob Pinaha, and Carl Gafford.
1   3   6

No. 4, May 1988, "Q's Day" by Michael Carlin, Pablo Marcos, Carlos Garzon, Arne Starr, Bob Pinaha, and Carl Gafford.
1   2   4

No. 5, June 1988, "Q Effects" by Michael Carlin, Pablo Marcos, Carlos Garzon, Arne Starr, Bob Pinaha, and Carl Gafford.
1   2   4

No. 6, July 1988, "Here Today" by Michael Carlin, Pablo Marcos, Carlos Garzon, Arne Starr, Bob Pinaha, and Carl Gafford.
1   2   4

Star Trek: The Next Generation: D.C. Comics Incorporated, 1989-present. Continuing adventures of the *STTNG* crew in comic form.

No. 1, October 1989, "Return to Raimon" by Michael Jan Friedman, Pablo Marcos, Bob Pinaha, and Julianna Ferriter.
1.50   3   5

	Issue	Fair	Mint

No. 2, November 1989, "Murder, Most Foul" by Michael Friedman, Pablo Marcos, Bob Pinaha, and Julianna Ferriter. **1.50 2 4**

No. 3, December 1989, "Derelict" by Michael Friedman, Pablo Marcos, Bob Pinaha, and Julianna Ferriter. **1.50 2 4**

No. 4, January 1990, "The Hero Factor" by Michael Friedman, Pablo Marcos, Bob Pinaha, and Julianna Ferriter. **1.50 2 3**

No. 5, February 1990, "Serafin's Survivors" by Michael Friedman, Pablo Marcos, Bob Pinaha, and Julianna Ferriter. **1.50 2 3**

No. 6, March 1990, "Shadows In The Garden" by Michael Jan Friedman, Pablo Marcos, Bob Pinaha, and Julianna Ferriter. **1.50 2 3**

No. 7, April 1990, "The Pilot" by Michael Friedman, Gordon Purcell, Pablo Marcos, Bob Pinaha, and Julianna Ferriter. **1.50 2 3**

No. 8, May 1990, "The Battle Within" by Michael Friedman, Gordon Purcell, Pablo Marcos, Bob Pinaha, and Julianna Ferriter. **1.50 2 3**

No. 9, June 1990, "The Pay Off" by Michael Friedman, Pablo Marcos, Bob Pinaha, and Julianna Ferriter. **1.50 2 3**

No. 10, July 1990, "The Noise of Justice" by Michael Friedman, Pablo Marcos, Bob Pinaha, and Julianna Feter. **1.50 2 3**

No. 11, August 1990, "The Impostor" by Michael Friedman, Pablo Marcos, Bob Pinaha, and Julianna Ferriter. **1.50 2 3**

No. 12, September 1990, "Whoever Fights Monsters" by Michael Friedman, Pablo Marcos, Bob Pinaha, and Julianna Ferriter. **1.50 1 2**

No. 13, October 1990, "The Hand of the Assassin" by Michael Friedman, Pablo Marcos, Bob Pinaha, and Julianna Ferriter. **1.50 1 2**

No. 14, December 1990, "Holiday On Ice" by Michael Friedman, Pablo Marcos, Bob Pinaha, and Julianna Ferriter. **1.50 1 2**

No. 15, January 1991, "Prisoners of the Ferengi" by Michael Friedman, Pablo Marcos, Bob Pinaha, and Julianna Ferriter. **1.50 1 2**

No. 16, February 1991, "I Have Heard The Mermaids Singing" by Michael Friedman, Bob Pinaha, and Julianna Ferriter. **1.50 1 2**

No. 17, March 1991, "The Weapon" by Michael Friedman, Ken Penders, Pablo Marcos, Bob Pinaha, and Julianna Ferriter. **1.50 1 2**

No. 18, April 1991, "Forbidden Fruit..." by Dave Stern, Mike O'Brien, Mike Manley, Robert Campanella, Bob Pinaha, and Julianna Ferriter. **1.50 1 2**

No. 19, May 1991, "The Lesson" by Michael Friedman, Peter Krause, Pablo Marcos, Bob Pinaha, and Julianna Ferriter. **1.50 1 2**

***Star Trek: The Next Generation* Annual:** #1, D.C. Comics Incorporated, 1990. "The Gift" by John de Lancie, Gordon Purcell, Pablo Marcos, Bob Pinaha, and Julianna Ferriter. Special comic edition co-written by actor John de Lancie (Q). **2.95 2 5**

Comic Books (Foreign And Translations) _____

Foreign collectible prices vary widely and assessing their value in this country is problematic. For this reason, only the issue price in pence (p), pounds sterling (£), or francs is given (if known).

Star Trek Annuals: United Kingdom, World International Publishing Ltd., (Manchester, England). British reprints of *Gold Key* comic stories in hardcover format. These volumes include full-color artwork, games, crosswords, and activities for children. Two Star Trek comics are featured per book. These are authorized editions released in association with Star Trek shows on BBC-TV.

(A) 1969, 96 pages. **60p 20 30**

(B) #0-7235-0083-5, 1970, 94 pages. **62p 20 25**

(C) #0-7235-0083-5, 1971, 96 pages. **65p 20 25**

(D) #0-7235-0109-2, 1972, 96 pages. **65p 15 20**

(E) #0-7235-0166-1, 1973, 76 pages. **65p 15 20**

(F) #0-7235-0213-7, 1974, 78 pages. **65p 10 15**

(G) #0-7235-0325-7, 1975, 77 pages. **70p 15 20**

(H) #0-7235-0361-3, 1976, 62 pages. **70p 10 15**

(I) #0-7235-0419-9, 1977, 77 pages. **75p 15 20**

(J) #0-7235-6506-6, 1978, 61 pages. **75p 15 20**

(K) #0-7235-6551-1, 1979, 62 pages. **— 15 20**

(L) #0-7235-6506-6, 1979, 64 pages. **— 15 20**

(M) #0-1-86030-350-0, Stafford Pemberton Publishers Ltd., 1983, 60 pages. **— 10 15**

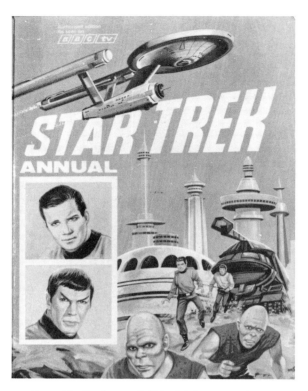

Star Trek Annual, World International
Publishing Ltd., United Kingdom.

Star Trek Television Picture Story Book,
P.B.S. Limited, United Kingdom, 1972

(N) #0-7235-6765-4, 1986, 61 pages.

—	10	15

Star Trek Comic Book: France, Mensuel #2,
Western Publishing Company, 1973. Paper comic.
5½" x 7½". —

Star Trek Comic Book: Mexico, Gold Key #13,
Western Publishing Company, 1973. Paper comic.
5½" x 7½". —

Star Trek Comic Book: Spain, Gold Key #13,
Western Publishing Company, 1973. Paper comic.
5½" x 7½". —

Star Trek Mighty Midget Comic: United
Kingdom, Polystyle Publishing, (London, England),
September 25, 1976, paperback, sixteen pages. Spe-
cial insert story featuring Star Trek.

—

Star Trek Mighty TV Comic: United Kingdom,
Polystyle Publishing (London, England), September
25, 1976, paperback, sixteen pages. Special edition
featuring Star Trek. —

Star Trek Television Picture Story Book: United
Kingdom, P.B.S. Limited, 1972, hardcover, 61 pages.

Special edition comic reprint of the Gold Key comic
"Sceptre of the Sun." Cover is red with artwork of
Kirk and Spock with Enterprise above.

65p	15	20

***Star Trek: The Next Generation* Comics:** United
Kingdom, Marvel Comics, 1990. British editions of
the American *STTNG* six-book mini-series. Includes
Mission Reports and *Starlog* episodes. Cover artwork
comes with a red canvas 1½" x 3" patch attached to
the front. Patch shows *STTNG* insignia on black circular background.

➤ #1, November 17, 1990, "...Where No Man Has
  Gone Before."
➤ #2, December 1, 1990, "Spirit In The Sky."
➤ #3, December 1990, "Factor Q."
➤ #4, December 29, 1990, "Q's Day."
➤ #5, January 19, 1991, "Q Effects."
➤ #6, January 1991, "Here Today."

Price for each.	55p	2	3

***Star Trek II: The Wrath of Khan* Annual:** United
Kingdom, #0-86030-350-0, Stafford Pemberton Publishers Ltd., 1983, hardcover, 60 pages. Special companion edition to the BBC annuals.

Comic Premiums

	Issue	Fair	Mint

Dan Curtis Give-A-Ways: Western Publishing Company, 1974. Comic premiums issued in a 3" x 6" format and containing nine assorted and abridged Gold Key Comic reprints, two of which were Star Trek comics. Comics came in sealed bags on newspaper stock.

(A) #2, "The Enterprise Mutiny," reprint of Gold Key Comic #14.   **Free   10   20**

(B) #6, "Dark Traveler," reprint of Gold Key Comic #13.   **Free   5   10**

Star Trek: The Motion Picture **Comic Strips:** MacDonald's, 1979. These were the Happy Meal premiums released in conjunction with the theater premiere of *STTMP*. Included paper comic strip cels packaged in silver or black plastic viewers. Five different strips were distributed. They came wrapped in a plastic bag with instructions.

Price for each comic strip.   **Free   4   6**

Dan Curtis Give-A-Ways, 1974.

Comic Specials

Star Trek TV Series

Elftrek: Part I, Dimension Graphics, July 1986. A black and white comic satire based on the characters of the TV series by Marcus Lusk, Mark Poe, Greg Legat, and Jayne Sisson.   **1.75   2   4**

Elftrek: Part II, Dimension Graphics, August 1986. Continuation of the TV Trek satire by Marcus Lusk, Mark Poe, Greg Legat, and Jayne Sisson.   **1.75   2   4**

Extremely Silly: No. 1, Volume 2, The Antarctic Press, 1986. "Chaos on the Enterprise" by Radio Bavaria, Ben Dunn, and Mike Cogliandro. The first of several black and white comic satires.   **1.25   2   4**

Enterprise Logs: #0-307-11185-7, Volume 1, Golden Press, 1976, tradepaper, 233 pages, Western Publishing Company. A compilation of Gold Key comic reprints containing Star Trek issues #1-8. Since a Boston warehouse fire destroyed half of the supply of this series intended for distribution in the United States, these are valuable collectibles. Volume 1 includes Kirk's psychofile, portrait of a starship, Scotty's diary, and Trek artist profile. **1.95   10   20**

Enterprise Logs: #0-307-11187-3, Volume 2, Golden Press, 1977, tradepaper, 224 pages, Western Publish-

	Issue	Fair	Mint

ing Company. A compilation of Star Trek issues #9-17.   **1.95   10   20**

Enterprise Logs: #0-307-11188-1, Volume 3, Golden Press, 1977, tradepaper, 224 pages, Western Publishing Company. A compilation of Star Trek issues #18-26. Also contains Spock's psychofile.   **1.95   10   20**

Enterprise Logs: #0-307-11189-X, Volume 4, Golden Press, 1977, tradepaper, 224 pages, Western Publishing Company. Includes Star Trek issues #27, 28, 30, 31, 32, 34, 36, and 38, despite the cover claim that the book contains comics #35 and 37 as well. Also includes Enterprise history.   **1.95   5   20**

Star Trek Dynabrite Comic: #11357, Whitman Publishing, 1978, 48 pages. Softbound reprint of Gold Key comics #41 ("The Evictors") and #33 ("The Choice") on heavy gauge bond. **.69   5   10**

Star Trek Dynabrite Comic: #11358, Whitman Publishing, 1978, 48 pages. Softbound reprint of Gold Key comics #36 ("A Bomb in Time") and #34 ("The Psychocrystals") on heavy gauge bond.   **.69   5   10**

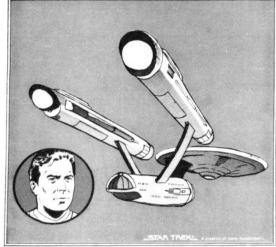

Voyages of the Enterprise, No. 1.

Voyages of the Enterprise, No. 6.

	Issue	Fair	Mint

Star Trek Movies

Stan Lee Presents *Star Trek: The Motion Picture*: Pocket Books, 1980, 250 pages. Special paperback comic adaptation of *STTMP* in conjunction with Marvel Comics Group.   **2.50   5   (10)**

Star Trek: #0-939766-00-0, Marvel Comics Group, paperback, 159 pages, by Stan Lee. Three stories told in comic format and which are reprints of original Marvel Comic #12 ("Eclipse of Reason"), #11 ("Like A Woman Scorned"), and #7 ("Tomorrow or Yesterday").   **2   5   10**

	Issue	Fair	Mint

Star Trek: The Mirror Universe: D.C. Comics, 1991, tradepaper. Reprints D.C. Comics #9-13 and includes the "Mirror, Mirror" sequel story which takes place fifteen years after the original TV episode and which features the Trek movie crew, including Saavik.   **19.95   20   22**

Star Trek: The Motion Picture: #02077, Marvel Super Special Magazine #15, Marvel Comics Group, December 1979, softbound, 130 pages. Official comic adaptation of *STTMP* which includes photos, art, and a new concordance glossary. The price tag printed on this comic is actually a printing error. The comic was meant to sell for $2.   **1.50   5   8**

Comic Syndications

B.C.: By Johnny Hart. A fearless ant from this syndicated comic reenacted a "Beam me up Scotty" routine upon finding himself hopelessly surrounded by hungry anteaters.

Bloom County: *The Washington Post*, by Berke Breathed. This comic has always been spotted with Star Trek references, the most memorable being when Breathed's penguin character Opus took a voyage to the premiere of *STTMP*.

Funky Winkerbean: By Tom Battiuk, 1979-81. In 1979, Battiuk's central cartoon character was an animated school computer which was obsessed with its devotion to Star Trek. In this long-running series, the computer not only waits in line to buy tickets for the *STTMP* premiere, but goes on to host a self-sponsored Trek convention in Toledo, Ohio.

John Darling: By Armstrong and Battiuk. In this comic strip, the artists satirized Leonard Nimoy's dislike at continually being identified with the legendary Mr. Spock.

Star Trek Comics: *Desert News*, by Michael C. Goodwin, 1977. Pen and ink overlays featuring ex-

Issue   Fair   Mint

terior shots of the Enterprise deep in space with humorous balloon captions. This serial produced by a local Salt Lake City newspaper ran from January to September 1977 and later became the collected tradepaper anthology entitled "My Stars!" published by Vulcan Books.

Star Trek Syndicated Comics: L.A. Mirror Time Syndicate, 1979. Series of newspaper comic strips released along with *STTMP* in December 1979. The first strips were drawn by California artist Thomas Warkentin, but Ron Harris and Sharman DiVono contributed as well. The strip ran in 600 newspapers across the country.

Voyages of the Enterprise: Nostalgia World, Connecticut. Newspaper stock reprints of the *L.A. Mirror*

Issue   Fair   Mint

Time syndicated Star Trek comic originally printed in daily newspaper editions. These compilations come in seven booklets with stapled covers. 8¼" x 10¾".

➤ #1, comics by Thomas Warkentin, blue cover with Kirk and Enterprise.

➤ #2, comics by Thomas Warkentin, green cover with Kirk, Spock, and Enterprise.

➤ #3, comics by Thomas Warkentin, purple cover.

➤ #4, comics by Thomas Warkentin.

➤ #5, comics by Thomas Warkentin.

➤ #6, comics by Ron Harris and Sharman DiVono, black cover.

➤ #7, comics by Ron Harris and Sharman DiVono.

Price for each booklet.   3   5   10

Communicator Kits And Props

Star Trek Communications Receiver: Starland, distributor, 1990. TV prop, elongated ear plug device as worn by Lt. Uhura on the TV series. Solid piece cast.   **24.95   25   30**

Star Trek Communicator Props (Life-sized):

(A) TV props from the 1970s. Numerous flip-top epoxy resin, metal, and polyurethane cast types of devices with varying degrees of detail and operability.

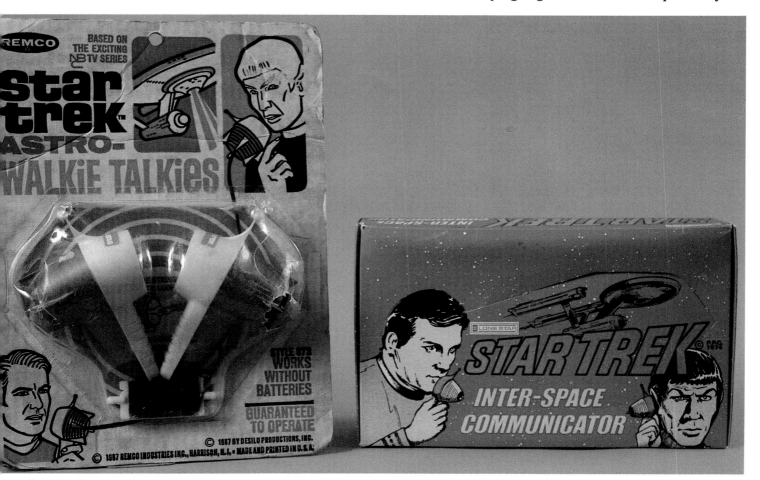

Star Trek Astro Walkie Talkies, Remco, 1967; and Star Trek Inter-Space Communicator, Lone Star, 1974.

	Issue	Fair	Mint

Based on the classic series, these units come assembled, sometimes with optional kits for electronic sound effects. Prices vary with functions.

➤ Assembled, non-working replicas.

	50	60	70

➤ With optional electronic kits. **60 70 80**

➤ Non-assembled, non-functional. **40 55 55**

(B) TV props of 1980s vintage, new improved model props built of polyurethane plastic with metal grids and flick-your-wrist action (flip your wrist and the lid swings up). Three styles:

➤ 1986, non-functional. **65 65 75**

➤ 1989, functional flashing lights only. LED's blink. Back unscrews to replace the required battery.

	100	100	110

➤ 1989, functional flashing lights with chirrup.

	125	125	130

Star Trek Communicator Prop (Miniature): #2727, Lincoln Enterprises, 1990. "Mini Classic Communicator," detailed miniature TV prop replica of the classic hand-held communicator. Top grid screen opens to show the controls below. Size 7/16" x 15/16".

	14.95	15	16

STTMP — **Belly Warmer:** #P2495, Richard Coyle, designer, Lincoln Enterprises, 1980. Movie vintage prop, close-range belt communications device as worn on the formal uniforms. Solid cast polyurethane cast

with snap-post fasteners. Size is approximately 2" x 4". **5.95 10 20**

STTMP — **Wrist Communicator:** #H-2493, Richard Coyle designer, Lincoln Enterprises, 1980. Hand-painted movie prop communicator that straps to the wrist with metal band. **30 40 65**

ST III — **Communicator:** #H-2492, Richard Coyle, designer, Lincoln Enterprises, 1980. Non-working movie prop device used in the third movie (return to classic-style communicator device) in polyurethane plastic with metal grill and trimmings.

	55	60	70

ST III / ST V — **Communicator:** New Eye, distributor, 1990. Non-functional movie version prop similar to original classic hand-held device with unique acid-etched flip grid. **75 75 80**

ST V — **Communications Receiver:** Winkie Electronic Jewelry, 1984. "Winkie Computer Friend Chip." Looks like the earplug prop used by Uhura in the movie. **— 10 12**

STTNG — **Communicator Insignia Pins:**
(A) 1989, *STTNG* pin prop. Non-functional. All of these replicas which are non-working pin-back accessories are listed in the **Pins** section.
(B) 1990, *STTNG* working prop. Working unit communications device is an encircled insignia. Unit produces a "dinging" sound when center is pressed.

	49.95	45	55

Communicator Toys

Star Trek Astro Walkie-Talkies: #872, Remco Industries, 1967. Oval, hand-held microphone set. 2" x 4" hand mikes have blue hand grips and a single, fixed antenna. Units interconnect with each other using string and communications occur through vibration. Paper decals read "Star Trek" and show the classic insignia designs. Waxboard blister-packed on 8¼" x 11" backing with blue outline drawings of the Enterprise, Kirk, and Spock playing with the toys. Two per set. **1 30 50**

Star Trek Communicators: #51214, Mego Corp, 1974. Working walkie-talkies. The classic communicator devices are replicated by this seven-transistor toy in blue and black plastic. Send and receive messages up to one-quarter mile. Twin warp sound, telescoping antenna. Two-tone plastic with silver and black insignia design. Each unit uses 9-volt battery and includes a belt clip. Boxed with artwork Spock holding toy, Kirk in background. Two per set.

	19	100	135

Star Trek Communications Command Console: Mego Corp, 1976. Working Base Control Station for use with the above communicator walkie-talkies. Blue plastic table station sends and receives signals. Five sound effects and flashing lights, with telescoping antenna. Uses one 9-volt battery. 13½" x 8" box with close-up artwork of Spock at station and smaller Kirk using communicator. **17.50 100 140**

Star Trek Inter-Space Communicators: #1340, Lone Star, England, 1974. Repackaging of the above 1967 Remco string-operated toys. Blue and gold plastic hand-held mikes interconnect by string. Blue flip-top box has cartoon of Kirk and Spock with toy, Enterprise above. Two per set. **— 20 35**

STTMP **Belt Communicator (Belly-Warmer):** #7904, South Bend, 1979. Non-working movie version belt communicator toy includes 32" clear vinyl belt. Buckle resembles the movie gear and has thermal sensor (cold-hot), I.D. card, and plastic insignia badge in

	Issue	*Fair*	*Mint*

packaging. Box is 9¼" x 3" with illustration of toy. Pop-up display back has photo of boy and girl in blue *STTMP* uniforms wearing the toy.

(A) Retail sales. **12 25 30**

(B) Heroes World, 1980. Marvel Comic Special Offer advertised in Star Trek Marvel Comic Issue #2. Coupon offer. **6.99 25 30**

STTMP Wrist Communicator: #91238, Mego Corp, 1980. Working walkie-talkie. Movie era wrist communicator toy that straps on and is powered by two 9-volt batteries carried in pack attached to the wrist. Flexible antenna sends and receives voices up to 20' indoors and 50' outdoors. 6½" x 3½" x 4¾" box illustrates boy with toy. Pop-up display header shows front view artwork of movie Enterprise.

12 150 200

ST V Communicator Premiums: Proctor & Gamble, manufactured by P. J. McNerney & Assoc., Inc., 1989. Working walkie-talkies. Dark gray molded plastic with flip-up clear lid with gold decal striping. Red- and white-painted buttons underneath. 13½" telescoping antenna. Uses two 9-volt batteries. Units measure 2¾" x 4¼". Premium packaged in plain heavy cardboard mailing box. Two per set.

(A) 1989 premium offer. Advertised in glossy Sunday newspaper supplement. Full-page flyer shows movie title logo and photos of boy and girl holding the toys. Product and mail-in coupons included (expired 8/21/89). Required two UPC symbols from Crest (4.6 oz. or larger) plus payment. **14.99 45 55**

(B) 1990 mail-order offer, Paramount Special Effects. **— 45 55**

Computer Prints

Creative Computing: Morristown, New Jersey, 1976. Black and white dot matrix prints show oversized photo reproduction busts of TV series characters: Kirk, Spock, McCoy, Scotty, Sulu, and Uhura, plus the Enterprise. Price for each. **1 3 4**

Lincoln Enterprises: #P2165, 1979. Five-color dot matrix photo reproduction of starboard profile of TV ship over reddish nebula effect. Detailed computer print measures 12" x 38" and is designed as a wall mural. **4 3 6**

Computer Software

Listings below are by software package titles.

EGA Trek: #197, Nels Anderson, 1989. Updated release of *ST V*. Fight Klingons and Romulans as Captain of the Enterprise. You can hail starbases, reallocate energy, raise or lower shields, mine for dilithium, use sensors, fire weapons, and repair damage. Full graphics software. IBM PC and compatibles. **10 10 12**

ENTREP, Starship Enterprise on Printer: PC-SIG Disk #44, 1985. Games #6. Diskette with twenty Basic games including a printer program for creating the starship and STAR TREK, an adventure game in 45K Version. **6 7 9**

Galaxy Trek: #197, Larry Jordon, 1982. *ST II* vintage software. You command the U.S.S. Columbia against your enemies — the Megatons. Character only display. No graphics. Sound effects are extensive with warp drive, torpedoes, phasers, and incoming phaser fire. Runs on PC compatibles. **10 10 12**

Galaxy Trek/EGA Trek: Disk #740, Book Warehouse, 1990. Low cost public domain software containing two Star Trek computer games on one disk. Made for IBM/PC/XT/AT compatibles. 5¼" floppy disc. **3 3 5**

MEGATREK: PC-SIG Disk #299, 1985. Mixture. Diskette with 22 simple utilities and assembler programs including Megatrek fame and Nutrek, a screen-oriented program. **6 7 9**

MS-Trek: #1221, Paul Alderdice, 1984. Destroy all enemy ships before they destroy you. Unusual game allows you to beam down and explore planets. Also has useful tracking devices, shuttlecraft landings, warp drive, impulse drive, scanners, and weapons. Monochrome characters only. **10 10 12**

NEWTREK: PC-SIG Disk #24, 1985. Another version of STARTREK. Games #3. Nine Basic games including Tic-Tac-Toe, pseudo PACMAN, moon survival, and a Trek adventure. **6 7 9**

PHASER: PC-SIG Disk #53, 1985. Sixteen sound effects programs, two of which are phasers. **6 7 9**

SPACEGAMES: #C10205, Repunch Software, 1990. Three space games: Creeps and Rebel Bomber, plus Trek 64 (captain the Enterprise and save the Federation from the Klingons). Commodore 64. **5 5 8**

Space Trek: #A10280, Keypunch Software, 1987. Disk with four games — Galactic Empire, Starway

153

Star Trek 3.5 software, 1981, for Atari.

	Issue	Fair	Mint

Trader, Space Rebels, and Space Trek (a Trek game battling Klingons). Cover art is Star Trek showing blue Earth with front view of TV Enterprise firing twin phasers. Apple II, II+, IIe, and IIc.

Note: The 1985 packaging for IBM compatibles included the games Invaders, Alien and Lunar Landing, plus Space Trek, and did not sport an Enterprise cover.

	6.99	7	9

SPACWR / "Space War": 1973 Digital Equipment Corp. Paperback manual entitled *101 Basic Computer Games* by David H. Ahl. Complete instructions for Basic-Plus. SPACWR program was the first version of the Super Star Trek game in Basic.

	6	8	10

STAR FLIGHT: Electronic Arts, 1990. General sci-fi cover art with Trek crossover theme: "Has Boldly Gone Where No Game Has Gone Before." Choose

	Issue	Fair	Mint

player parts of Captain, Science Officer, Communications Officer, Navigator, Medical Officer, or Chief Engineer to battle aliens. IBM compatibles.

	23.99	15	21

Starship Commander: UPTIME Vol. 1, No. 6, Viking Technologies, 1986. A disk monthly. IBM PC compatibles. Software containing eight educational and "For fun" programs including this Trek program. Disk is packaged in blue vinyl slipcase with *STTMP* Enterprise on the cover, 8½" x 11".

	14.95	15	18

Star Trek: #0-87626-166-7, Winthrop Publishers, 1979. Paperback manual titled *Computer Games for Business, Schools and Homes* by J. Victor Nahigian and William S. Hodges. Instructions for Basic games. "Star Trek" game on pages 123-127 involves battle sequence with Klingons, warp drive, phasers, and diminishing life support.

	8	9	12

Star Trek 3.5: Lance Micklus, 1981. Adventure International (Division of Scott Adams, Inc.). 35K Star Trek theme game for use as an Atari conversion.

	—	10	15

Star Trek Evolution: Share Data, Inc., 1986. Disk with no manual required. Klingons attack a Federation home base and must be eliminated before they overrun the known universe. Three levels of play — Beginner's ST, ST Junior, and ST Senior. Plastic pocket package. For Commodore 64 and 128 computers.

	6.50	7	9

Star Trek: First Contact:

(A) 1989. Captain the Enterprise to Gothica with a two-fold mission: deliver a group of diplomats and avoid Klingons as you make first contact with a new civilization. Interactive graphics, Captain's Log, databank files, and sound effects. Bookcase portfolio cover shows rear view of TV Enterprise in warp approaching planet. Available in Apple version and for IBM and compatibles.

	39.95	30	42

(B) Simon & Schuster and Science Fiction Book Club. Interactive fiction software including graphics display of locations, objects and aliens, expandable Captain's Log, historical files to Enterprise, the databanks, and sound effects. Packaged in hardbound slipcover.

➤ #011742, IBM software.
➤ #012351, Apple software.

Price for each.	39.95	40	45

Star Trek: The Kobayashi Alternative: Simon & Schuster Software, Micromosaics Products, Inc., 1986. Disk detailing routine mission in the Trianguli sector when Lt. Sulu's ship vanishes. Enterprise must find him and neutralize the Menace. Bookcover case is

Simon & Schuster bookcased software: First Contact (1989), The Kobayashi Alternative (1986), and The Promethean Prophecy (1986).

	Issue	*Fair*	*Mint*

32-page spiral bound with drawings, mission briefings, bios, and ship stations.

➤ #0-671-55771-8, IBM PC, PC/XT, PC AT, and PC Jr.

➤ #0-671-57770-X, Apple II+, IIe and IIc.

➤ #0-671-557772-6, Commodore computers.

| Price for each. | **39.95** | **30** | **42** |

Star Trek: The Promethean Prophecy: Simon & Schuster Software, 1986. Story disk detailing the badly-damaged Enterprise and Kirk as he unravels the enigmatic Promethean culture to save the crew. One of the "lost adventures of the Starship Enterprise." Bookcover case shows fanciful planetscape and crew.

(A) #0-13-842782-8, IBM PC, PC/XT, PC AT, and PC Jr.	**39.95**	**35**	**42**
(B) #0-13-842766-6, Apple II+, IIe, and IIc.	**39.95**	**35**	**42**
(C) #0-13-842774-7, Commodore 64 and 128.	**32.95**	**30**	**35**

Star Trek Phaser Strike: #4973, Milton Bradley, 1979. Interchangeable cartridge for the Microvision game. You battle attacking Klingon Warships. Graphics are cube-shaped ships of varying sizes and speeds, adjustable firing locations, and speed controls. Ending score appears on screen. Includes an instruction booklet. Ages 8 to adult. Boxed 4" x 9" with

	Issue	*Fair*	*Mint*

STTMP Star Trek title logo in white on black, magenta, and yellow cardstock box.

	19	**15**	**25**

Star Trek: The Rebel Universe: Simon & Schuster, 1989. A Klingon-aided mutiny has broken out on Federation ships. Kirk and crew must halt the rebellion. Unique full-color graphics, navigation screens, and simulated battles. Warp and impulse power, weapons, and transporter beams with sound effects. Bookcase portfolio cover shows artwork collage of Spock, Kirk, McCoy, and crew over front view of TV Enterprise on gridwork.

Note: Magazine advertisements for this product's release included a silver inflatable Enterprise mobile as a premium with the purchase of this software (see **Mobiles**).

(A) Atari ST.	**39.95**	**35**	**40**
(B) IBM.	**49.95**	**45**	**50**
(C) Commodore 64.	**33.95**	**35**	**40**
(D) Tandy Compaq.	**33.95**	**35**	**40**

Star Trek: The Rebel Universe: Simon & Schuster and Science Fiction Book Club. Interactive fiction software including full-color graphic screens which display navigation screens and simulated battles. Also contains engines with warp speeds and impulse power, photo torpedoes and phaser banks, transporter beams, and sound effects. Packaged in hardbound slipcover.

	Issue	Fair	Mint
(A) #010124, IBM software.	49.95	50	55
(B) #011395, Atari software.	39.95	40	45

Star Trek Strategic Operations Simulator: Sega Enterprises, 1983. Official arcade version video game cartridge for home computers and video consoles. One player or two, strategies. Three-way viewing screen; functions include thrust, warp drive, photo torpedoes, phaser banks, and energy fields with exclusive combat control overlay, joy-stick control or keyboard control. Box has cartoon of the movie Klingons at the helm sighting in on the starship Enterprise.

Note: A Proctor & Gamble store display coupon contained rules for obtaining this software package at the special price of $9.95 plus Proofs of Purchase from any three: Crisco (3-pound can), Crisco Oil (48-ounce bottle), Duncan Hines Cake Mix or Frosting, or Pringles Potato Chips. Coupon, printed on 3" x 5" paper on tear-off store pads, expired 9/30/84.

➤ Atari 2600
➤ Atari 5200
➤ Coleco Gemini
➤ Coleco Vision Expansion Module
➤ Commodore 64 or Vic-20
➤ Sears Tele-Games 400/800/1200

Price for each.	29.99	25	35

STARTREK: PC-SIG Disk #178, 1985. Seven Basic programs including color chess, space travel, and super color version of Trek.

		6	7	9

STARTREK, Another Game: PC-SIG Disk #71, 1985. Eight Basic programs including memory game, speller, and this Trek adventure game.

		6	7	9

STARTREK, The Game of: PC-SIG Disk #2, 1985. Spoolers. Basic program with mostly printer, file, and graphics utilities, a simply Trek game.

		6	7	9

STARTREK, Questions: PC-SIG Disk #329, 1985. Questions to play Trek trivia game.

		6	7	9

STARTREK, Starship Enterprise: PC-SIG Disk #13, 1985. Three Basic programs. Trek action game to rid the galaxy of Klingon menace by destroying their invasion force. You have 40 solar years to complete the mission. Instruction screen and sound effects for space battle.

		6	7	9

STARTREK2: PC-SIG Disk #17, 1985. Ten Basic games on disk including a Trek adventure with overlay module.

		6	7	9

Star Trek The Motion Picture: General Consumer Electronic, VEXTREX Arcade System Cartridge, 1982. For one to two players, features black hole, enemy

	Issue	Fair	Mint

Klingon mothership, enemy Romulans, and Federation refueling space station. Abilities for laser weapons and shields, includes 7" x 8½" plastic screen overlay. Boxed.

(A) Cartridge with screen overlay.

		29	25	35

(B) #HO-4110, screen overlay only.

		2	1	2

Star Trek V The Final Frontier: Midescape, Level Systems, Inc., 1989. Sybok takes control of the Enterprise. You, as Kirk, must stop him. Bookcase box illustrates front view of Enterprise, busts of Kirk and Spock, and Klingon Klaa with movie title logo. For IBM PC, XT, AT, and PS/2.

		39	30	35

Star Trek Trivia: PC-SIG Disk #1278, Scott Miller, 1990. Volume 1 in a series of ten trivia games (only the first is on Shareware). Set of 100 questions about Trek TV includes episode titles, alien races, dialogue, and character information with multiple choice answers. If you answer correctly, game rewards with extra information and one bonus point for every ten right answers. Wrong answers lose credits.

		4	4	5

Note: For a description of the other Star Trek Trivia volumes see the listing below titled Trek Trivia, Apogee Software Productions.

SUPER STAR TREK: #0-89480-052-3, Workman Publishing Co., 1978. Editor David H. Ahl. Tradepaper sequel to *101 Computer Games*. Titled *Basic Computer Games — Micro-computer Edition*. Super Star Trek instructions for programming on pages 157-163. Microsoft 8K Basic Version 3.0 and higher. This Trek gaming program appeared in the magazine *Creative Computing*.

	7.95	8	10

SUPERTREK: PC-SIG Disk #457, 1985. Full sound effects game plus vocal module that gives voice instructions from Spock, Sulu, etc. Plays the *Star Trek* theme song and provides phaser and photon effects, as well as Klingon territory alarm siren.

		6	7	9

SUPERTREK, Another Version for Trekkies: PC-SIG Disk #16, 1985. Six Basic games including chess, craps, communications, and undated version of the Trek game on Disk #13.

		6	7	9

3-D Star Trek: Norton Software, 1985. Program designed for the TI-99/4A computer. Here is an undated version of the classic space war game using TI graphics to add a new twist to the Trek adventure:

Issue Fair Mint

(A) #10975, cassette format. TI Basic/Ext. Basic.

| | 9.95 | 10 | 15 |

(B) Disk #14994. TI Extended Basic with expansion.

| | 9.95 | 8 | 10 |

TI-TREK: Texas Instruments, 1980. Commercial package designed for the TI 99/4A computer. Game of skill that used the speech capabilities of the TI-99 console. You are responsible for the safety of a galaxy and have the ability to fire phasers and torpedoes to destroy the enemy. A warp control is provided. Comes as a module hook-up and plugs into the gaming console. Part number PHD 5002.

| | 15 | 10 | 20 |

Transinium Challenge: Transfiction Systems, 1989. Digitized, fully animated and never-seen-before aliens, icons, and hotspots in this *STTNG* game. Terrorists have taken over the Aguila Star System. You are Wil Riker in command. For IBM, Tandy, and PC compatibles. Boxed. **49.95 50 55**

Trek Net: Starfleet Fan Club, 1990. Special computer bulletin board services (BBS) established nationwide allowing users to communicate about Star Trek, Starfleet, and other science fiction organizations. Use depends on ownership of a computer and a modem. Free/shareware BBS software is also available. **N/A N/A N/A**

Trek: #0-89303-349-9, Softsync, Brady Communications Co. Tradepaper book collection of short programs in Basic by John W. Stephenson entitled *Brain Games for Kids and Adults Using the Com-*

Issue Fair Mint

modore 64. "Trek" is a geometry game where the goal is to coordinate your starship back home. Pages 132-137. **9 10 12**

TREK (Yet Another Star Trek Game): PC-SIG Disk #27, 1985. Four Basic games including Trek that uses a color graphics monitor. Has four utility programs and three printer spools.

| | 6 | 7 | 9 |

TREKRUN: PC-SIG Disk #197, 1985. Utilities. Exclusive Trek games that work on color graphics or mono screens. Includes complicated games MS-TREK and Galaxy Trek using official SEC advice and command codes. **6 7 9**

Trek Trivia: Apogee Software Productions, 1990. Ten volumes of Trek questions including bonus points of extra information for correct answers. (First volume is on Shareware. See Star Trek Trivia PC SIG Disk #1278). Apogee programs use Turbo Pascal version 3.0 or version 5.0. Volumes 1 through 10.

| | 4 | 4 | 5 |

Note: Volume 1 of this ten-part series was also offered through public domain Shareware. See listing above titled Star Trek Trivia, PC-SIG.

Trivial Trauma: PC-SIG, 1988. Disk requiring computer graphics CGA or Hercules. Programs include TREK and TREKPIK trivia, plus others. **19.95 19 22**

Contests

Star Trek fans have enjoyed contests and competitions since the 1960s when *Star Trek* and its cast were favorite topics of the popular movie star and teen star magazines. Contestants were asked only token questions with winners being randomly selected by drawings to earn very nominal gifts. Sometimes the mail-in readership and viewer responses served the higher purpose of providing feedback to the program's producers and sponsors, but usually all the trivial facts and humorous exploits were designed simply as interactive fun. In recent years, local television networks and radio stations have participated in a variety of Trek-A-Thons (mail-in and phone-in contests) offering local contestants a shot at free movie passes to Star Trek theater premieres and other special Paramount promotional events. There has also been an upsurge in sponsorship from the food industry where manufacturers are involved in promotional packagings with Star Trek themes that can include

box-panel and insert flyer contests. Some of these have tantalized collectors with the chance to win limited edition prizes. From picking up the phone and "talking with the crew" and queries through polls and ballots to winning an all-expenses-paid trip to vacation cities, today's Star Trek contests are more inventive and challenging than ever.

Chronological Listing Of Contests

1967 Bill Shatner Contest

"Star Trek's Bill Shatner asks for your help! Suggest five to ten songs you'd like to hear Bill sing at his first recording session! If you match five, you win."

Entries: *T.V. Star Parade Magazine,* expired October 30, 1967.

Spread: One full page with coupon.

Judging: Ideal Publishing Corp. Editorial Staff

Early teen magazine contest from _FAVE_ magazine, 1968.

Prize: First pressing of Bill's Gold Star record album. Winner to be announced in February 1968.

Note: This album under the Gold Star Label was never released.

1967 Star Trek's Design-A-Costume Contest

"Design a costume for any one of the _Star Trek_ stars or even something you'd like to see a guest star wear. Use the weirdest designs you can think of! Note exactly what fabric is being used and the colors."

Entries: _T.V. Star Parade Magazine_, expired December 30, 1967.

Spread: Two full pages with coupon, rules, and photo layout of some of _ST_'s provocative female attire.

Judging: Bill Theiss (_ST_ Costume Designer) and Ideal Publishing Corp. Editorial Staff.

Prizes: A shirt like those worn by Shatner, Nimoy, Kelley, Doohan, or Takei, or a Yeoman's uniform.

1968 Is There Anything Star Trek Has That You Would Like To Have?"

This coupon/suggestion contest (quoted in the introduction to this book) was really a query originated by

Bill Theiss and Gene Roddenberry. It stands as the historical forebear to the Roddenberry's Star Trek / Lincoln Enterprises catalogue sales.

Spread: One-third page column with photo of the bridge crew.

Judging: Bill Theiss and Gene Roddenberry.

1968 Mr. Spock's Computer Contest!

"Leonard Nimoy and Mr. Spock now have so many dedicated fans it's getting very hard to keep track of them all! But Leonard has found a way: Mr. Spock's Computer Contest!" Fans were to fill in the coupon computer card facsimile provided and send in a personal photograph. "Your personal information card will be added to the Star Trek Computer's Memory Tapes — which never forget anything! Then whenever Mr. Spock wants to know about you, he asks the Computer and, ZING! There you are!"

Entries: _FAVE_ magazine, running one month.

Spread: One full page with computer card coupon and photo of Spock at the computer console.

Judging: By random drawing of 50 cards.

Prizes: First — three new portable record players, a personal message from Leonard Nimoy, and an autographed copy of the album "Mr. Spock's Music From Outer Space." Next 47 cards drawn win autographed copy of the new album only.

Note: Winners were announced in a full-page spread along with their photos and pictures of the _ST_ cast.

1968 Star Shadow Contest

"Dick Clark meets Mr. Spock!" was the title of this contest which included the very original poetry:

Spock's mood has changed, it appears
The Vulcan hasn't laughed so in years!
Spock's enjoying the show
But he wants to know
If you'll guess who is wearing his ears!"

Entries: _Flip_ magazine, expired July 30, 1968.

Spread: One full page with photo of Leonard Nimoy, Dick Clark as host, and an unnamed mystery guest whose only recognizable features are a large pair of pointed ears.

Judging: _Flip_ Editorial Staff.

Prizes: Ten in total, none described.

Answer: Paul Revere of Paul Revere and the Raiders.

1968 Double Giveaway Contest

Contest to win Leonard Nimoy's newest hit album by

guessing the number of songs Leonard sings on "The Way I Feel" or by guessing the color of Barbra Streisand's "Funny Girl" movie blouse.

Entries: *Movie Stars* magazine, expired November 30, 1968.

Spread: One full page. Photos of both stars and includes a double coupon with three possible correct answers each.

Judging: *Movie Stars* Editorial Staff.

Prizes: Copy of Nimoy's album or a duplicate blouse.

1968 Pick Your Choice — Spock vs Barnabas!

A character popularity contest pitting ears against fangs. Spock versus Barnabas Collins, the vampire from ABC's TV hit *Dark Shadows*. Coupon choices read "Mr. Spock is the only one for me! How could anyone like a vampire?" or "Barnabas is the greatest. How could anyone like a Vulcan?"

Entries: *Movie Life* magazine, expired December 31, 1968.

Spread: One full page with photos of each of the characters and a coupon.

Judging: Editorial Staff, with a drawing from each category.

Prize: Autographed photo.

1969 Pick Your Choice — Rematch Spock vs Barnabas

This contest was too close to count! Barnabas won the first match by a very narrow margin. This rematch featured the same photos and coupon as listed above. Judging and prizes remained the same, with the addition of a magazine feature article to appear on the grand character winner.

1969 Outasite Space Joke Contest

Star Trek *FAVE* space jokes. "Mr. Chekov got together with this boss, Mr. Spock, and let us Outasiters in on the laffs goin' round in Outaspace! Know any space jokes? Send in the coupon. The jokes that break up the Enterprise crew most will win a groovy prize!"

Entries: *FAVE* magazine, expired March 30, 1969.

Spread: Two pages, including sample jokes, a photo of Chekov and Spock, and an album list of space top-tens, such as "Spock! In The Name of Love!"

Judging: *FAVE* Editorial Staff.

Prize: Five dollars cash.

Note: Okay, all you 60s Trekkers, decode for the newcomers all the hip slang in this contest!

Movie Life's **Pick Your Choice contest, pitting Vulcan against vampire, 1968.**

1973 Star Trek Essay Contest

Student's achievement essay contest with Trek theme.

Entries: *Scholastic Voice* magazine, February 5, 1973. Vol. 54, #2.

Spread: Magazine article page.

Prizes: Meritorious award. Winners announced April 30, Issue #12.

1978 Starlog Records Ballot

Help Starlog Records determine which previously unrecorded movie and TV soundtrack scores you would like to see released as records in the future. Check five favorite movie scores and three favorite TV themes.

Entries: *Starlog* magazine.

Spread: Coupon ballot including 27 soundtrack titles and fifteen TV themes, one of which was *Star Trek* by Courage and Roddenberry. Check box on ballot reads: "I am eager to see these scores released in record album format and would be willing to pay $6.95 to $7.95 each."

1979 Star Trek Pinball Art Contest

"Design your own pinball backglass art." Backglass is the upright box at the top of the playfield on arcade pinball machines. Original artwork contest was solicited from amateur artists.

Entries: *Starlog* magazine, expired September 14, 1979.

Spread: One page of rules and prize descriptions, photo of Bally pinball table.

Judging: *Starlog* Staff Members.

Prizes: First — Bally Professional Pinball Machine, Second — (5) *STTMP* Collector set of nine Pocket Books, Third — (10) Bradley Time *STTMP* Watch #5743 DFE4, Fourth — (15) AMT / Lesney *STTMP* Enterprise Model Kits, Fifth — (15) four Bantam paperbacks in gift-box edition, Sixth — (25) 1980 *STTMP* Pocket Books Calendar, Seventh — (30) *Starlog* magazine Issue #1 glossy cover print, Eighth — (100) *STTMP* novelization by Roddenberry.

1983 Science Fiction Celebrity Treasure Hunt #6

Identify the sci-fi celebrity from *Starlog* back issues and use the ABC crossword clues in remaining squares to make a word. The words have been hidden somewhere in this issue (excluding ads). The number beneath each word line indicates that word's order in making a complete sentence. The three words from Treasure Hunt #6 combine with Hunt #5 to make the final solutions. The three clues provided with celebrity picture are:

A. Turning death into life (seven words).

B. TV ghost story (seven words).

C. Not a war or a log (four words).

Entries: *Starlog* magazine, expired March 31, 1983.

Spread: Partial photo of mystery celebrity Gene Roddenberry.

1984 Rebuilding of the Enterprise Contest

"Your new orders from Starfleet Command are to design the new Enterprise II, Constitution Class III, using the latest Trans Warp technology." Submit illustrations (preferably ink on bristol board), NASA and M.I.T. Engineers are invited to submit, too.

Entries: *Starblazer* magazine, begins in November 1984 issue.

Spread: Two full pages with two black and white photos of Enterprise and one art drawing of Excelsior.

Judging: Editorial staff. Illustrations are property of the magazine and not returned. Winner's design and photo to be published in future issue.

Prizes: First — copy of tradepaper *Star Trek Compendium*, Second — Ertl Company model kit U.S.S. Enterprise, Third — (3) copies of the *ST III* novelization.

1985 Star Trek 20th Anniversary Favorite Episode Poll

Postcard entry format was used for voting for your favorite classic Trek episode. Winner drawn by random based on overall favorite selected.

Entries: *D.C. Comics*, expired November 30, 1985.

Spread: Page ad in Comic Issue #22, January 1986 cover date.

Judging: Editorial Staff.

Prizes: First — complete set of 26 Trek novels from Pocket Books including *Star Trek Quiz Book* and an original plot and dialogue from Issue #22 comic signed by Tona Isabella with one-year subscription to D.C., Second — (4) Trek novels including *Final Reflection*, *My Friend My Enemy*, and *Tears of the Singers*. Plus one-year subscription to D.C.

1986 Star Trek IV Trivia Contest

Three basic trivia questions: 1) What is the serial number on the saucer of the Enterprise, 2) Who was the first Captain of the Enterprise, and 3) What does the "T" stand for in James T. Kirk?

Entries: Star Trek The Official Fan Club, expired October 15, 1986.

Spread: *D.C. Comics* Issue #33 — 20th-Anniversary Special; or Publication #51 of the Fan Club.

Judging: Random drawing from correct submissions on 11/1/86.

Prizes: Grand — trip for two for two days, one night in New York City for advance screening of the *ST IV* movie; plus tour of D.C. Comics by the Editor. First — (39) West End Star Trek Adventure Role Playing Game, Second — (125) Pocket Books updated *Star Trek Compendium*, Third — (125) Pocket Books 1987 ST Calendar, Fourth — (1,000) Paramount *ST IV* Movie promo poster. Grand Winner Dwight McKay announced in D.C. Issue #37.

1988 Most Knowledgeable Trekkie Fan in the World

Promotional contest affiliated with the Trekkie Trivia Game Card set by Line of Sight. Winner through contestant elimination. Phone call for questions and the most answered correctly in consecutive order will win.

Entries: Trekkie Trivia Card Game produced by Line of Sight.

Expired February 14, 1988.

Spread: Contest advertised in *Starlog* magazine.

Prize: One week vacation for two in Hawaii, including hotel and airfare. No purchase necessary.

1988 *STTNG* American Diabetes Association Bike Ride Plus (Missouri Affiliate, Inc.)

Bike-A-Thon for charity. Mail-in entry brochure describes details of the marathon and choice of nine routes through Kansas City/St. Joseph, Missouri. Walk/ride through checkpoints from 10 a.m. to 3 p.m. with sponsor mileage pledges.

Entries: Kansas City/St. Joseph. Race on May 7, 1988.

Spread: Advertised in national magazine. Brochure mailed.

Judging: Highest mileage/donations achieved.

Prizes: Grand — trip for two on Braniff round trip to Los Angeles. A day on the set of *STTNG*. Meet and lunch with the stars and get VIP Paramount tour. Three nights paid hotel accommodations. First — Suzuki Shuttle (moped), Runners-Up — host of brand name gifts.

1988 *STTNG* General Mills Cheerios Package Contest

STTNG photo stickers included inside specially-marked boxes of Cheerios brand cereal with peel-off contest backings. Find the right sticker to win the contest.

Entries: Second Chance mail-in only. Expired May 31, 1988.

Spread: Box-backs of 15-ounce and 20-ounce Cheerios and Honey Nut Cheerios cereal boxes. Full-color back and one side panel display. Contest in conjunction with coupon poster premium and inside sticker set.

Judging: Instant Win through peel-off stickers.

Prizes: Grand — one week trip for four to Hollywood with $2,000 spending money, a tour of Paramount Studios, and the opportunity to appear as an extra on one episode of *STTNG*. First — Instant Win, one of 75,000 limited-edition plastic Next Gen NCC-1701-D ships. (See **Ship Toys**.)

1990 Starlog Magazine

Advertisement in Issue #159, October 1990. Mail-in postcard to be eligible to win a hardcover copy of the novel *Prime Directive* by Judith and Garfield Reeves-Stevens. Must write in the exact date in 1966 for the first network broadcast of Star Trek, the classic series.

Entries: Mail to *Starlog* magazine, expired October 15, 1990.

Judging: Winner selected by random postcard drawing.

Prizes: (25) Hardcover book, identified above.

Convention Booklets And Bags

	Issue	Fair	Mint
August Party: 1976-81. Five years of program booklets. Price for each.	N/A	4	8
Bicentennial 10: New York, 1976. Guests included William Shatner, DeForest Kelley, James Doohan, Nichelle Nichols, George Takei, Walter Koenig, and Grace Lee Whitney. Included booklet and bag.			
(A) Booklet with full-color, vignette cover. 8½" x 11".	N/A	4	8
(B) Bag, 13¾" x 15".	N/A	3	5
Boston Star Trek Convention: 1976. Full-color vignette cover booklet. Features Kelley, Doohan, Nichols, and Takei. 48 pages.	N/A	5	8

Equicon / Filmcon Series: 1973-76. These two conventions merged in 1975 and became a large West Coast convention series with a production staff composed of John and Bjo Trimble, Rita Ratcliffe, and D. C. Fontana. Booklets are memory books with sten-

	Issue	Fair	Mint
ciled covers, progress bulletins, and flyers.	N/A	5	10

International Star Trek Convention: New York, 1973. Promo items included a booklet and bag.

	Issue	Fair	Mint
(A) ISTC booklet, large format program with black cover, and color photo inserts of Sulu and Scotty. Includes the comic "Star Truckin'" by Howski Comix and a program schedule insert. 39 pages, 8½" x 11".	N/A	10	15
(B) ISTC bag, yellow plastic with black Spock's head and convention logo.	N/A	4	5

International Star Trek Convention: New York, 1974. Promo set includes convention book, special program schedule pamphlet, and convention bag. Convention goers also received a pen and paper specialty gift.

	Issue	*Fair*	*Mint*

(A) ISTC book, cover photo (close-up) of Spock. Includes stills from the Bloopers reel. 40 pages, 6" x 9". **N/A 5 10**

(B) ISTC program schedule, pamphlet with "Welcome to the 1974 ISTC," and a portion designated to autographs. Illustrated cover shows planet, Enterprise, and Spock's head with the slogan "Star Trek Lives!" **N/A 2 4**

(C) ISTC bag, plain black plastic. **N/A 2 4**

(D) Special ISTC notepaper and pen set, 5" x 6" notepaper with the ISTC slogan and outline drawing of planet and Enterprise. Pen is a black and silver ballpoint with ISTC logo imprinted on it. Price for both. **N/A 2 4**

International Star Trek Convention: New York, 1975. Booklet with color cover photo of seated Kirk with McCoy and Spock beside him. No lettering. Guests included Shatner, Doohan, and Koenig. 24 pages, 8½" x 11". **N/A 5 8**

International Star Trek Convention: Philadelphia, 1975. Special convention book with cover display of the Starfleet Command recruiting poster showing Kirk pointing a finger at you. Reverse shows a Klingon recruiting poster. Cover art by F. Biochet. Also contains bios, classified ads, and many black and white photos. Twenty pages, 8½" x 11". **N/A 5 8**

International Star Trek Convention: New York, 1976. Memory book containing photos, bios, etc. **N/A 5 8**

International Star Trek Convention: Washington, DC, 1976. Memory book with photos and information. **N/A 5 8**

Autographed convention program and memory book from the first Star Trek Convention in NYC, 1972.

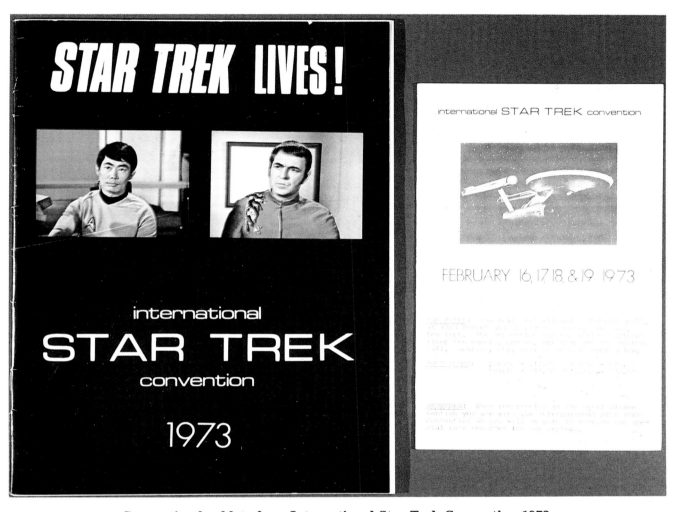

Convention booklets from International Star Trek Convention 1973.

	Issue	Fair	Mint

KWest Con: 1974. Booklet featuring program scheduling, photos, and information.
N/A 3 6

Media West Con: Michigan, 1981-90. Program schedules and information. N/A 2 5

Miamicon: 1975. Program booklet with artwork cover by Adams Bode and Kirby. Cover design by Jack Kirby. Guest was James Doohan. 36 pages, 8½" x 11". N/A 5 8

Odyssey One: Milwaukee, 1978. Full-color photo cover. Guests were Koenig and Takei. Twelve pages.
N/A 3 5

Omnicon: Miami, 1976. Artwork, event schedules and bios. Guest was DeForest Kelley.
N/A 5 10

Palm Beach Con 1: West Palm Beach, Florida, 1975. Program with cover art by Jack Kirby. Other artists include Adama and Bode. James Doohan was the guest. 36 pages, 8½" x 11". N/A 3 5

Pittsburgh Star Trektacular: 1975. Information, pictures, and bios. N/A 4 8

Shoreleave: Maryland, 1979-90. Artwork, photos, and information. N/A 2 5

Shuttlecon Columbus: 1978. Photos, bios, and program schedules. N/A 4 6

Space Con 4: Los Angeles, California, 1977. Full-color vignette cover. Guests were Shatner, Kelley, Grace Whitney, and Harlan Ellison. 48 pages. 8½" x 11". N/A 3 5

Space Con 7: Los Angeles, California, 1978. Guests were Shatner, Takei, Nichols, and Harlan Ellison. 30 pages. 8½" x 11". N/A 3 5

Space...The Final Frontier: Oakland, California, 1974-78. One of the largest Star Trek cons on the West Coast. Programs included *STTMP* movie news, bios on Trek cast, Trek animation articles, and information on space exploration. 5½" x 8½".
N/A 5 8

	Issue	*Fair*	*Mint*

Star Con: Dallas, 1979. Information and bios. Grace Lee Whitney guested. 48 pages.

| | N/A | 3 | 5 |

Star Trek America: 1977-80. Program scheduling, artwork, and general information.

(A) Program booklet. N/A 3 5

(B) Bag, 13¾" x 15". N/A 1 2

Star Trek Bi-Centennial-10: New York, 1976. Guests were Shatner, Kelley, Doohan, Nichols, Takei, Koenig, and Whitney. 32 pages. 8½" x 11".

| | N/A | 5 | 10 |

Star Trek Cleveland: 1979. Artwork and information on the con. N/A 3 5

Star Trek Convention: New York, 1972. Black cover with Enterprise. Interior black and white photos. Small format booklet. N/A 20 30

Star Trek Convention: New York, 1975. Included program booklet, schedule booklet, and bag.

(A) Program book, cover photo of Kirk with Enterprise model in background. 6" x 9".

| | N/A | 5 | 10 |

(B) Program schedule, plain white cover with blue stenciling. 8" x 11". N/A 2 4

(C) Bag, blue plastic with picture of Kirk's and Spock's heads in black. N/A 2 4

Star Trek Convention: New York, 1976. Included packet with booklet, pocket program, and bag.

(A) Program book, shows color close-up of McCoy outside of Cochrane's home from the TV episode "Metamorphosis," plus black and white photos. 6" x 9". N/A 5 8

	Issue	*Fair*	*Mint*

(B) Pocket program, large format schedule with white cover and blue lettering. 8½" x 11".

| | N/A | 2 | 4 |

(C) Bag, silver plastic with black, elongated oval STC emblem with a stylized starburst and Enterprise silhouette. N/A 2 4

Star Trek Expo: Washington, DC, 1976. Information, artwork, and pictures. N/A 2 5

Star Trek Houston: Texas, 1975.

| | 2.50 | 3 | 6 |

Star Trek Orlando: Florida, 1976. Pictures and information. N/A 3 5

Star Trek Philadelphia: 1977. Artwork, bios, and information. N/A 3 5

Star Trek Space Expo: 1978. Schedule information and photos. N/A 3 5

Stellar Voyage: 1982. Schedule information and artwork. N/A 3 5

T'Con: 1978. Schedule information and photos.

| | N/A | 3 | 5 |

Toronto Star Trek: 1976. Artwork and photos.

| | N/A | 3 | 6 |

Trekcon 1: West Palm Beach, Florida, 1975. Program cover art by C. C. Beck. Guests were Kelley, Takei, Freas, and Noel Neill. 32 pages.

| | N/A | 3 | 5 |

Trekruise East: 1987. Souvenir program from the special cruise trip from May 15-18, 1987.

| | N/A | 4 | 6 |

Ultimate Fantasy: Houston, Texas, 1982. A special con with laser light show and an orchestrated cast performance billed as the Star Trek Con of all time. Included the full cast from *STTMP*.

| | N/A | 5 | 10 |

Costumes

This section includes adult- and child-sized Halloween or party dress-up costume sets fabricated from cloth, and plastic and latex molded face masks. Listings of authentic prop-quality TV and movie replica tunics (both prefabricated uniforms and patterns) are in the section listing **Uniforms**. Vulcan ear slip-ons are listed as **Ears**.

Classic Costumes

Gorn Head Mask: Rubie's Costumes, Don Post creations, 1990. Full head mask in latex polymer is hairless and green-skinned Saurian alien (from the episode Ar). Features spine ridges, white bulbous eyes, and rows of sharp shark-like teeth.

| | 60 | 60 | 70 |

Kirk Head Mask: Rubie's Costumes, Don Post creations, 1990. Full head mask in latex polymer with wool hair and eyebrows for dressing as the Captain.

| | 60 | 60 | 70 |

Kirk: "Kirk — Star Trek Costume." #244, Ben Cooper, 1975. Long black pants, shirt sleeves. Ornamentation is blue, yellow, red, and black. Cartoon of Kirk's head and inaccurate TV insignia on shield. "Star Trek" lettering across the Enterprise saucer. Mask is pink with highlighted hair. 10" x 12" win-

Mr. Spock Deluxe Costume, #505-14506, Ben Cooper, 1975.

	Issue	*Fair*	*Mint*

dow-cut box front cartoon has portraits of Kirk, Klingon, McCoy, and Spock with phaser. Shuttlecraft below with upper Enterprise orbiting the Moon. Side-panel bust of Spock and Enterprise.

	3.98	25	35

Klingon: #245, Ben Cooper, 1975. Beatnik-style goatee and widow's peak face mask similar to TV's original fair-skinned Klingons. Long black pants, shirt sleeves. 10" x 12" window-cut box cartoon is same as Kirk #244 above. **3.98 25 35**

Mugatu Head Mask: Rubie's Costumes, Don Post creations, 1990. White wool hair (fur) over latex polymer with unicorn spike and ape-ish appeal (from the episode PWL). **60 60 70**

Salt Monster Head Mask: Rubie's Costumes, Don Post creations, 1990. Gray-skinned alien from the first televised classic episode MT. White wool hair, yellow eyes, and lamprey-like suction mouth.
60 60 70

Spock:
(A) "Spock — Super Hero Costume." #254, Ben Cooper, 1973. Knee-length black pants, shirt sleeves. Ornamentation is blue, silver, yellow, and black. Cartoon on shield of stylized standing Spock with communicator, sketchy outline of the Enterprise, a lunarscape, and an inaccurate TV version insignia.

	Issue	*Fair*	*Mint*

Mask is pink with blue-highlighted hair, full pink lips, heavy eyeshadow, and long, exaggerated pointed ears. 10" x 12" window-cut box has lightning bolt. Side panels shows cartoon of a big-eared Spock, Batman, *Planet of the Apes* star, and Superman.

	3.98	30	35

(B) "Spock — Star Trek Costume." #246, Ben Cooper, 1975. Long black pants, shirt sleeves. Ornamentation is identical to Spock #293 below — shield and mask. Pants are without cuffs. 10" x 12" window-cut box front cartoon is same as artwork character and ship collage on Kirk #244. **3.98 25 35**

(C) "Mr. Spock — Deluxe Costume" (uniform). #505-14506, Ben Cooper, 1975. Sturdy-play, deluxe boxed costume in heavy cardboard box with flip-top lid. No window-cut or Trek art on lid. All-fabric suit follows actual TV blue Sciences uniform design — blue shirt with gold insignia, black pants, boot cuffs. Mask is plastic and the same as other Ben Cooper masks.

	10	50	70

(D) "Mr. Spock — Science Fiction Costume." #293, Ben Cooper, 1975. Long black pants with heavy vinyl cuffs to simulate boots. Sleeveless. Ornamentation is blue, yellow, red, and black. Shield shows cartoon of Spock's head and inaccurate TV insignia. "Star Trek" lettering across the Enterprise saucer. Mask is pink, red-highlighted black hair, long ears, and heavy

	Issue	*Fair*	*Mint*

eye shadow. 10" x 12" window-cut box is blue with cartoon giant insect, astronauts with American flag, moon, and satellite.   **3.98**   **25**   **30**

(E) "Spock — Super Hero Face Mask" (Adult). Ben Cooper, 1976. Plastic mask. Pink-complexioned face and lips, long ears, solid black hair, and eye liner.   **.79**   **7**   **10**

Star Trek (Generic) Mask: #2800, Lincoln Enterprises, 1984. One mask of 24 original felt, fabric, embroidery, and thread designs by Maureen Culligan and distributed by Lincoln. Only one of the series is designated to be Star Trek affiliated. Red and purple starburst-style creation.   **19.95**   **4**   **6**

Movie Costumes

STTMP — **Ilia:** #2490-E151, Collegeville Flag Mfg., 1980. Sleeveless yellow girl's shift dress with cloth front ornamentation in pink, brown, and black. Cartoon on shield of standing Ilia and her name beneath encircled movie insignia and logo. Mask is pink, bald, full-lipped, with black eyeliner and gray eyeshadow. 10" x 12" window box with rainbow design movie poster on lid.   **4.49**   **15**   **25**

STTMP — **Kirk:**

(A) #2491-E148, Original Release, Collegeville Flag, 1980. Long silver pants, shirt sleeves. Ornamenta-

tion in neon-glo pink and green, plus silver, black, and yellow. Photo on shield shows Kirk seated with Spock and Ilia standing, encircled insignia, front view of Enterprise, and solar flare. Movie title logo. Mask is pink-complexioned without facial etching. Auburn hair with black highlights. 10" x 12" window-cut with "Rainbow."   **4.49**   **15**   **25**

(B) #2491, Collegeville Flag, 1980. Above costume packaged on plastic hanger.   **4**   **10**   **15**

(C) #2476-9776, Collegeville Flag, 1984. Re-release. Long silver pants, shirt sleeves. Ornamentation returns to the *STTMP* styling with deletions: *STTMP* title logo is gone. Ilia remains. Mask shows fuller hair with blue highlights. Flesh-complexioned with some etching in darker pink. 10" x 12" window.   **4.99**   **10**   **15**

STTMP — **Klingon:** #2489-E150, Collegeville Flag, 1980. Long-legged pants, shirt sleeves. Ornamentation in neon-glo pink and yellow with green, silver, and black. Shield cartoon shows detailed movie race Klingon equipped with holstered disrupter. Pants are olive green in pseudo-suede. Mask is pink, gray, black, blue with yellow skull ridge, and orange facial highlights. Bearded. 10" x 12" window-cut box with rainbow art.   **4.49**   **15**   **25**

STTMP — **Klingon Head Mask:** Rubie's Costumes, Don Post Creations, 1990. Full head mask in latex

Movie costumes by Collegeville Flag: *STTMP* Spock (1980) and *ST II* Kirk (1982).

Issue Fair Mint

polymer with movie vintage skull ridge and wispy, coarse hair in wool. Full lips show wide, prominent teeth between Fu-Manchu beard. **60 60 70**

STTMP — **Spock:**

(A) #2488-E149 Original release, Collegeville Flag, 1980. Long silver pants, shirt sleeves. Ornamentation and shield are the same as *STTMP* Kirk above. Mask is dark pink with heavy etching, blue-highlighted black hair and short ears. 10" x 12" window-cut box has rainbow art. **4.49 15 25**

(B) #2488, Collegeville Flag, 1980. Above costume packaged on plastic hanger. **4 12 15**

(C) #2488-9788, re-release, Collegeville Flag, 1984. Long silver pants, shirt sleeves. Ornamentation and shield return to the *STTMP* styling with deletions:

Issue Fair Mint

STTMP movie title logo is gone. Ilia remains. Mask is flesh-complexioned, black hair with blue highlights, sky blue heavy eyeshadow, and some pink etching. 10" x 12" window-cut box. **4.99 10 15**

STTMP — **Spock Head Mask:** Don Post Studios, 1980. Latex mask slips over the head. Adult-sized Mr. Spock in "Vulcan Novice" mode — with wool hair eyebrows and simulated mat of hair. **51.95 75 85**

STTMP — **Vulcan Master Head Mask:** Don Post Studios, 1980. Latex slip-on head mask in adult size. Bald-headed male Vulcan priest as seen in the first movie. **36.95 60 70**

ST II — **Kirk:** #2476-9576, Collegeville Flag, 1982. Long silver pants, sleeveless shirt. Ornamentation colors and face mask are the same as *STTMP* Kirk.

Ben Cooper *STTNG* alien costumes: Lt. Worf and Ferengi (1987).

Issue   Fair   Mint

Shield is different. Ilia is removed from the circle and there is a rear view of the Enterprise to left of *ST II* movie title logo. 10" x 12" window-cut box.

4.49   15   20

ST II — Spock: #2488-9588, Collegeville Flag, 1982. Long silver pants, sleeveless. Ornamentation and shield same as *ST II* Kirk above. Mask is similar to *STTMP* Spock but with all facial etching removed. 10" x 12" window-cut box.   4.49   15   20

Star Trek: The Next Generation

STTNG — Ferengi: #22290, Ben Cooper, 1987. "Super Hero Costume." Brown plastic Ferengi mask

Issue   Fair   Mint

with sleeveless vinyl jumpsuit. Top is fur, spotted black and brown. Bottom is brown with leggings. Reads "Star Trek The Next Generation" over left chest. Window-cut box, 8½" x 11½".

4.99   10   15

STTNG — Lt. Worf: #22290, Ben Cooper, 1987 (same as above Ferengi). "Super Hero Costume." Black bearded mask. Sleeveless jumpsuit has black trim on orange with black leggings. Reads "Star Trek The Next Generation" in gold across chest. Silver insignia in circle on left. Window box, 8½" x 11½".

4.99   10   15

Credit Cards

Star Trek The Enterprise Mastercard: Associates National Bank, 1989. Standard credit card features

TV Enterprise against black starfield. Membership includes a credit line up to $3,000, cash advances of

Star Trek Enterprise credit card applications for MasterCard and VISA.

Top: **Theatre promo cups for *ST V* (1989) and *STTMP* (Coca Cola, 1979). Bottom: Set of four cups for *ST IV* (Coca Cola, 1986).**

Issue Fair Mint

$750 or more, ATM access, Convenience Check Access, low monthly payments, car rental discounts, and easy credit qualification. Those who received credit approval by a specified date also received a free copy of the audio-cassette "Enterprise, The First Adventure" by Vonda McIntyre and an exclusive black T-shirt with the TV enterprise amidst comet field on reverse. Included in the glossy bridge scene promotional envelope were a cut-out communicator, a Vulcan Mind Meld questionnaire, a Vulcan Analysis Application, and a 16" x 22" fold-out poster of movie Enterprise with the legend "Where No Man Has Gone Before." The promotional package itself is a nice collectible. Annual fee of $30 with an annual percentage rate of 19.8 percent.   — **N/A N/A**

***Star Trek: The Next Generation* Enterprise VISA Card:** Associates National Bank, 1988. Standard-sized credit card features the *STTNG* Enterprise warping out of a glowing nebula. Membership in-

Issue Fair Mint

cludes an opening credit line up to $2,500, cash advances, ATM access, car rental discounts, $100,000 travel accident insurance, convenience checks, and easy credit qualification terms. Annual fee of $20 with an annual percentage rate of 21.9 percent.
                                       — **N/A N/A**

***Star Trek: The Next Generation* Videocassette — Charter Account Card:** Columbia House Video, 1991. Standard-sized credit card is laminated cardstock and features photo of front view of *STTNG* Enterprise orbiting blue planet with starfield on left. Title logo in yellow box above with name and charter membership charge account number embossed on the bottom. Active membership includes ten-day preview of the videocassette "Encounter At Farpoint" for payment of $4.95, plus handling. At four-six week intervals other *STTNG* videocassettes arrive for the price of $19.95 — keep only the ones you want with no minimum purchase.   — **N/A N/A**

*STTNG promo cups. Top center: KCOP-TV promo (Pepsi, 1989) and set
of five ICEE cups (1987).*

Cups And Cup Holders

	Issue	Fair	Mint

This section lists the promotional/advertising plastic cups released in conjunction with the Star Trek movies and *Star Trek: The Next Generation* TV series. For listings of plastic dinnerware see **Dish Sets**.

Beam Me Up Scotty Cup Holder: Koozie, circa 1980s. Standard style foam cup holder for drinks and cans. Pink with black lettering. Reads "Beam Me Up Scotty" with black zoom-in stripes behind and "There's no intelligent life down here" below. 3" diameter x 4½" high.

	Issue	Fair	Mint
	1	2	4

STTMP Coca-Cola Promo Cups: Coca-Cola Company, 1979. Large four-tone promotional cup sold with purchase of a coke at movie theaters premiering *STTMP*. White plastic with busts of Decker, Spock, Kirk, McCoy, and Ilia in aqua, brown, and black drawings. Movie title logo above, movie ship with blurb below. 4" diameter, 5½" tall, 32-ounce.

	Issue	Fair	Mint
	1	5	10

ST IV Coca-Cola/Stop 'N Go Stores Glow-Cup Promos: Coca-Cola (Classic), manufactured by Giacona Container, 1986. Promo cup distributed by Stop 'n Go Stores. Set of four 28-ounce cups with artwork collages on green-tinted plastic. Orange, yellow, red, green, blue shades, and purple, 4" diameter, 6¾" tall. Issue cost included a fill-up of Classic Coke.

➤ Crew Cup — McCoy, Spock, Kirk/Sulu, Chekov, Uhura, and Scotty in two panels.

➤ Kirk Cup — Admiral with portside ship.

➤ Spock Cup — Vulcan in robes and bust shot.

➤ Klingon Bird of Prey — starboard below plane.

	Issue	Fair	Mint
Price for each.	1.59	8	10
Price for set of four.	—	25	40

ST V Paramount Theater Promo Cup: 1989. Promo cup sold in the premiere movie release theaters. Red plastic with black-, red-, and gold-outlined movie insignia design logo. Movie title logo in gold and black shows below the insignia design and

Top: Action Scene curtains (Stephens), Classics (Pacific Mills). Bottom: Coordinates (Aberdeen).

	Issue	Fair	Mint

appears alone on cup's reverse. 3¾" diameter, 6¾" tall.   **4 5 7**

STTNG ICEE Promo Cups: 1987, distributed by ICEE-U.S.A. Set of five large capacity white plastic cups sold with ICEE drinks in a limited regional promotion. Fronts show full-color photo busts, reverses feature *STTNG* split letter logo and caption in red, blue, and black, 3¾" diameter, 6" tall.

(A) Captain Jean-Luc Picard   **2 5 7**

(B) Commander William Riker   **2 5 7**

	Issue	Fair	Mint

(C) Lieutenant Geordi LaForge, Counselor Deanna Troi, Lieutenant Commander Data   **2 5 7**

(D) Dr. Beverly Crusher and Wesley Crusher   **2 5 7**

(E) Lieutenant Commander Tasha Yar   **2 10 12**

Price for set of five.   **— 25 35**

STTNG KCOP TV Promo Cup: Pepsi, 1989. Plastic cup features full-color *STTNG* crew portraits and television network affiliate logo. Distributed in a regional promotion in conjunction with Pepsi.
— 6 10

Curtains

Star Trek Shower Curtain: #RN 33152, 1986. Standard twelve-ring vinyl shower curtain has black border with clear panel center and red, yellow, and white front view of Enterprise over right-hand planet sunrise. "STAR TREK" title logo, 70" x 72".
14.95 30 40

Star Trek Window Curtains:

(A) *Star Trek* Action Scene, Stephens. Standard window-width curtains in 83" length show artwork running figure of TV Kirk and Spock, plus starboard profile of the TV Enterprise. Pastel blue background with dark blue, yellow, and red planets and white stars. Plastic-bagged.

Note: These drapes match the Stephens sheets. See section listing **Bed Linens**.   **— 30 40**

(B) *Star Trek* Classics, Pacific Mills, 1976. Blue backdrop fabric featuring Kirk and Spock over starry field with Enterprise. Pocket rod curtain style.

Note: These curtains match the Pacific Mills bed sheets (see **Bed Linens**).   **— 30 40**

(C) ST-20 Coordinates, Aberdeen Mfg., 1986. Navy background with colorful repeating row patterns of art showing starboard TV Enterprise with green *ST III* movie Klingon Bird of Prey ship; yellow-lettered "Star Trek/Beam Me Up Scotty"; and space port with orange, yellow, and gray transporter-effect block. Kodel polyester/cotton. Pinch pleat shorties and drapes with rings, poly- bagged.

Note: These curtains and drapes match the Aberdeen bed sheet sets. See section listing **Bed Linens**.

➤ #A5794-3, measures 48" x 36".   **— 15 20**
➤ #A5794-4, measures 48" x 45".   **— 15 20**
➤ #A5794-5, measures 48" x 54".   **— 15 20**
➤ #A5794-6, measures 48" x 63".   **— 20 25**
➤ #A5794-8, measures 48" x 84".   **— 30 35**

Water-mount decals, Star Trek/Lincoln Enterprises.

Decals

	Issue	Fair	Mint

Star Trek Adventure Decal: Universal Studios, 1988. Star Trek logo commemorating the 20th anniversary. **2.95 3 5**

Star Trek College Decals: New Eye Studios, 1984. Special transparent decals designed for placement inside car windows. 2½" x 18".

➤ "Romulan Military Academy"

➤ "Starfleet Academy"

➤ "Vulcan Science Academy"

Price for each. **2 2 3**

Star Trek Decals: Star Trek / Lincoln Enterprises, 1968-80. Set of eight, two-tone, water-mount decals in assorted themes. Each black and silver decal set comes on a 4" x 9" backing with removal instructions.

	Issue	Fair	Mint

(A) #1801, insignia designs: three styles of uniform insignias plus miniature aliens. **.75   5   10**

(B) #1802, spacecraft: Enterprise, Klingon warship, Galileo, and standing figures. **.75   5   10**

(C) #1803, gadgetry: communicator, phaser, and 3-D chess game. **.75   5   10**

(D) #1804, NCC-1701 letter logos: Enterprise call letters in assorted sizes. **1.25   5   8**

(E) #1805, monster portraits: eight oval portraits of Trek aliens. **1.95   5   8**

(F) #1806, crew portraits: four oval busts of Kirk, Spock, McCoy, and Scotty. **1.50   5   8**

(G) #1807, crew portraits: oval busts of Uhura, Sulu, Chekov, and Chapel. **1.50   5   8**

(H) #1806 and #1807, sold as double set. **3   10   15**

(I) #1807A, head portraits: Spock, Chapel, Kirk and McCoy. **1.50   5   8**

***Star Trek: The Motion Picture* Instant Stained Glass Decals:** Aviva, 1979. Set of six full-color transparencies that may be applied to windows and used over and over again. Packaged on 6½" x 8" blue cardstock back with starfield design. Shrink-wrapped. Decal sizes approximately 5" x 6".

➣ Admiral Kirk, cut-out portrait with command insignia

➣ "Live long & prosper," Spock in Vulcan robe

➣ Mr. Spock, Spock portrait cut-out with science insignia

➣ U.S.S. Enterprise, Enterprise against blue starfield and yellow planet

➣ Vulcan salute, encircled hand

➣ Vulcan salute, Spock portrait and hand

Price for each. **2   4   6**

Star Trek V: The Final Frontier Decal: Ad Art, 1989. Special promotional decal sold at theaters for the premiere of *ST V*. Shows *ST V* logo with movie Enterprise. **2.95   3   5**

Decanters And Accessories

Mr. Spock Decanter: Grenadier Spirits Company, 1979. *STTMP* vintage porcelain ceramic bust of Spock. Fully-painted decanter is filled with 25.4 ounces of 49-proof Ceilo Liqueur. Box has cellophane

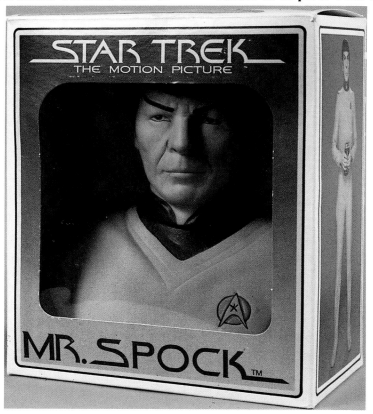

Mr. Spock Decanter, Grenadier Spirits Company, *Star Trek: The Motion Picture*, 1979.

Star Trek: The Motion Picture Spock Decanter, limited edition, Ceilo, 1979.

Tombstone decoration by Partyworks, 1989.

	Issue	Fair	Mint
window cut-out for easy viewing. Cardstock edges feature data on Star Trek, Leonard Nimoy, and Mr. Spock.			
(A) Decanter without liqueur.	—	25	35
(B) Decanter with liqueur.	—	75	100

Saurian Brandy Bottle: Dickel Whiskey Company, 1964-69 and 1980. This genuine whiskey decanter was used as a prop in several of the TV episodes and earned itself a permanent place in Star Trek fandom. The bottle is powder horn-shaped with a leather stopper and handle strap assembly. In 1980 Dickel began manufacturing these bottles once again, but the newer decanters have all-vinyl straps in lieu of the old leather ones. Bottle came without any contents.

	Issue	Fair	Mint
(A) Miniature bottle.	—	20	30

	Issue	Fair	Mint
(B) Fifth bottle.	—	45	55
(C) One quart bottle.	—	60	85

Saurian Brandy Bottle Label: Joy-Miller Enterprises. Silver-toned Federation Seal of Approval for Galactic Distribution. This self-sticking label is made for application onto the Dickel Saurian Brandy bottles instead of the standard George Dickel Tennessee Sour Mash label which comes with the decanter.

	.50	3	6

Spock Decanter: Ceilo, 1979. Limited edition decanter of *STTMP* vintage. Full-figure statue on molded base of Spock with front right hand raised up in Vulcan salute. Decanter is metallic gold-glazed porcelain. This rare collectible is packaged in a styrofoam envelope within a blue satin box with brass hinges. Comes empty, but is designed to hold 750L

	Issue	Fair	Mint

of 48 proof Ceilo Liqueur. Also comes with a numbered sticker and a matching certificate of authenticity. Only 1200 of these decanters were made. 13½" high. — **600 1000**

Decorations

Star Trek Tombstone: Over the Hill Birthday Parties, Partyworks, 1989. Gray styrofoam table party standee with etched lettering which reads "Beam Me Up Scotty." Packaged in plastic bag with cardstock header. 12" x 9". **2.95 3 5**

Diplomas

Star Trek Diplomas: April Publications, 1984. Diplomas lithographed in gold and suitable for framing. 8½" x 11".
➤ Doctorate of Space Medicine
➤ Klingon War Academy
➤ Starfleet Academy
➤ Vulcan Master
➤ Vulcan Science Academy
Price for each. **1 1 2**

Star Trek Diplomas: T-K Graphics, 1984. Black lettering on white cardstock. Has gold foil seal and the appearance of a standard diploma. Blank place

Star Trek: The Motion Picture Dish Set by Deka Plastics, 1979.

	Issue	Fair	Mint

for your name. 8" x 10". Not to be confused with the smaller diplomas of later issue.
(A) Star Fleet Academy, unframed.
    .75   2   4
(B) Star Fleet Academy, framed with heavy artist's board. **2.75** 5 8
(C) Vulcan Space Academy, unframed.
    .75   2   4
(D) Vulcan Space Academy, framed with heavy artist's board. **2.75** 5 8

Star Trek Diplomas: T-K Graphics, 1984. Diplomas are printed in black on white cardstock with gold foil seal and a place for personalizing with your name. Come plain or framed with heavy artist's board. 5½" x 8½".
(A) Star Fleet Academy, unframed.
    .75   1   2

(B) Star Fleet Academy, framed.
    2.75 3 5
(C) Vulcan Space Academy, unframed.
    .75   1   2
(D) Vulcan Space Academy, framed.
    2.75 3 5

***Star Trek: The Next Generation* Diplomas:** Lincoln Enterprises, 1988. Special diplomas issued to Starfleet Academy graduates.
(A) #1405, standard diploma. **1.25** 1 2
(B) #1406, deluxe diploma. **2.50** 3 5

Temple Of Trek Diploma: Temple of Trek, 1988. A diploma naming bearer as an Extraordinary Master of Trek from the Praise Trek University. Comes with Handbook with the Books of Roddenberry, the Trekker's Creed, etc. **10** 10 12

Dish Sets

Paper Birthday Dish Set: Tuttle Press, 1976. The classic title logo used in this set follows in the mode of the Gold Key Comics Star Trek letter logo. This was a popular and often repeated style of lettering during this period.

(A) Cake Toppers. Tuttle packaged two different sets of edible candy cake toppers to match its paper dish

set. These items are listed in the section titled **Food Packages**.
(B) Cups. Cellophane-wrapped set of eight disposable 7-ounce party cups featuring cartoon busts of McCoy, Kirk, and Spock with TV Enterprise.
    1.50 7 9
(C) Napkins. Wrapped sets of paper napkins with ac-

Star Trek aliens by Mego Corporation, 1975: Romulan, Keeper, Talos, and Cheron.

	Issue	Fair	Mint

tion scene of running cartoon figures captioned "Dr. McCoy," "Captain Kirk," and "Mr. Spock" with three-quarter rendition of the TV starship overhead.

➤ Cocktail, 6½" x 6½" (set of twenty)
| | 1 | 6 | 9 |

➤ Dinner, 13" x 13¼" (set of sixteen)
| | 1 | 7 | 10 |

(D) Plates. Wrapped set of eight party plates in white with cartoon action scene the same as (C) above.

➤ Cake, 6" diameter
| | 1.50 | 7 | 9 |

➤ Dinner, 8" diameter
| | 2 | 8 | 10 |

(E) Tablecloth. Disposable paper tablecloth with repeating cartoon action scene as above, except that individual Kirk, Spock, and McCoy busts are added to the running figure scenes. Sized to fit a 54" x 88" table.
| | 5 | 15 | 20 |

Plastic Children's Dish Sets: Deka Plastics.

(A) *Star Trek* set, 1975. Child's plastic place setting with color decal bust cartoon of "Mr. Spock," "Captain Kirk," and "Dr. McCoy" with the TV Enterprise in starboard profile in between. Originally packaged

both as a set and sold individually.

	Issue	Fair	Mint
➤ Cup (14-ounce)	—	4	6

➤ Mug (10-ounce), with squared handle
| | — | 5 | 7 |

| ➤ Bowl, #07208 (20-ounce) | — | 6 | 9 |
| Price for set. | — | 20 | 25 |

(B) *Star Trek: The Motion Picture* set, 1979. Child's plastic dish set with versatile place-setting combinations. Imprinted design on white features elaborate rainbow background, front view of *STTMP* Enterprise, and photo busts of Decker and Ilia and Spock, Kirk, and McCoy. Sold individually and packaged in different combination sets.

➤ Bowl #580 (14-ounce)	—	5	8
➤ Bowl (20-ounce)	—	5	8
➤ Cup (14-ounce)	—	3	5

➤ Divided Dinner Plate #07208 (9" diameter)
| | — | 10 | 12 |

➤ Mug (10-ounce)	—	3	6
➤ Tumbler #530 (6-ounce)	—	2	3
➤ Tumbler #540 (11-ounce)	—	3	4

Dolls And Play Sets

This section lists posable vinyl and cloth dolls complete with clothing and accessories and includes plastic and vinyl play sets scaled for doll use. Smaller articulated play figures are listed in the **Action Figures** section.

Star Trek aliens by Mego Corporation, 1975: Andorian, Neptunian, Mugato, and Gorn.

Doll Figures

Star Trek Dolls (8-Inch): Mego Corporation, 1975. Vinyl dolls with articulated limbs and movable heads. Removable cloth uniforms and plastic boots. Classic accessories include plastic utility belt, tricorder, pistol phaser, and communicator. Detailed faces and painted hair (with exception of Uhura, which has page boy-style fiber hair). Dolls are plastic-bubbled to 9¼" x 8½" cardstock with artwork portraits of TV characters. Back panel advertises the Mego Flight Deck playcase and Mego Communicators.

Note: Mint prices below are for MIP (Mint In Package) dolls. Many of these dolls are available in many conditions (e.g. from excellent condition/no box, all the way down to no accessories, and even damaged wares). Collectors are advised that such gradations affect prices significantly.

	Issue	Fair	Mint
(A) 1974-75 United States releases.			
➢ #51200/1, Captain Kirk	2.99	25	35
➢ #51200/2, Mr. Spock	2.99	25	35
➢ #51200/3, Dr. "Bones" McCoy	2.99	75	95
➢ #51200/4, Lt. Uhura	2.99	65	75
➢ #51200/5, Scotty	2.99	75	95
➢ #51200/7, Klingon	2.99	50	60
(B) 1975-76 European releases (hard to find).			
➢ #51203/1, Neptunian	—	110	140
➢ #51203/2, Keeper	—	110	140
➢ #51203/3, Gorn	—	160	175
➢ #51203/4, Cheron	—	175	200
➢ #51203/5, Andorian	—	175	250
➢ #51204/1, Romulan	—	450	600
➢ #51204/2, Talos	—	175	250
➢ #51204/4, Mugato	—	225	275

Spock and Kirk, Grammy's Little Trekkers by Berry Patch Dolls, 1986.

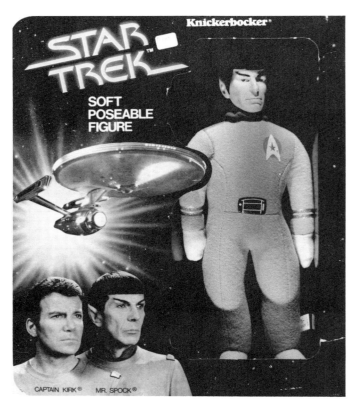

Star Trek: The Motion Picture Spock,
Knickerbocker, 1979.

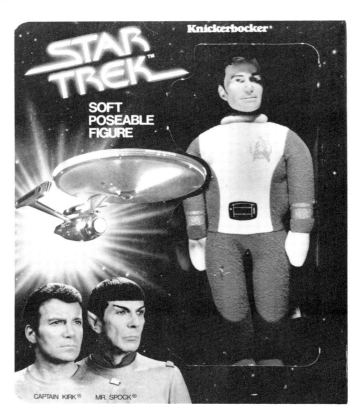

Star Trek: The Motion Picture Kirk by Knickerbocker, harder to find than the Spock doll.

	Issue	Fair	Mint

***Star Trek* Dolls (11-Inch) Grammy's Little Trek-
kers:** Berry Patch Dolls, 1986. Hand-sewn, soft cloth
body dolls. Removable uniforms in classic TV styling.
Patterned after the Cabbage Patch Kids.
➢ Kirk
➢ Spock

	Issue	Fair	Mint
Price for each.	49.95	60	70

***Star Trek* Dolls (14-Inch) Porcelain Collector
Series:** R. J. Ernst Enterprises, 1987-present.
Limited edition series of 19,500 per release. Hand-
painted porcelain heads with custom-tailored fabric
TV uniforms. Detailed faces, pre-posed arms, painted
hair. Offered through Hamilton Collection, originally;
and direct through Ernst. Mailed in white cardstock
box with heavy packing and Trek theme tissue paper.
➢ Mr. Spock
➢ Captain Kirk
➢ Dr. McCoy
➢ Scott
➢ Uhura
➢ Chekov
➢ Sulu

	Issue	Fair	Mint
Price for each.	75	100	150

	Issue	Fair	Mint

***STTMP* Dolls (12½ Inch):** Mego Corp., 1979.
Movie vintage cloth uniforms on vinyl dolls with articulated limbs. An assortment of plastic accessories
are included. Window-cut cardstock box shows the
same illustrations as those found on the packages for
3¾" *STTMP* Action Figures by Mego. Cartoons of
six dolls on front and photos of characters from the
movie on rear.

	Issue	Fair	Mint
(A) #91210/1, Kirk (gray and white uniform)	10	75	85
(B) #91210/2, Spock (Science Officer uniform)	10	65	75
(C) #91210/3, Decker	10	65	80
(D) #91210/4, Ilia (in shirt-dress)	10	55	65
(E) #91210/5, Klingon (with skull-ridge)	10	100	130
(F) #91210/6, Arcturian (fleshy head)	10	55	65

***STTMP* Dolls (14-Inch) Soft Posable:** Knicker-
bocker, 1979. Stuffed flannel dolls for young children.
Vinyl heads are non-movable. Velcro strips along the
body allow for posing of the limbs. Fabric is sewn to
simulate movie uniforms.

Star Trek Mission to Gamma VI play set, #51226, Mego Corporation, 1976.

	Issue	Fair	Mint

➤ Kirk (gray and white fabric)
➤ Spock (blue-gray fabric)

Price for each.	4	25	35

Doll Play Sets (Scaled for 8-Inch Dolls)

Star Trek **Enterprise Flight Deck:** #51210, Mego Corporation, 1975. Washable vinyl playcase for carrying the 8-inch dolls. Replicates the flight deck/bridge with Captain's chair, navigations console with seats, and transporter alcove which spins by means of a dial to allow dolls to disappear. Six interchangeable cardboard viewscreen panels attach to front screen. 11½" x 16½" x 11" boxed. Box shows photograph of the opened playcase with dolls.

	12	85	150

Star Trek **Enterprise Transporter Room:** #22608, Palitoy/Bradgate, 1974. English Mego release. Plastic transporter alcove (identical to the one included as part of Flight Deck above). Lone chamber is a stand-alone play set with same button-control action. Boxed 11" x 5¼" with photo of actual toy on side panels.

	—	45	55

Star Trek **Mission to Gamma VI:** #51226, Mego Corp., 1976. Mountain terrain alien landscape action play set including an acto-glove to operate moving jaw on the "Vaal" idol. Includes a man-eating plant and a secret trap door. Boxed 17½" x 19" x 7¾". Cover has cartoon of a child playing with the set.

	12	450	650

Star Trek **Telescreen Console:** #51232, Mego Corp, 1976. Command action play set scaled for eight-inch dolls. 5" diagonal viewscreen operates with four D-cell batteries and targets beep when hit. Plastic console has Captain's chair for Kirk doll. Features phaser aiming controls and battle sounds, scoring device light, and projection targets. 14¼" x 9½" box with cartoon head of Spock and photo of actual toy.

	15	200	325

Star Trek Telescreen Console play set, #51232, Mego Corporation, 1976.

Doorknob Hangers And Signs

	Issue	Fair	Mint

Beam Me Up Scotty Door Hanger: #46, H & L Enterprises, 1986. Standard style "Do Not Disturb" sign for doorknobs. White plastic card with 2½" diameter hole at top and multicolored design. Two color types. 4" x 8".

➤ "Beam Me Up Scotty" legend in blue lettering at bottom with yellow streak and blue and mauve speckling along the sides.

➤ "Beam Me Up Scotty" legend in black lettering with yellow streak and black and red speckling along the sides.

Price for each.   **1.29**   **2**   **4**

Beam Me Up Scotty Door Hanger: #D026, Antioch Publishing Company, 1986. Laminated cardstock door sign in red, yellow, green, and white. "Beam Up Scotty — there's no intelligent life down here" ap-

From left to right: Beam Me Up Scotty doorknob hangers by H & L Enterprises and by Antioch.

	Issue	Fair	Mint

pears in red on a yellow bullet-shaped patch. Borders are green with a design of stars and planets throughout. Reverse features standard "Please Do Not Disturb" notice in blue. 4" x 9".

1.99   2   4

	Issue	Fair	Mint

Beam Me Up Scotty Door Sign: #27, H & L Enterprises, 1986. Small plastic door sign which reads, "Beam Me Up Scotty, There's no intelligent life down here." White lettering on red. 2½" x 4".

1.29   2   4

E

Earrings

	Issue	Fair	Mint

Classic Earrings

Enterprise Design: Aviva.
(A) Starship outlined in black on a clear Lucite block. Pierced. **1 6 9**
(B) 3-D replica in clip-on, or dangling from chain on post, silver-plated or gold-plated. **6 6 9**

IDIC Design: Lincoln Enterprises.
(A) #2305A, 1976. Lightweight gold- and silver-plated symbols in clip-on style. **7.50 10 14**
(B) #2305B, 1976. Same as above, but pierced with wire loop. **8.50 10 14**
(C) #2311GA, 1987. 14K solid gold, pierced. **150 145 155**

Insignia Design: Lincoln Enterprises.
(A) #2355, 1976. Pierced, dangle, gold-plated. **8 10 12**
(B) #2365, 1976. Pierced, dangle, sterling silver. **15 25 35**
(C) #2354, 1976. Pierced, post, gold-plated. **8 10 12**
(D) #2364, 1976. Pierced, post, sterling silver. **15 25 35**
(E) #2353, 1976. Clip, dangle, gold-plated. **8 10 12**
(F) #2363, 1976. Clip, dangle, sterling silver. **15 25 35**
(G) #J2373G, 1987. 14K gold, dangle with diamond. **150 145 155**
(H) #J2378GD, 1987. 14K gold, pave diamond, pierced. **600 575 625**
(I) #J2478F, 1987. Clip, ½" wire design. **10.95 10 12**
(J) #J2478H, 1987. Pierced, ½" wire design. **10.95 10 12**

(K) #J2478B, 1987. Clip, ¾" wire design. **12.95 12 14**
(L) #J2487C, 1987. Pierced, ¾" wire design. **12.95 12 14**

Movie Earrings

STTMP **Enterprise:**
(A) #J2404B, Lincoln Enterprises, 1987. Movie ship in 3-D, ¾" gold-plated, clip-on. **14.95 12 16**
(B) #J2404C, Lincoln Enterprises. Pierced with loop, otherwise same as (A). **14.95 12 16**
(C) #J2404G, Lincoln Enterprises. Pierced with loop, 14K gold, otherwise same as (A). **250 225 275**
(D) Intergalactic, 1990. Silver-plated, pierced with loop. **9.95 10 12**

Star Trek: The Next Generation
Earrings

STTNG **Enterprise Design:**
(A) #J2405B, Lincoln Enterprises, 1987. 3-D miniature in gold plate, clip-on. **14.95 12 16**
(B) #J2405C, Lincoln Enterprises, 1987. 3-D miniature in gold plate, pierced loop. **14.95 12 16**
(C) #J2405G, Lincoln Enterprises, 1987. 3-D miniature, 14K solid gold, pierced. **250 245 255**
(D) #J2405GD, Lincoln Enterprises, 1987. 3-D miniature, 14K solid gold with .25 carats of diamonds rimming the saucer edge, pierced. **600 550 650**
(E) Intergalactic, 1990. Silver-plated, 1" pierced. **14.95 12 16**

Star Trek Spock ears (1986), *STTMP* Spock ears (Aviva, 1979), *ST II* Vulcan ears (Don Post, 1982).

Ears

This section describes costume-quality Vulcan ears molded in flexible latex or hard solid plastic. It does not include authenticated one-of-a-kind prop ear tips such as those worn by Mr. Spock and the other Vulcans and Romulans of Star Trek. In the past, such rare and valuable "Mr. Spock ears" have been made available at fan conventions and auctioned by Paramount representatives in dedicated charity drives. Prop ears come with a numbered certificate of authenticity and on occasion command prices of $1,000 or more. In the Costume Ears listing, more often than not, it is the novelty in the packaging and its affiliation (classic versus movie) that distinguishes the product. Ears are generally fabricated to adult size, measuring roughly 2¼" x 4¼".

	Issue	Fair	Mint

Ear Tips: Star Child, distributor, 1988. Costume ear tips that look Vulcan and are made of thin latex. Non-Trek packaging. Plastic-bagged with cardstock header showing filmstrip display of assorted ghouls and fantasy creatures wearing the ear tips and reading "Woochie Facial Additions." Ear tips are good adult costume apparel. Require spirit gum adhesive.

	7.95	8	10

Star Trek Mr. Spock Vulcan Ears: Paramount Pictures Corporation, 1986. Bagged rubber ears with package photo of Spock. Ears are actually red! Also sold as "Mr. Martian Space Ears," without Trek packaging.

	4.95	10	12

Star Trek Vulcan Ears: #3295, Franco, 1975. Flesh-toned pointed ears molded in latex. Bagged

	Issue	Fair	Mint

with orange cardstock header showing artwork illustration of Spock, shuttlecraft, and planet.

	2	6	10

STTMP **Spock Ears:** #833, Aviva, 1979. Soft plastic flesh-toned ears blister-packed to black cardstock with large cut-out photo of movie Spock on right. Package lettered "Live Long and Prosper" above movie title logo.

	3	18	25

	Issue	Fair	Mint

STTMP **Vulcan Ears:** 1980. Flesh-toned latex molds bagged in plastic with white paper header illustrating a Vulcan Master over planetscape.

	2	5	10

ST II **Vulcan Ears:** Don Post Studios, 1982. Molded latex ears packaged in cup on cardstock with photographs of the bridge crew from *ST II*.

	7	15	20

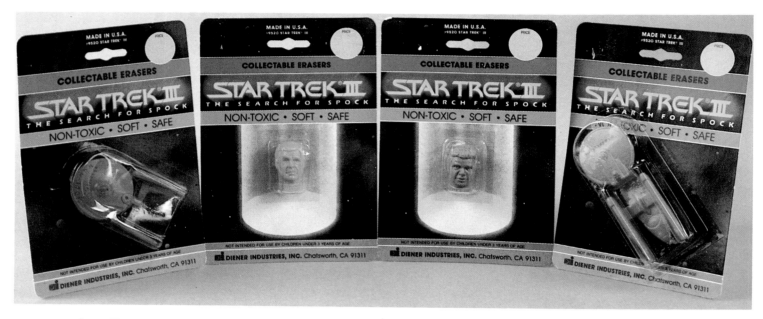

***Star Trek III:** The Search for Spock* erasers with cardstock backings, Deiner Enterprises, 1984.

Eight-Track Tapes

Inside Star Trek: #TC8 PCA 34279, Columbia Records, 1976. Narratives produced by Ed Naha and Russ Payne. Gene Roddenberry tells tales and anecdotes about Star Trek. TT 56:04.

	8	10	15

Star Trek: The Motion Picture: #JSA-36334, Columbia Records, 1979. Cartridge featuring music from the motion picture soundtrack as composed and conducted by Jerry Goldsmith. TT 37:47. Slipcover case.

	7.98	10	15

Two Sides of Leonard Nimoy: #DLP 5835, Dot Records, 1969. Nimoy sings songs written by Charles Grean with Spock overtones. TT 21:10.

	3.79	15	25

William Shatner Live!: #NU 9408, Imperial House, 1978. Canadian recording compiled from Shatner's one-man shows across college campuses.

	7.95	10	15

Erasers

Enterprise Eraser: Rectangular block eraser in assorted colors with portside profile of the TV Enterprise imprinted on the top.

	.50	1	2

Star Trek III: The Search for Spock **Eraser Tips:** Deiner Enterprises, 1984. Small pencil toppers in

seven different mold styles. Colors are magenta, lime green, yellow, and sky blue. Come individually in packages.

➢ Enterprise

➢ Excelsior

	Issue	*Fair*	*Mint*

➤ Kirk's head

➤ Kruge's head

➤ McCoy's head

➤ Scotty's head

➤ Spock's head

Price for each.   .40   1   2

Events

Cruise a la Trek: Cunard, 1987. Special Trek cruise, May 10-14, 1988, aboard the Cunard Princess that departed from Vancouver, stopped at San Francisco, and debarked at Los Angeles, California. The cruise host was James Doohan and the Her-A-Canes, plus guests Richard Arnold, Majel Barrett, Bibi Besch (Dr. Carol Marcus), William "Trelayne" Campbell, Walter Koenig, Mark Lenard, Susan Sackett, Grace Whitney, and Bill "Argyle" Yeager (*STTNG*). Price per person.   **650-750**

Seatrek '89: Admiral Cruises, Inc., 1987. Special four-day Trek cruise, May 12-15, 1989, aboard the S.S. Emerald Seas that departed from Miami, stopped in the Bahamas and Little Stirrup Key (private island), and debarked back at Miami. Guest stars included Majel Barrett, Robin Curtis, James Doohan, Michael Dorn, Jonathan Frakes, Walter Koenig, Mark Lenard, Nichelle Nichols, Andy Probert, Gene Roddenberry, Marina Sirtis, George Takei, and Grace Whitney. The cruise also featured cast photo sessions, autograph sessions, informal Q & A panels, Trek trivia games, Trek of Fortune, a gala beach party and BBQ, costume party, talent contests, a dealer's room, plus a souvenir cruise book with a surprise gift. Price per person.   **495-750**

Seatrek '91: Chandris Fantasy Cruises, 1991. Three-day special Silver Anniversary cruise, May 26-31, 1991, aboard the U.S.S. Britanis which departed from Miami, Florida and disembarked again in Miami. Stops included Key West (Florida), Playa Del Carmen, Yucatan, and Cozumel (Mexico). Special guest stars included Majel Barrett, William Campbell, Denise Crosby (Yar), Robin Curtis, Joan de Lancie (Q), James Doohan, Walter Koenig, Mark Lenard (Sarek), Nichelle Nichols, Gene Roddenberry, Marina Sirtis, George Takei, Wil Wheaton, and Grace Lee Whitney. The cruise also featured guests Mike Okuda, Ann C. Crispin, Jeanne Dillard, Richard Arnold, David McDonnell, and Arne Starr. Special activities were the Gala Launch party, post-cruise Trek-Fari to Disneyland, question and answer sessions, beach party, dealer's room, movies, talent contest, Trek cabaret, and a complimentary package of photos autographed by the guests, along with a souvenir cruise book. Price per person.   **595-1,185**

Star Trek Adventure Space Station: Paramount Pictures and Universal City Studios, Inc., June 19, 1988. Grand opening of the Star Trek Space Station tour. The first 1,000 people presenting a special mail-out invitation got in free and received a tour of the life-sized Trek sets used in making special audience participation videos. Selected guests may star in an original Star Trek featurette and portray Enterprise crew members, Klingons, or aliens in full costumes designed by Robert Fletcher. The participants learn their parts and act them out on detailed sets of the Enterprise bridge, the engine room, the transporter room, a Klingon Bird of Prey bridge, and the planetscape of Akumal 7 with special effects produced by Industrial Light and Magic. They may purchase a video copy of their group's performance at the conclusion of the tour. The theater seats 2,000 people. Six shows per day run from 12:05 p.m. to 6:40 p.m. One show is entirely in Spanish. (For information on the Star Trek Adventure video, see **Video Cassettes**.)

Star Trek East-West Cruises: 1986. Two special four-day Trek cruises offered on opposite coasts at different times.

(A) Trek Cruise East, Eastern Cruise Lines, May 15-18, 1987. Cruise was aboard the S.S. Emerald Seas which departed from Miami, stopped in the Bahamas and Little Stirrup Key, and debarked at Miami. Trek guest included Majel Barrett, Robin Curtis, James Doohan, Walter Koenig, DeForest Kelley, Mark Lenard, Nichelle Nichols, Gene Roddenberry, George Takei, and Grace Whitney. Cruise consisted of photo sessions, parties, movies, TV episodes, deck sports, games, and dancing. Price per person.   **370-595**

(B) Trek Cruise West, Western Cruise Lines, September 11-14, 1987. Cruise was aboard the S.S. Azure Seas which departed Los Angeles, California, stopped at Ensenada, Mexico, and debarked at Los Angeles. Trek guests included Majel Barrett, Robin Curtis, James Doohan, Walter Koenig, DeForest Kelley, Mark Lenard, Nichelle Nichols, Gene Roddenberry, George Takei, and Grace Whitney. Cruise consisted of photo sessions, Star Trek theater, costume parties, a dealer's room, and singing performances by Nichelle Nichols and Grace Whitney. Price per person.   **440-595**

Star Trek Opera: Paramount Pictures Corporation and New York City Opera, October 1990. The official announcement as made by *USA Today* revealed that an operatic version of Gene Roddenberry's Star Trek was in the works as part of the 25th Anniversary Celebration coming up in 1991. (A recent report in *The New York Times* indicated that the plans for the opera have fallen through.)

Star Trek Postage Stamp: Citizen's Stamp Advisory Committee, U.S. Postal Service, Washington, DC, 1985. A nationwide campaign petitioning the postal service to issue a postage stamp in honor of the space shuttle Enterprise and the U.S.S. Enterprise from Star Trek. The stamp would be designed to show both space vehicles as a representation of present and future technology, as well as a tribute to America's commitment to manned space exploration. The chairman of the Citizen's Stamp Advisory Committee is Mr. Belmont Faries.

Trekfest: Future Birthplace of Captain James T. Kirk, Riverside Area Community Club, Riverside, Iowa, 1983. A municipal promotion where proceeds were supposed to go towards the construction of a permanent statue commemorating Kirk's birthplace in Riverside, Iowa. To help fund the venture, containers of dirt from behind the barbershop where Kirk would be born were sold, along with a numbered certificate of authenticity suitable for framing.

Price for vial of dirt.   **4   4   8**

Exhibits

Official Star Trek exhibits probably had their beginnings during the early 1970s which heralded the heyday for large-scale fan-sponsored Star Trek conventions. The very first Star Trek Con, which was held in January 1972 in New York City, proudly showcased its cherished Star Trek mementos (one of Spock's pointed ears and a superbly handcrafted miniature replica of the Galileo 7 Shuttlecraft) by exhibiting them under glass for the public viewing. That was, of course, only the beginning. Over the past 25 years, Star Trek exhibits have been cultivated to the point of professional sophistication. Commercial exhibits devoted to Star Trek can be seen at wax museums and in the halls of the renowned Smithsonian Institution. Private clubs and city halls alike have participated in constructing replica models.

The Star Trike, as exhibited and photographed by Loch David Crane.

Recently, Paramount Studios has also sent along authentic movie uniforms and costumes in conjunction with the releases of its home video tapes for viewing at select store locations. From placards to billboards to stage-set reproductions, Star Trek displays are as large as life!

Star Trek Exhibits and Locations

Bridge Set Replica: Starfleet Chapter XIV, U.S.S. Kasimar, Bangor, Maine. The SFC organization fan club for Maine, New Hampshire, Vermont, Massachusetts, Rhode Island, Connecticut, and eastern Canada. The club handcrafted a full-size working mock-up of the TV series bridge with over 400 lights, a 4' x 5' main viewscreen, and a wraparound sound system. Set measures approximately 30' x 37'.

Enterprise Prop: Smithsonian Institution, Air & Space Museum, Washington, DC. The Enterprise prop from the TV series. This 11-foot filming model, constructed of wood and plastic, was donated to the museum in 1974. It has appeared in numerous titled displays at this museum. Also in storage are filming models of the Klingon Battle Cruiser, the Tholian Scout (episode TW), and the miniature Enterprise in plastic cube (episode CP). The Smithsonian is planning a special 1991 Star Trek Anniversary exhibit featuring artifacts to commemorate the series.

Enterprise Ride: Hauss Manufacturers, Germany. Traveling circus amusement ride originally from Germany in 1968, appearing at carnivals and state fairs around the United States. A fast Ferris wheel ride with cabs that spin and elevate to upside-down position. Mural backdrop varies, but the general theme is a classic space battle between TV Enterprise starship and Klingon Cruisers. Some murals show artwork derived from the Bantam Book covers. Lighted marquee reads "The Enterprise." Eight rides are presently touring the United States.

Enterprise "Star Trike": Designer/owner Loch David Crane, California. Construction began in 1976. Operational three-wheel trike replica of the TV Enterprise. Consists of 1600cc engine mounted on a half-frame from a 1968 Volkswagen Squareback and a Honda CB 360 front end. Starship's saucer and secondary hull are fiberglass over plywood; nacelles (which function as twin 2½" gallon gas tanks) are capped in auto head lamps. Features include deck lights, bridge dome lights, and navigational markers. Averages 38 mpg and warps at 100 mph. In-dash stereo plays Star Trek tapes. A fully-licensed and street-legal vehicle, the Star Trike makes regular appearances at custom motorcycle shows and charity parades around the west coast.

Galileo '7 Shuttlecraft Prop: Owner/restorer Stephen Haskins. This full-sized prop used in the TV series was originally made for Paramount by AMF Phoenix at a cost of $65,000. Recent refurbishing included restoring the interior. Donated to the California Museum of Space & Technology.

Star Trek Wax Displays:

(A) "Bridge of the Enterprise" Exhibit — Movieland Wax Museum, Bueno Park, California. Wax figures of the seven classic Trek characters: standing Spock, Uhura, McCoy, and Scotty; seated Kirk, Chekov, and Sulu. The figures are at their station posts on a detailed platform replica of the studio bridge set. The exhibit includes illuminated sensor monitors and lighted consoles, turbo lift doors, chairs, and railings in an authentic reproduction. Brochure fold-outs (11" x 17"), postcards, and special museum slides and Viewmasters are available as souvenirs of this exhibit.

(B) "Star Trek Stars" Exhibit — Hollywood Wax Museum, Hollywood, California. Exhibit features wax sculptures of Mr. Spock (seated) and Captain Kirk (standing with his hand on Spock's shoulder). Backdrop is a painted panel with graphic designs, lighted boards, and dial inserts to simulate the engineering section. Brochures are available as 9" x 11¾" fold-outs with close-up color photo of the exhibit.

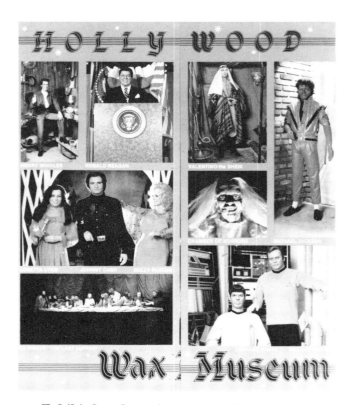

Exhibit brochure from the Hollywood Wax Museum.

U.S.S. Riverside Starship: Riverside Area Community Club, Riverside, Iowa. To-scale TV starship mounted on triangular trailer base. Replica is over 20' long. This model is used in local parades and is focal point for the annual Trek Fest celebration held at Riverside each June. Proceeds from souvenir sales and fees are to go towards the construction of a statue of Captain James T. Kirk erected by the city of Riverside — "the Future Birthplace" of the Captain.